THE CULTURE OF INTERPRETATION

The Culture of Interpretation

Christian Faith and the Postmodern World

Roger Lundin

WILLIAM B. EERDMANS PUBLISHING COMPANY
GRAND RAPIDS, MICHIGAN

To Sue,
for all things

Copyright © 1993 by Wm. B. Eerdmans Publishing Co.
255 Jefferson Ave. S.E., Grand Rapids, Michigan 49503
All rights reserved

Printed in the United States of America

Library of Congress Cataloging-in-Publication Data

Lundin, Roger.
   The culture of interpretation: Christian faith and the postmodern world /
Roger Lundin.
      p.   cm.
   Includes index.
   ISBN 0-8028-0636-8 (pbk.)
    1. Deconstruction. 2. Postmodernism — Religious aspects — Christianity.
3. United States — Civilization — 1970-   4. Christianity and culture.
I. Title.
BT83.8.L86   1993
261'.0973 — dc20   93-6750
                                                 CIP

CONTENTS

v

ACKNOWLEDGMENTS

O_{F THE MANY} people who have helped me at some point in the writing of this book, three friends deserve special thanks. One is Mark Noll, who read most of these chapters in one form or another and gave me the benefit of his vast learning, his keen theological sense, and his unerring editor's eye. I am also grateful to Alan Jacobs, who is a constant source of striking insights and delightful conversation and who gave the entire manuscript a careful reading; his comments were enormously helpful as I prepared my final draft. Finally, I want to thank Chuck Van Hof, the managing editor at Eerdmans. Chuck's criticism of the first draft of the manuscript was astute and was delivered with his characteristic good cheer.

As I have worked on this book over the past several years, many others have helped me by commenting on one or more chapters. Some of those who have helped have been friends of long standing, while others are scholars I was fortunate to meet at two conferences sponsored by the Pew Foundation. For their words of appreciation and their instructive criticism, I thank William Abraham, Stephen Evans, Gabriel Fackre, Os Guinness, William Hasker, James Davison Hunter, George Marsden, Thomas Oden, Neal Plantinga, Eleonore Stump, Clare Walhout, Mark Walhout, David Wells, and Tom Werge.

My project editor at Eerdmans, Jennifer Hoffman, gave timely advice and prompt attention to the manuscript. A grant from the Aldeen Fund at Wheaton College helped to defray some of the costs of preparing my final draft.

ACKNOWLEDGMENTS

In a significantly different form, portions of several chapters were published earlier in the *Reformed Journal*, the *Christian Scholar's Review*, and *Religion and Literature*. A section of one chapter appeared in *Evangelicalism and Modern America*, edited by George Marsden (Grand Rapids: Eerdmans, 1984). I am grateful to the respective publishers for permission to use that material in revised form in this book.

I wish to thank especially each of the members of my family — my son, Thomas, for his high spirits and, whenever I grew weary of writing and revision, for the delightful diversion of his countless park district soccer and baseball games; my daughter, Kirsten, for her creative spark and for the assistance she gave me in tracking down references; and my son, Matt, for carefully checking scores of sources and quotations and for serving as a sounding board for many of my ideas about contemporary American culture and the Christian faith. I have noted elsewhere in this book my greatest debt, which is to my wife, Sue. Throughout the years she has been my deepest source of encouragement and my best critic; for me, Sue has always been that "Gentle Reader" described by Nathaniel Hawthorne more than a century ago as "that one congenial friend, that all-sympathizing critic" whom every author seeks to find.

INTRODUCTION

A S I SIT DOWN to write this introduction, I have just finished perusing an issue of *The New Republic* that came in the afternoon mail. Its cover consists of a picture of Geraldo Rivera overlaid by the headline "The Idiot Culture." The cover article laments the sorry state of public discourse in contemporary America. Written by Carl Bernstein of Watergate reportorial fame, it concludes: "Today the most compelling news story in the world is the condition of America. Our political system is in a deep crisis; we are witnessing a breakdown of the comity and the community that has in the past allowed American democracy to build and to progress. . . . We are in the process of creating, in sum, what deserves to be called the idiot culture."[1]

Those are strong, sobering words to consider at the outset of a book entitled *The Culture of Interpretation*. But as I think about Bernstein's indictment of contemporary America, it strikes me that he is raising many of the very issues that this book, in a decidedly different way, attempts to address. What kind of culture do we inhabit in the modern West, and how did this culture come into being? What conceptions of the true and the good are dominant in contemporary culture? Furthermore, what are the implications of these conceptions of truth and virtue for our lives as citizens in this culture — whether we think of ourselves, broadly, as members of the civil commonwealth or more specifically as professing members of the Christian church?

1. Bernstein, "The Idiot Culture," *The New Republic,* 8 June 1992, pp. 28, 25.

I

The Culture of Interpretation is an attempt to take an account of contemporary culture by exploring the historical background to some of its central beliefs and by considering the ethical and theological implications of those beliefs. Though I have written this book from a self-consciously Christian perspective, the issues it engages should be relevant to people far beyond the orbit of the Christian faith. I have no desire to conceal my commitments as a Christian scholar; at the same time, however, I have attempted to show my respect for those with whom I disagree by taking them seriously enough to engage them in a dialogue about vital matters.

Because contemporary education is a focal point for many of the conflicts in the larger culture, the opening chapter examines competing arguments in the debate about the nature and purpose of the university. With those present-day arguments as a backdrop, the book then moves back in time, so to speak, for three chapters in an effort to understand several historical developments that have led to our contemporary disputes; those chapters lay out the central arguments of the book about the main reasons for and implications of the growth of "the culture of interpretation." Chapters 5 and 6 attempt to assess the specifically American context of contemporary cultural developments by looking in depth at two nineteenth-century American authors, Ralph Waldo Emerson and Nathaniel Hawthorne. From those chapters, the book proceeds in Chapters 7 and 8 to consider the connections between deeply ingrained American habits of mind and two of the more powerful movements in contemporary literary and cultural theory: Marxism and poststructuralism — or deconstructionism, as it is sometimes called. The final two chapters examine more explicitly and systematically several key implications of the history outlined in the book for the practice and proclamation of the Christian faith.

As the argument of *The Culture of Interpretation* develops, there are several terms that will continue to weave their way through the chapters that follow. To prepare for that argument, I thought it might be best to conclude this introduction with a few brief definitions of key terms that the book will make use of repeatedly. The purpose in doing so is not to attempt to be definitive; rather, it is simply to offer an explanation of the way in which this book will be employing problematic words that have complex connotations for the understanding of contemporary cultural and intellectual life.

The first of those words comes from the title of this book — *culture.*

It is a word of which the esteemed English scholar Raymond Williams has written, "*culture* is one of the two or three most complicated words in the English language. This is so . . . mainly because it has now come to be used for important concepts in several distinct intellectual disciplines and in several distinct and incompatible systems of thought."[2] With almost all of its early uses having to do with the *tending* of something — typically crops or animals — *culture* only gradually began to be applied, early in the modern period, to human development in a general sense. The exceedingly complicated history of the modern usage of the word *culture* indicates, in Williams's words, "a complex argument about the relations between general human development and a particular way of life, and between both and the works and practices of art and intelligence."[3]

In the sense that I have in mind in this book, *culture* designates that complex, interlocking network of symbols, practices, and beliefs at the heart of a society's life. While fully acknowledging the existence of myriad ethnic, religious, and regional subcultures within American society, I will argue in this book that there is a dominant cultural pattern deeply embedded in the American past and the American character. Furthermore, because of the power of the market economy and the pervasiveness of the mass media, there are in contemporary America striking similarities between the preoccupations of popular culture and those of the intellectual elites. It is hardly a coincidence that so many of the chapters in this book begin with an image or story from sports, the media, or advertising and then move on to discuss matters of history and theory. The chapters unfold in that manner because of my conviction that relationships between what we classify as "high" and "low" culture are closer than many of us have been accustomed to suspect.

One of the terms used frequently in this book to describe contemporary culture is *postmodern*. A key to this term is the hyphen buried within it — "post-modern." In architecture, literature, and theory, *postmodern* culture focuses upon contemporary culture as an advance upon, or an abandonment of, the *modernist* movement that was at the center of Western culture in the first five or six decades of this century. If modernism represented a desperate effort to have art and culture fill the void created

2. Williams, *Keywords: A Vocabulary of Culture and Society* (New York: Oxford University Press, 1976), pp. 76-77.

3. Williams, *Keywords*, pp. 80-81. An excellent recent study of the arguments over the meaning and nature of "culture" in contemporary America is James Davison Hunter's *Culture Wars: The Struggle to Define America* (New York: Basic Books, 1991).

by the decline of religion in the West, then postmodernism stands as the affirmation of the void, as the declaration of the impossibility of ever filling it. In an influential book, Jean-François Lyotard argues that "the word *postmodern* . . . designates the state of our culture following the transformations which, since the end of the nineteenth century, have altered the game rules for science, literature, and the arts." The definition of *postmodern*, Lyotard writes, is, "simplifying to the extreme, . . . incredulity toward metanarratives."[4]

The *metanarratives* toward which the postmodern temperament responds with incredulity are the stories of progress and development that have given shape to the Western experience over the last several centuries. As several chapters in this book will elaborate, there are clear overlapping concerns shared by Christian orthodoxy and postmodernism: both camps are skeptical of the claims made on behalf of reason in the Enlightenment and on behalf of the imagination in romanticism; they are suspicious about the faith placed in the power of self-conscious intentions to control and direct the course of history; and Christians and postmodernists alike have ample cause to be critical of the confidence the Western mind has had, at least since Descartes, in its ability to know the truth with scientific certainty. When Christian philosopher Nicholas Wolterstorff writes, "On all fronts foundationalism is in bad shape,"[5] he is, in effect, saying something very close to what Lyotard is saying when he defines *postmodernism* as "incredulity toward metanarratives."

In pointing to this connection between postmodernism and the *Enlightenment* and the *romantic* movement, I am making the first of many references that will appear throughout this book to the two great cultural movements of the eighteenth and nineteenth centuries. As it was defined by its greatest spokesman, the German philosopher Immanuel Kant, the "Enlightenment [was] man's leaving his self-caused immaturity. Immaturity is the incapacity to use one's intelligence without the guidance of another. . . . *Sapere Aude!* Have the courage to use your own intelligence! is therefore the motto of the enlightenment."[6] The Enlightenment devoted

---

4. Lyotard, *The Postmodern Condition: A Report on Knowledge*, trans. Geoff Bennington and Brian Massumi (Minneapolis: University of Minnesota Press, 1984), pp. xxiii, xxiv.

5. Wolterstorff, *Reason Within the Bounds of Religion* (Grand Rapids: Eerdmans, 1976), p. 52.

6. Kant, "What Is Enlightenment?" trans. Carl J. Friedrich, in *The Philosophy of Kant*, ed. Carl J. Friedrich (New York: Modern Library, 1949), p. 132.

itself to the task of discovering the full potential of reason and employing it to establish justice and happiness in the historical world.

Although the Enlightenment differed markedly in a number of respects from the romantic era that followed in its wake, these two movements shared a distinct perspective upon the place of the self in nature and society. Both emphasized the self as an entity in isolation, equipped in its solitude with a panoply of powers. In the Enlightenment, to be sure, faith was centered upon rationality as the instrument of power, while in romanticism it was the intuition or imagination that promised to deliver humans from their bondage to ignorance and injustice. But the adherents of the Enlightenment and romanticism were more united by their unshakable faith in the self than they were divided by their disagreements about the mechanisms through which that self did its work.

While orthodox Christians and postmodernists alike are critical of many aspects of the Enlightenment and romantic heritages, they are very likely to part company over the question of truth in those traditions. Though many Christians might be sympathetic to postmodernist skepticism about the powers of rationality, not many would agree with postmodern conclusions about the nature of truth. To most Christians, the collapse of the Cartesian project does not mean that the search for truth must be abandoned; if rationality and the imagination cannot supply certain access to the truth, the Christian may turn — or return, as the case may be — to the Bible, to the church, and to tradition for the truth. The postmodernist, on the other hand, is far more likely to abandon the search for truth altogether and turn instead to a therapeutic understanding of human experience.

In speaking of a *therapeutic understanding,* I am referring to what Philip Rieff has brilliantly described as "the unreligion of the age, and its master science." According to Rieff, in a therapeutic understanding of the world there is "nothing at stake beyond a manipulatable sense of well-being."[7] The model of the therapeutic has great explanatory power for American culture because of the manifold ways in which therapeutic categories have become central to public discourse and personal experience in contemporary America. A *therapeutic culture* is one in which questions of ultimate concern — about the nature of the good, the meaning of truth, and the existence of God — are taken to be unanswerable and hence in

---

7. Rieff, *The Triumph of the Therapeutic: Uses of Faith After Freud* (New York: Harper & Row, 1966), p. 13.

some fundamental sense insignificant. A therapeutic culture focuses upon the management of experience and environment in the interest of that "manipulatable sense of well-being" described by Rieff.

According to Rieff, few things suit the therapeutic ideal better than the "prevalent American piety toward the self. This self, improved, is the ultimate concern of modern culture."[8] As the following chapters will argue, the history of the aggrandizement of the self in America helps to explain the appeal of postmodernist thinking in the theoretical reaches of the American university as well as in the popular culture of the marketplace and media. Lyotard's definition of postmodernism as "skepticism toward metanarratives" means, among other things, that the postmodern self is free to see itself as neither defined nor confined by the historical or communal narratives that make a claim upon it. The *therapeutic self* considers itself free of the obligations of truth and the claims of ethical ideals. "In our culture," argues Alasdair MacIntyre, "truth has been displaced as a value and replaced by psychological effectiveness."[9]

To point to the pervasiveness of the therapeutic model in contemporary culture is not to deny the appropriateness of that model in psychological and pastoral care. It is simply to question the wisdom of extending therapeutic methods and ideals to the whole of cultural experience. In a therapeutic culture, there is no room for a Christian conception of truth and the ethical life. If personal well-being and psychological effectiveness are the defining criteria of the spiritual life, then there is no place for the claims of the true and the good. While there may be some initial benefits that accrue to the church when it tailors the gospel to make it "relevant" to a therapeutic culture, in the long run the therapeutic ideal enervates the church, its faith, and its practices.

In short, this book is an attempt to understand certain aspects of contemporary American culture and to offer one account of how we have come to this point. Further, it is an effort to assess several crucial implications of postmodern culture for the profession and practice of the Christian faith. Its goal is to initiate a dialogue — both within the Christian church about the relationship of Christ to contemporary culture and outside the Christian fold about the nature of the self and truth. For the church, and for the culture, dialogues of this kind are nothing short of essential.

---

8. Rieff, *Triumph of the Therapeutic,* p. 62.

9. MacIntyre, *After Virtue,* 2nd ed. (Notre Dame: University of Notre Dame Press, 1984), pp. 30-31.

CHAPTER I   *Diversity and Desire*

A FTER TWO DECADES of relative tranquility, American college and university campuses at the end of the 1980s had become the scene of noisy disputes whose rumblings were heard beyond the cloistered halls and ivy walls. Virtually for the first time since the end of the Vietnam War, the events of campus life seemed to fix the attention of the American media and public. To be sure, in the 1970s and 1980s there were occasional stories about provocative commencement speakers, such as Aleksandr Solzhenitsyn at Harvard in 1978; the obligatory newspaper stories and television reports had appeared about the trends in student behavior, especially attitudes toward drugs, alcohol, and sex; and, of course, over the past two decades the explosive growth of college sports programs has placed highly selective images of universities constantly before the American public. But in the main, when it came to undergraduate education, for almost two decades the American public had appeared to be content with a policy of benign neglect. To a significant extent, the parents of American young people seemed content to deposit their children before the gates of the great American educational factories and to return four years later to see what the intellectual assembly line had produced. What went on during the process of production seemed beyond their control and out of their area of expertise.

Then something happened. In the middle part of the last decade, books such as Allan Bloom's *The Closing of the American Mind* and E. D. Hirsch's *Cultural Literacy* weighed in with sharp indictments of American higher education.[1] At the same time, newspapers such as the *Wall Street Journal* and *The New York Times* began reporting on significant curricular changes at such prestigious institutions as Stanford and Duke. Events on those campuses brought the seemingly arcane matters of literary and cultural theory dinning into the ears of the American public.

But though the furor may have sounded like that of the 1960s, the issues had a distinctly different ring to them than those of the earlier era. In place of protests against the Vietnam War and segregation, and in favor of sexual freedom, American campuses in recent years have heard loud disputes about curricular requirements, literary canons, and restrictions on offensive speech. The debates have been divisive, with a number on one side arguing that because of the racist, sexist, and homophobic legacy of Western culture, higher education must work to reform society and serve as an agent of liberation for those oppressed by the entrenched ideologies. At the same time, the opponents of the radical reformers have resisted dramatic curricular and canonical reform and have frequently construed recent changes as acts of capitulation by humanist scholars to a series of narrow political concerns. Again and again, these opponents have warned against the pernicious effects of contemporary theories of language, knowledge, and interpretation that have been imported from Europe.

In the midst of this debate, the Christian critic of culture may find it difficult to know where to take a stand. On the one hand, within the Christian church there is a rich tradition of advocacy on behalf of the dispossessed. Throughout the modern period, for instance, progressive Christians have been among the leaders of the fight against slavery and the struggle for equal rights. Should the contemporary Christian appropriate that legacy and side with those who argue that theories of language and literature ought to be pressed into service to free those who have been held so long in bondage? Does not the Bible command the Christian to side with the powerless and oppressed? If literary theory and a reformed curriculum might help to fulfill the mandate for liberation, why should Christians not form strategic alliances with Marxists, feminists, and poststructuralists?

But on the other hand, some will ask, should not the Christian critic

---

1. Bloom, *The Closing of the American Mind: How Higher Education Has Failed Democracy and Impoverished the Souls of Today's Students* (New York: Simon and Schuster, 1987); Hirsch, *Cultural Literacy: What Every American Needs to Know* (New York: Vintage Books, 1988).

stand with traditionalists? Because of their respect for texts handed down from the past, their veneration of the written word, and their civility, traditional humanists may appear to have more in common with Christians than do strident proponents of contemporary theories of interpretation and culture. As people who encounter God through the reading of a canonical text, should not Christians ally themselves with those who seek to protect the integrity of the past from the cynical theories of the present? Is not the Christian obliged to join with those who affirm the validity of religious belief and the sanctity of morality against the chic amorality of gays, lesbians, and neo-Marxists?

For the Christian critic, the problem is that both sides in this argument express a measure of the truth. Since the beginning of history, religious language has frequently been employed to deceive, to conceal, and to oppress. In the Western experience specifically, from the Crusades of the Middle Ages, through the European conquest and settling of America, to the establishment and maintenance of a system of chattel slavery, the Bible and Christian language have often been pressed into the service of brutal practices. Any honest appraisal of our use of language will show that we use words to conceal the truth as well as to reveal it, that we are just as capable of covering our sin with words as we are of confessing it. The act of exposing hidden corruption, which is central to the efforts of many demystifying contemporary theorists, can have an illuminating power for those who only dimly see the corruption of their own practices.

At the same time, however, the Christian may understandably regret that contemporary theories of literature, language, and culture appear to be so intrigued by the deceptive possibilities of language that they are always in danger of forgetting its power to reveal the truth. The Christian student of history cannot help but conclude that, for all the ignorance and oppression lodged in the past, that past was also the scene of God's activity to redeem humanity. The gospel itself is a message that we can receive only because it has been handed down to us from the past. Our rootedness in history is something for which we ought to be thankful as well as something from which we are called, in certain instances, to set ourselves and others free.

Faced with lively cultural arguments about the nature of language and the truth, Christians have the challenge to enter into a vigorous dialogue with the prominent voices in the contemporary debates. Yet by *dialogue* I do not intend meanings frequently associated with the word. A dialogue is not a conversation in which one party remains unnaturally deferential because of a sense of shame or inadequacy. In the conversations of contemporary theory, Christian belief and practice are frequently ridiculed as naive or oppressive, and such characterizations make a certain sense. They are plausible because of the undeniable fact, in the words of a philosopher sympathetic to Christian belief, that "high ethical and spiritual ideals are often interwoven with exclusions and relations of domination. . . . The great spiritual visions of human history have also been poisoned chalices, the causes of untold misery and even savagery."[2] The Christian critic should not gainsay the folly and abuse that have been a significant part of the history of the church.

There is another reason, however, besides that of indignation over the ethical legacy of the Christian faith, for the tendency of contemporary theorists to dismiss or ridicule Christian belief, and this reason also can contribute to the hesitancy of Christians to enter into a genuine debate. It has to do with the simple fact that Christian claims to the truth go against the grain of contemporary skepticism in epistemology and ethics. By conceiving of human action as a response to truth and to the demands of an ethical ideal, Christian thought runs counter to some of the most deeply held tenets of this postmodern age. In entering into dialogue with those who disparage or disregard Christian belief, Christian critics ought to be clear about the ethical and epistemological assumptions of their adversaries and ready to respond to charges against the faith.

If a dialogue is not a passive listening to a litany of accusations or complaints, neither is it simply hearing what contemporary thinkers have to say about sin and society, about language and life, and then selecting those elements compatible with Christian belief, while rejecting the unacceptable ones. Such an approach to culture and the intellectual life has too frequently informed and thus weakened the practices of Christians in the modern academic world. By employing a selective process of appropriation and rejection, the Christian thinker fails to engage contemporary theories at the deepest level and contributes nothing distinctly Christian to the intellectual conversation of the day. To be an intelligent and principled participant in the dialogue of contemporary intellectual life, the Christian must have a firm sense of the history behind present disputes and a clear idea of the relevance of Christian doctrine for the arguments of the day.

---

2. Charles Taylor, *Sources of the Self: The Making of the Modern Identity* (Cambridge: Harvard University Press, 1989), pp. 518-19.

Left vs. Right: The "Political Correctness" Debate

Three very different works published in recent years bring into focus the issues in contemporary debates about the nature of interpretation, language, and culture. Together they represent widely divergent responses to developments of the past several decades. To some degree, all three of these books have the contemporary college or university as their subject matter, yet each moves far beyond the walls of the academy in the claims it makes and in the implications of the theories it propounds.

The Left: Liberal Education

The first of these works, originally published as a special issue of *The South Atlantic Quarterly* in 1990 and subsequently published in book form with the title *The Politics of Liberal Education,* speaks effectively on behalf of those who have called for the university to become an agent of radical change in American culture.[3] Versions of the essays in this volume were delivered at a 1988 conference sponsored by Duke University and the University of North Carolina. The tone for that conference was set by the opening remarks of the leaders of the two schools. Paul Hardin, chancellor of the University of North Carolina, welcomed the guests and told them that they were meeting "against a background of harsh and unloving criticism." He accused William Bennett, then Secretary of Education, and Allan Bloom, author of *The Closing of the American Mind,* of "too much romanticizing over the ancient writers of Western civilization" and of desiring to "close the canon." Hardin's counterpart, H. Keith Brodie, president of Duke University, reminded these victims of "harsh and unloving criticism" that "a university is, after all, meant to be a subversive institution; is meant to overthrow entrenched attitudes of inhumanity, arrogance, and intolerance."[4]

These juxtaposed introductory remarks say a great deal about the state of debate in the contemporary academy. President Brodie tells the members of the conference audience that they are in the vanguard of "subversives" dedicated to "overthrow entrenched attitudes," while Chan-

---

3. *The Politics of Liberal Education,* ed. Darryl L. Gless and Barbara Herrnstein Smith (Durham, NC: Duke University Press, 1991); first published in *The South Atlantic Quarterly* 89, 1 (Winter 1990).

4. *The Politics of Liberal Education,* pp. 1, 2, 4.

cellor Hardin complains that those who embrace those "entrenched" values are cruel and "unloving" because they object to relentless attacks upon their most basic beliefs. By the logic of the president and chancellor, those whose values are under assault have no right to defend themselves but should accept with gratitude assaults upon all that they hold most dear.

This demand — that the subjects of harsh attacks respond with nothing but tolerance, respect, and appreciation — has become commonplace among cultural critics today. At the height of the recent furor over "political correctness," for instance, *The Chronicle of Higher Education* ran a front-page article under the headline "Reeling From Harsh Attacks, Educators Weigh How to Respond to 'Politically Correct' Label." The article quoted Gene Ruoff, director of the Institute for the Humanities at the University of Illinois at Chicago: "Mr. Ruoff admitted that professors would have a hard time convincing the public of the merit of contemporary scholarly approaches to literature, such as Marxism and deconstruction, since 'we are in opposition to what I would essentially call religious values.'"[5] Apparently Mr. Ruoff is offended that members of the taxpaying public object to the fact that their money is funding institutes whose stated purpose is to subvert beliefs and values they cherish.

Stung by criticism, many of the radical theoreticians have sought to put themselves at a distance from their own records of aggression and attack. In the first paragraph of his article in the Duke conference volume, for example, Henry Louis Gates, Jr., described himself as a member of "the cultural left — . . . that uneasy, shifting set of alliances formed by feminist critics, critics of so-called 'minority' discourse, and Marxist and poststructuralist critics generally, the Rainbow Coalition of contemporary critical theory."[6] He went on in that paragraph to compare William Bennett and Allan Bloom to, among others, George Wallace and Orville Faubus, two racist governors who were avowed supporters of segregation in their day. With visions dancing before their eyes of Bennett standing on schoolhouse steps, with his arms folded and nose upturned to block the path of federal marshalls and helpless minority children, it is unlikely that many at the conference rose to defend such a despicable man and his deplorable ideas.

---

5. "Reeling From Harsh Attacks, Educators Weigh How to Respond to 'Politically Correct' Label," *The Chronicle of Higher Education,* 12 June 1991, p. A-17.

6. Gates, "The Master's Pieces: On Canon Formation and the African-American Tradition," in *The Politics of Liberal Education,* p. 89.

More than three years later, Gates sounded a very different tone in an article in *The Chronicle of Higher Education*. The article had to do with a series of meetings at the 1991 Modern Language Association convention devoted to "a long-overdue counteroffensive against charges that their discipline is a seedbed of 'political correctness' and leftist ideology." After a decade of having proudly proclaimed their leftist ideals, the scholars at these meetings complained of being on the defensive against charges that they were exactly what they had claimed themselves to be. Such disingenuousness, coming from scholars who have until very recently proudly claimed the name of "radical," "leftist," or "Marxist," makes one sympathetic to Roger Kimball's complaint: "The MLA may have to be credited with spawning a new sub-variety of political correctness that consists in subscribing to all the politically correct pieties while loudly denying that such a thing exists."[7] A perfect example of this is Gates's lament in *The Chronicle* article dealing with the San Francisco convention: "I'm tired of crazy people on both the right and the left. It is time to chart out a center space and to get beyond the polarities and the name-calling that have torn us apart."[8] Gates seeks the shelter of a centrist position — and complains about extremism of the left and right — only after public criticism has been leveled against him and others for "leftist" positions that they had openly espoused.

At the Duke conference in 1988, there seemed to be no limit to the scorn that the speakers held for the prominent critics of recent changes in the curriculum and theory. Barbara Herrnstein Smith claimed that Bloom and Bennett are "fueled not by reverence for the past, but by an aggressive desire to lay hold of the present and future," and she complained that E. D. Hirsch's proposals are "vague and muddled" and "patently absurd." Henry Louis Gates, Jr., alleged that in their defense of the humanities, Bloom and Bennett "symbolize the 'antebellum aesthetic position,' when men were men, and men were white, . . . and when women and persons of color were voiceless, faceless servants and laborers, pouring tea and filling brandy snifters in the boardrooms of old boys' clubs." Henry Giroux stated that Bloom and Hirsch represent a "new conservative public philos-

---

7. Kimball, "The Periphery v. the Center: The MLA in Chicago," in *Debating P.C.: The Controversy over Political Correctness on College Campuses,* ed. Paul Berman (New York: Laurel, 1992), p. 70.

8. "Literary Scholars Mount a Counteroffensive Against a Bad Press, Conservative Critics," *The Chronicle of Higher Education,* 15 Jan. 1992, pp. A-9, A-12.

ophy" under which "intellectuals are cheerfully urged to take up their roles as clerks of the empire." And Eve Kosofsky Sedgwick argued that Christians and others who oppose homosexual behavior are "homophobic" people whose views display a "thoroughgoing, coercive incoherence," with Christians being especially guilty of "degrading" subtle arguments about the social construction of reality and turning them into the "blithe" edict that "people are 'free at any moment to' (i.e., must immediately) 'choose' to subscribe to a particular sexual identity (say, at a random hazard, the heterosexual) rather than to its other."[9]

In the final essay of the volume, Richard Rorty places *The Politics of Liberal Education* clearly on the political landscape. In assessing what transpired at Duke in 1988, he admits:

> our conference has been, in part, a rally of [the] cultural left. The audience responded readily and favorably to notions like "subversive readings," "hegemonic discourse," "the breaking down of traditional logocentric hierarchies," and so on. It chortled derisively at mentions of William Bennett, Allan Bloom, or E. D. Hirsch, Jr., and nodded respectfully at the names of Nietzsche, Derrida, Gramsci, or Foucault.[10]

For the speakers and audience at this "rally of the cultural left," the purpose of education appeared to be liberation, with scholars and teachers delivering students from the bondage of their roles as oppressed and "marginalized" people. "We need a language that defends liberal arts education not as a servant of the state or an authoritarian cultural ideology but as the site of a counterpublic sphere where students can be educated to learn how to . . . 'break existing public forms,'" argued Henry Giroux. "This is a utopian practice . . . in which the curriculum is not reduced to a matter of cultural inheritance, but is posed as part of an ongoing struggle . . . [to develop] the potentialities of democratic public life."[11]

While the authors in *The Politics of Liberal Education* are clear about the sources of oppression from which education must liberate men and

9. Smith, "Cult-Lit: Hirsch, Literacy, and the 'National Culture'"; Gates, "The Master's Pieces"; Giroux, "Liberal Arts Education and the Struggle for Public Life: Dreaming about Democracy"; and Sedgwick, "Pedagogy in the Context of an Antihomophobic Project," in *The Politics of Liberal Education*, pp. 84, 89, 119, 146, 147.

10. Rorty, "Two Cheers for the Cultural Left," in *The Politics of Liberal Education*, p. 227.

11. Giroux, "Dreaming about Democracy," in *The Politics of Liberal Education*, pp. 133-34.

women, they give little indication of the goal of the liberation they so avidly promote. They seem confident that they know the source of the oppression from which they seek to free their students and their culture, but they say very little about the ends to which they would have those students aspire. It is apparent that the educators in *The Politics of Liberal Education* do not desire that their students seek truth, justice, or righteousness — unless one defines truth as the process of uncovering the biases of others, justice as the protection of personal preference, and righteousness as the pursuit of desire.

The authors in *The Politics of Liberal Education* espouse a wide variety of theoretical positions, and yet they appear to be united in their understanding of the nature and function of language. They see it as a most useful tool to be employed by the desiring and acquiring self; the vision of life promoted at the conference might best be called a "therapeutic pragmatism." Richard Rorty seems to be writing on behalf of many in this particular volume and in the contemporary academy when he praises Friedrich Nietzsche and William James, who, "instead of saying that the discovery of vocabularies could bring hidden secrets to light, . . . said that new ways of speaking could help us get what we want."[12] The underlying assumption of the majority at the "Liberal Education" conference appears to be that the only truth of which we can be certain is that there is nothing deeper in human life than preference and desire. In a curious irony of contemporary theory, the radicals appear to promote a crass, marketplace vision of the ethical and intellectual life, even as they bewail the corrupting tyranny of capitalist practice.

"All preferences are principled" — this is how Stanley Fish of Duke pithily and approvingly summarizes the pragmatism at the heart of much contemporary cultural theory.[13] A just society is one in which men and women have the right to pursue their desires most fully and to exercise their choices most freely. "An ideal liberal society is one which has no purpose except freedom," writes Rorty. "It has no purpose except to make life easier for poets and revolutionaries while seeing to it that they make life harder for others only by words, and not deeds."[14] Like Chancellor

12. Rorty, *Consequences of Pragmatism* (Minneapolis: University of Minnesota Press, 1982), p. 150.

13. Fish, *Doing What Comes Naturally: Change, Rhetoric and the Practice of Theory in Literary and Legal Studies* (Durham, NC: Duke University Press, 1989), p. 11.

14. Rorty, *Contingency, Irony, and Solidarity* (Cambridge: Cambridge University Press, 1989), pp. 60-61.

Hardin and President Brodie, Rorty positions himself as the champion of those who desire to attack established institutions from a position of invulnerable security. While not necessarily sharing the more radical opinions of his fellow scholars on the "cultural left," Rorty happily presents himself as their defender and promoter, as one who "has no purpose except to make life easier for poets and revolutionaries." In Rorty's "ideal liberal society," those revolutionaries are busy proclaiming that to be righteous is to espouse correct opinions, to welcome "subversive readings," and to commend attacks on "hegemonic discourse" and "logocentrism," while scorning those ideas or practices summarily judged to be "racist," "sexist," or "homophobic."

Like the radical reformers of the Enlightenment who are their forebears, members of the "cultural left" in the contemporary academy are correct to call attention to the manifold uses of language as a tool of deception and oppression throughout history. Unquestionably, base motives have consistently worn the masks of high ideals. Because of the enormous power we have to deceive others and ourselves, what Paul Ricoeur has aptly labeled "the hermeneutic of suspicion" ought to be part of every responsible critic's interpretive scheme.[15] After the work of the likes of Nietzsche, Marx, and Freud, it is intellectually irresponsible to ignore the powerful roles played in human affairs by biological forces, economic motives, and sexual drives.

But at the same time, neither is it responsible to ignore the considerable power of moral and spiritual ideals over human action. The authors in *The Politics of Liberal Education,* however, appear to disparage such ideals regularly, except when they are imagining utopias in which men and women never have to be burdened with moral and spiritual ideals again. By letting a "hermeneutic of suspicion" all but determine their readings of texts and actions, they have made themselves and those they instruct incapable of understanding a wide range of the human experience. "Have you noticed," asks the normally cynical Mr. Compson in William Faulkner's *Absalom, Absalom!* "when we try to reconstruct the causes which lead up to the actions of men and women, how with a sort of astonishment we find ourselves now and then reduced to the belief, the only possible belief, that they stemmed from some of the old virtues?"[16] To which one can only imagine most of the contributors to *The Politics of Liberal Edu-*

---

15. Ricoeur, *Freud and Philosophy: An Essay on Interpretation,* trans. Denis Savage (New Haven: Yale University Press, 1970), pp. 32-36.

cation responding, "No, that hadn't occurred to me, nor does your mentioning it *cause* it to occur to me."

The Right: Traditionalists

Conferences such as the one that led to the publication of *The Politics of Liberal Education* have helped to fuel the debates on American campuses over curricular change and acceptable speech. These debates have in turn led to a number of critical studies, one of the best known of which is Dinesh D'Souza's *Illiberal Education: The Politics of Race and Sex on Campus,* the second of the three works we are considering in this chapter. Through an examination of race relations, admissions policies, and curricular principles on six major American campuses — Berkeley, Stanford, Howard, Michigan, Duke, and Harvard — D'Souza constructs an argument about what he calls the "academic revolution" that has led to the "transformation of American campuses" where "a new worldview is consolidating itself." This revolution is being led by intellectuals in the humanities and social sciences, with the support or acquiescence of administrators. It is "conducted in the name of those who suffer from the effects of Western colonialism in the Third World, as well as race and gender discrimination in America. It is a revolution on behalf of minority victims." The goal of the revolution is to put an end to the bigotry that allows social injustice to persist, to rectify the inequities of the past, and to "advance the interests of the previously disenfranchised."[17]

In his examination of different institutions, D'Souza discusses such things as the effects of affirmative action on admissions standards at Berkeley, where admissions officers employ a complex academic scale on which a black student must score 4,800 out of 8,000 to be admitted, a white student 7,000, and the average Asian student even higher; the debate at Stanford University over the Western civilization requirement, which was highlighted by, among other things, a group of Stanford undergrads, wearing "blue jeans, Los Angeles Lakers T-shirts, Reeboks, Oxford button downs, Vuarnet sun glasses, baseball caps, [and] Timex and Rolex watches" and chanting "Hey, hey, ho, ho, Western culture's got to go"; the ban at the University of Michigan on "any behavior, verbal or physical, that

16. Faulkner, *Absalom, Absalom!* (New York: Vintage Books, 1972), p. 121.

17. D'Souza, *Illiberal Education: The Politics of Race and Sex on Campus* (New York: The Free Press, 1991), pp. 2, 13.

stigmatizes or victimizes an individual on the basis of race, ethnicity, religion, sex, sexual orientation, creed, national origin, ancestry, age, marital status, handicap, or Vietnam-era veteran status"; and the situation at Duke University, where members of the English department boast of their "line-up of home run hitters" and "academic superstars," and where the academic provost says of these professors with six-figure incomes: "Look, what we wanted was academic excitement, and these fellows sure knew how to generate that. They are cutting-edge. Whatever they're doing, they get attention. That's our objective."[18]

While D'Souza is able to document any number of oddities and excesses in the political world of the contemporary university, he has difficulty in articulating a convincing claim about the mission of that university. He appears to assume that there is in the West a unified cultural tradition as well as privileged rational and empirical methods of inquiry that the university must protect. Any criticism of that tradition, or of the rationalism and empiricism supposedly embedded within it, is taken by D'Souza to be tantamount to an anarchist's assault on holy order.[19] One of the most disappointing sections of *Illiberal Education* is that in which he surveys briefly a wide range of contemporary theories of knowledge and human understanding. In describing the many schools of literary criticism that he claims are "based on the denial of textual meaning," D'Souza lumps together many disparate theoretical approaches: "formalism, hermeneutics, psychoanalytic theory, semiotics, structuralism, Marxism, deconstructionism."[20] He claims that each of these theories aggrandizes the reader at the expense of the text and reduces truth to a matter of opinion. Such a charge distorts the truth by failing to acknowledge the great degree to which these theories disagree about first principles.

While blurring the dramatic differences between these schools of criticism, D'Souza's argument also distorts the nature of contemporary thinking about truth. By representing the state of literary theory and epistemology as he does, D'Souza gives the impression that there are only

18. D'Souza, *Illiberal Education*, pp. 59, 142, 159, 161.

19. John Searle's criticism of Roger Kimball's *Tenured Radicals* would seem to apply to D'Souza's *Illiberal Education* as well: "He simply takes it for granted that there is a single, unified, coherent tradition, just as his opponents do, and he differs from them in supposing that all we need to do to rescue higher education is to return to the standards of that tradition. But the situation is not that simple" (Searle, "The Storm over the University," in *Debating P.C.*, p. 103).

20. D'Souza, *Illiberal Education*, p. 177.

two alternatives — either the opaque formlessness of relativism or the clear rigidity of a rational, scientific ideal of knowledge. "What is the goal of liberal education if not the pursuit of truth?" he asks. "If education cannot teach us to separate truth from falsehood, beauty from vulgarity, and right from wrong, then what can it teach us worth knowing?"[21]

The pursuit of truth, beauty, and goodness is a noble ideal for a liberal education, but D'Souza's oversimplification of contemporary ethics and epistemology weakens his argument on behalf of that ideal. He appears to operate on the basis of a naive scientific realism, which assumes that a faithful study of the facts of nature and the structures of the human mind will disclose universal values and truths. Recent works in epistemology, hermeneutics, and the history of science have discredited such naive realism. There are very few contemporary thinkers of any theological, philosophical, or political persuasion who would hold to D'Souza's faith in the ethical and epistemological powers of the solitary observer. Yet D'Souza shows little awareness of the intellectual history behind the contemporary theories he deplores. By failing to acknowledge the disarray in the Enlightenment epistemological and moral traditions, he can offer only a tepid response to the ideological blandishments of the theorists he condemns.

Confessing Faiths: The University and Tradition

The third work we will consider in this chapter is the most recent book by moral philosopher Alasdair MacIntyre. In this book, entitled *Three Rival Versions of Moral Enquiry: Encyclopaedia, Genealogy, and Tradition*, MacIntyre addresses many of the same questions as D'Souza, but he gives very different answers. Indeed, MacIntyre's approach in this book puts both the theorists of "liberal education" and D'Souza to the test, setting the schools of thought represented by D'Souza and the authors of *The Politics of Liberal Education* in historical perspective and finding both of them to be wanting.

Most of the authors in *The Politics of Liberal Education* would be considered representatives of what MacIntyre calls the "genealogical" school of criticism; they tunnel beneath Western ideals and institutions in order to demolish the foundations of oppression and exclusion upon which modern Western culture has been built. MacIntyre describes the self-appointed task of the genealogist as that of writing "the history of those

21. D'Souza, *Illiberal Education*, p. 179.

social and psychological formations in which the will to power is distorted into and concealed by the will to truth."[22] The genealogists, all of whom are in some way the descendents of Nietzsche, seek to expose the devious compulsion that cowers behind the ethical and ideological masks of the self. In a disenchanted age, the cynicism of the genealogical approach is bound to have a strong appeal.

D'Souza, on the other hand, embodies the values of what MacIntyre calls the "culture of the encyclopedia." This is the culture that for two centuries has touted the virtues of human rationality and that until recent decades captured the allegiance of the large majority of the educated class. The encyclopedist operates with the "belief that in all enquiry, religious, moral, or otherwise, the adequate identification, characterization, and classi- fication of the relevant data does not require . . . any prior commitment to some particular theoretical or doctrinal standpoint. The data, so to speak, present themselves and speak for themselves."[23] Rationalism and empiricism are the guiding philosophies of the "culture of the encyclopedia."

In *Three Rival Versions of Moral Enquiry*, as in the two books that preceded this work,[24] MacIntyre develops a complex narrative of intellectual history. He traces the "encyclopedic" culture back to the Enlightenment and considers its central premise to be the belief that in all matters of moral and theological significance a rational consensus can be reached by individuals committed to the search for truth. The modern liberal university is one of the products of this culture of the encyclopedia, and it was guided in the early stages of its development by the conviction that minds freed from the constraints of religious and moral tests would make irreversible progress in intellectual enquiry. The encyclopedist believed that the truth about all that matters most deeply to humans would emerge inevitably from the process of rational enquiry to which the university had dedicated itself. But as MacIntyre laments, "the subsequent history of the liberal university has been one of increasing disarray generated in key part by this initial error" of believing in the power of unaided reason to discover the truth.[25]

According to MacIntyre's narrative depiction of the development of

22. MacIntyre, *Three Rival Versions of Moral Enquiry: Encyclopaedia, Genealogy, and Tradition* (Notre Dame: University of Notre Dame Press, 1990), p. 39.

23. MacIntyre, *Three Rival Versions of Moral Enquiry*, p. 16.

24. MacIntyre, *After Virtue*, 2nd ed. (Notre Dame: University of Notre Dame Press, 1984); and *Whose Justice? Which Rationality?* (Notre Dame: University of Notre Dame Press, 1988).

25. MacIntyre, *Three Rival Versions of Moral Enquiry*, p. 225.

modern intellectual life, the work of the contemporary genealogist has been made easy by the "lack of self-knowledge [that] has been systematically institutionalized" in the culture of the encyclopedia. That is, in their inability to recognize the degree to which self-interest guided their supposedly disinterested quests for truth, the encyclopedists made the advent of genealogy inevitable. By tracing all human aspirations, ideals, and truth claims back to their hidden sources within the human will, the genealogists make it their goal to expose the falsehood of all claims to truth made by the culture of the encyclopedia. The only thing that can be presumed to be "fixed and binding about truth" to the genealogist "is an unrecognized motivation serving an unacknowledged purpose."[26] When the encyclopedist announces the discovery of a moral certainty or a spiritual truth, the genealogist responds with the charge that the encyclopedist has discovered nothing more than what he or she has projected. In the world of the genealogist, the primary certainties have to do with the will to power and personal preference.

Though MacIntyre does not discuss at length the events of the 1960s, that decade might be seen in his terms as the period in which genealogists began to wrest control of the universities away from the encyclopedists. The paternalistic liberal humanism that had ruled American schools for decades proved unequal to the challenge mounted by the subversive power of genealogical critique. "The rejection of the liberal university which was signaled by the revolt of the 1960s," writes MacIntyre, "was a response to the barrenness of a university which had deprived itself of substantive moral enquiry."[27]

According to MacIntyre, that revolt exposed the poverty of Enlightenment rationality and the reigning methods of analysis in the humanities and social sciences. The collapse of the liberal consensus, in turn, has led to a proliferation of competing methods of analysis and interpretation. In the study of literature, for example, "unconstrained and limitless absence of agreement has gradually become the order of the day. . . . What is observable is change of fashion rather than progress in enquiry."[28] In the fashionable world of genealogical critique, it is hardly surprising that what excites the Duke provost about his faculty is that "these fellows sure [know] how to generate" academic excitement. "They are cutting-edge. Whatever they're doing, they get attention."

26. MacIntyre, *Three Rival Versions of Moral Enquiry*, p. 35.
27. MacIntyre, *Three Rival Versions of Moral Enquiry*, pp. 235-36.
28. MacIntyre, *Three Rival Versions of Moral Enquiry*, p. 225.

According to MacIntyre, the contemporary university is profoundly fragmented and confused. For him, neither the cynicism of the Nietz-schean genealogists nor the misguided sincerity of the Enlightenment encyclopedists bodes well for the future of Western culture and moral reflection. The encyclopedists have been unable to provide convincing rational criteria for resolving any of the important quandaries of truth or morality. Furthermore, barred by their own understanding of the rational self from exercising any theological or political authority over their educational institutions, the encyclopedists appear to be doomed to watch the genealogists assume control of their world. The genealogists, on the other hand, have little to offer to the ethical debate save the rhetoric of liberation and the promises of preference. Since their duty is to expose "an unrecognized motivation serving an unacknowledged purpose," the genealogists do not have to labor to prove their theory of truth. Instead, they appear to assume that the culture will adopt their definition of men and women as appetitive creatures who employ language to conceal their primary desires.

The genealogists may have fewer truths to which they are committed, but they also have fewer reservations about exercising the power they have acquired. While D'Souza may express alarm about the overtly ideological atmosphere of the contemporary university, most genealogists greet these developments with relish and a clear conscience. In a world of nothing but preferences, the genealogist can tolerate anything but the belief that truth or virtue exists independent of the ungrounded choices of individuals. In the genealogist's world, you may prefer anything you wish, as long as you do not prefer to live in — or establish through your ethical and intellectual efforts — a society with a yearning for truth rather than opinions, with a commitment to ethical standards rather than personal preferences. What MacIntyre calls the "institutional tolerance of limitless disagreement" encounters in morality and theology a refusal to accept the blank indifference of unprincipled tolerance. For this reason, moral and theological discourse "have to be at best exiled to the margins of the internal conversations of the liberal university. . . . It [the liberal university] has successfully excluded substantive moral and theological enquiry from its domain."[29]

There are ironies aplenty in the relationship between this exclusion of theological and moral enquiry from the university and the recent turmoil

29. MacIntyre, *Three Rival Versions of Moral Enquiry*, pp. 225-26.

over political correctness and the restriction of speech on the nation's campuses. Mary Louise Pratt inadvertently provides insight into those ironies in her essay in *The Politics of Liberal Education*. A professor of comparative literature at Stanford, Pratt describes the debate that took place at Stanford in 1987 and 1988 over the revision of the Western civilization requirement at that university. In the fall of 1987, a Stanford committee issued a report calling for major changes in the core requirement. Focusing as they did upon the European tradition, the existing core courses, in the words of the task force, seemed "to perpetuate racist and sexist stereotypes and to reinforce notions of cultural superiority that are wounding to some and dangerous to all in a world of such evident diversity." As she describes the campus debate over this proposal, Pratt herself calls for "nonhierarchical, relational approaches to culture" and quotes with approval the comments made by one of her colleagues during the Stanford debate:

> The notion of a core list is inherently flawed, regardless of what kinds of works it includes or excludes. . . . A course with such readings creates two sets of books, those privileged by being on the list and those not worthy of inclusion. Regardless of the good intentions of those who create such lists, the students have not viewed and will not view these separate categories as equal.[30]

In his review of *The Politics of Liberal Education*, John Searle finds himself all but speechless in the presence of this complaint: "I find this an amazing argument." If accepted, the argument would invalidate "any set of required readings whatever" and would deny one of the most basic facts of common sense: "any list you care to make about anything automatically creates two categories, those that are on the list and those that are not."[31]

As much as they proclaim themselves to be advocates of preference and diversity, the members of Gates's and Rorty's "cultural left" repeatedly make it clear that there are certain preferences that they would forbid and particular expressions of diversity that they cannot tolerate. To support her claims concerning the need for curricular diversity, for example, Pratt cites two incidents that took place at Stanford at the time of the academic debates. One involved a group of fraternity brothers staging a silent vigil while wearing hoods and carrying candles, and the other had to do with

30. Pratt, "Humanities for the Future: Reflections on the Western Culture Debate at Stanford," in *Politics of Liberal Education*, pp. 17, 14.
31. Searle, "The Storm over the University," pp. 96-97.

a sorority "rush" dance that took place outside the campus Native American center. Though she advocates "nonhierarchical, relational approaches to culture," Pratt is understandably disturbed about the racist overtones of these acts; and by linking them to the need for a new curriculum, she demonstrates the impossibility of avoiding some form of hierarchy and the exercise of authority in communal life. She may deplore the very idea of a *core* list that deems some books "not worthy of inclusion," but it is clear that she wants the curriculum to assist the university to declare certain offensive beliefs and actions "not worthy of inclusion" in its life.

To his credit, Stanley Fish has recognized the seeming inconsistency of a professing *inclusiveness* that is in reality as theoretically and practically *exclusionary* as any other system of belief and practice. In an essay that surveys the campus disputes of the late 1980s, Fish argues for the right to censor "racist and hate speech" on the basis of his belief that "all affirmations of freedom of expression are . . . dependent for their force on an exception that literally carves out the space in which expression can then emerge." He claims that without "an in-built sense of what it would be meaningless to say or wrong to say," there could be no assertions or any reasons for making them. Speech cannot be "an independent value, but is always asserted against a background of some assumed conception of the good to which it must yield in the event of conflict." When any institution ("be it church, state, or university") comes up against a behavior that is "subversive of its core rationale, it will respond by declaring" that it cannot tolerate such action.[32]

Fish attempts to buttress his argument by saying that he is only claiming for universities the rights of prohibition that have historically belonged to religious institutions, be they churches or colleges. "All educational institutions rest on some set of beliefs — no institution is 'just there' independent of any purpose — and it is hard to see why the rights of an institution to protect and preserve its basic 'tenets' should be restricted only to those that are religiously controlled."[33] While he would hardly agree with the theological or ethical assumptions undergirding Christian educational enterprises, Fish recognizes that it is only against a background of prohibition that permission has meaning and that tolerance makes sense only in light of that which is taken to be unmistakably intolerable.

32. Fish, "There's No Such Thing as Free Speech and It's a Good Thing, Too," in *Debating P.C.*, p. 233.
33. Fish, "There's No Such Thing as Free Speech," p. 239.

Where Fish would differ from Christians of any stripe in his understanding of prohibition is in his oft-stated conviction that there are no standards to which one can appeal in deciding what to permit or prohibit. Since all principles are preferences — and only preferences — they are nothing but masks for the will to power, which is the ultimate source of what we call "values." Instead of appealing to authority outside ourselves, we can only seek to marshall our rhetorical abilities to wage the political battles necessary to protect our own preferences and to prohibit expressions of preference that threaten or annoy us. Fish is candid about the groundlessness of his own beliefs and about his willingness to wage political battles to silence those of whom he disapproves. When someone warns you, he writes, about the slippery slope and predicts that prohibition of one kind of speech will inevitably lead to further restrictions, you should reply: "Some form of speech is always being restricted; . . . we have always and already slid down the slippery slope; someone is always going to be restricted next, and it is your job to make sure that the someone is not you."[34]

Fish's incisive essay has the virtue of telling a truth that many university administrators and their defenders are unwilling to acknowledge. It is simply that in spite of its Enlightenment claims about truth, tolerance, and diversity, the secular university has all but abandoned the substance of its Enlightenment ideals. While proclaiming that it wishes to be inclusive of all beliefs and practices, it labors incessantly to do the necessary work of identifying itself through its exclusions; while it officially espouses the virtues of diversity — of such things as Mary Louise Pratt's "nonhierarchical, relational approaches to culture" — it finds it very hard to resist the temptation to turn the worship of diversity into a new and chilling mandate for uniformity; and while it still speaks of the search for "knowledge and truth," it explicitly endorses moral and historical understandings that proclaim that nothing undergirds human experience but personal preference and acquisitive desire.

In light of these developments in the contemporary university, MacIntyre calls for a plain acknowledgment of the actual state of affairs and for a vigorous debate between the partisans of the new cultural orthodoxies and the adherents of older religious traditions. His prescription for the *dis-ease* of the university involves what he calls "reconceiving the university and the lecture." Because the lecturer does not speak "with the voice of a single acknowledged authoritative reason," MacIntyre would have all lec-

---

34. Fish, "There's No Such Thing as Free Speech," p. 244.

turers become explicit about the partisan nature of their work. As advocates of particular traditions of thought, lecturers would work to advance enquiry from within their own traditions and would engage in debate with adherents of other traditions. Universities would become, in MacIntyre's scheme of things, centers of "constrained disagreement," where proponents of systems of belief and values took it as a "central responsibility . . . to initiate students into conflict."[35]

MacIntyre's argument is attractive on several counts. First, it provides a way of arguing for the truth without obligating one to have Enlightenment expectations about the nature or power of rationality. While D'Souza may have correctly identified many of the inconsistencies and injustices of the contemporary university, his solutions do not satisfy. Like many traditionalists of the past decade, D'Souza responds to the epistemological and moral challenges of postmodernism with the platitudes of modernism. In MacIntyre's terms, D'Souza is an encyclopedist who is trying to counter the arguments of genealogy by relying upon the very assumptions that set the stage in the first place for the devastating genealogical critique.

In addition, MacIntyre offers a way of assessing the demise of Enlightenment modernity that does not require one to embrace the relativism of postmodernism. In *Whose Justice? Which Rationality?* he especially presses this point. He takes "post-Enlightenment relativism and perspectivism" to be the "negative counterpart of the Enlightenment, its inverted mirror image." The power of relativism in contemporary intellectual life derives from its "inversion of certain central Enlightenment positions concerning truth and rationality." With the bankruptcy of the Enlightenment "view of truth and rationality" evident in the academic disciplines and in public life, "the protagonists of post-Enlightenment relativism and perspectivism claim that if the Enlightenment conceptions of truth and rationality cannot be sustained, theirs is the only possible alternative."[36]

MacIntyre's point is brilliantly illustrated in the opening section of an essay by the critic Robert Hughes. Not only does Hughes capture the differences between the two sides of the political correctness debate, but in his own attempts to mediate the dispute he shows, however unwittingly, how limited are the options available to the contemporary critic of culture and, by implication, how powerful a Christian critique of culture might be.

---

35. MacIntyre, *Three Rival Versions of Moral Enquiry,* pp. 230-31.
36. MacIntyre, *Whose Justice? Which Rationality?* p. 353.

Hughes opens his essay by crediting W. H. Auden with "having achieved what all writers envy: making a prophecy that would come true."[37] He finds that prophecy "embedded" in a speech by Herod in a long poem called *For the Time Being*. At that point in the poem, Herod is musing about the unpleasant prospect of "The Massacre of the Innocents." He does not wish to order the slaughter but is distraught about the prospects for his province if he fails to undertake the mass killings. Even though there is "no visible disorder" in his realm ("Soft drinks and sandwiches may be had in the inns at reasonable prices. Allotment gardening has become popular. . . . There are children in this province who have never seen a louse") there is no real happiness either, for "so many are still homesick for that disorder wherein every passion formerly enjoyed a frantic licence." Herod complains, "I have tried everything," and nothing has worked. Neither prohibition nor legislation has rid his land of superstition, and even "reason is helpless" against the barbaric demands of the people for passion and disorder.[38]

Into this time and place of discontent has come word of a miraculous birth. The "trio . . . with an ecstatic grin on their scholarly faces" has reported: "God has been born, . . . we have seen him ourselves. The World is saved. Nothing else matters." The irrationality of the wise men terrifies Herod, and this helps him to justify to himself the massacre.

It is Herod's attempt to rationalize his decision to kill innocent children that Hughes quotes at length. If this child lives and the rumors about him spread,

> Reason will be replaced by Revelation. Instead of Rational Law, objective truths perceptible to any who will undergo the necessary intellectual discipline, and the same for all, Knowledge will degenerate into a riot of subjective visions — feelings in the solar plexus induced by undernourishment, angelic images generated by fevers or drugs, dream warnings inspired by the sound of falling water. Whole cosmogonies will be created out of some forgotten personal resentment, complete epics written in private languages, the daubs of school children ranked above the greatest masterpieces.
>
> Idealism will be replaced by Materialism. . . . Life after death will be an eternal dinner where all the guests are twenty years old. . . .

37. Hughes, "The Fraying of America," *Time*, 2 Feb. 1992, p. 44.
38. W. H. Auden, *For the Time Being*, in *Collected Poems*, ed. Edward Mendelson (New York: Random House, 1976), pp. 301-2.

Justice will be replaced by Pity as the cardinal human virtue, and all fear of retribution will vanish. . . . The New Aristocracy will consist exclusively of hermits, bums, and permanent invalids. The Rough Diamond, the Consumptive Whore, the bandit who is good to his mother, the epileptic girl who has a way with animals will be the heroes and heroines of the New Tragedy when the general, the statesman, and the philosopher have become the butt of every farce and satire.[39]

What Herod foresaw, according to Hughes, was "America in the late 1980s and early 90s. . . . A society obsessed with therapies and filled with distrust of formal politics, skeptical of authority and prey to superstition, its political language corroded by fake pity and euphemism." The "demagogues" on the right and the "pushers of political correctness" on the left have trivialized the issues while debasing the language in their strident attacks upon one another and upon the common culture.[40] Herod's nightmarish vision of Revelation has become the glaring reality of the present day.

Yet for all of his considerable wit and insight, Hughes hardly does justice to Auden's poem. Hughes uses *For the Time Being* to make his point, but in doing so he all but completely ignores Auden's own intentions. By setting up Herod's vision as a prophecy of our contemporary "irrational" age, Hughes implies that Herod's liberal rationality might serve as a plausible alternative to the banal barbarianism of our present age. Nothing could be farther from the truth for Auden.

For the Time Being was the first long poem that Auden wrote after his return to Anglican orthodoxy. In it he was beginning to explore the possibilities of moving beyond the impasses of the Enlightenment and romanticism by returning to Christian belief. To Auden, the Enlightenment heritage offered no way of resolving the unbearable tensions it had itself engendered between the literary and the scientific, the radical and the reactionary, or the rational and the intuitive. As one movement supplants another ever more rapidly in the Enlightenment tradition, the new solutions do not seem to solve the old problems but only to compound them.

Hughes says that Herod does not want to massacre the innocents "because he is a liberal." For Auden, it would be closer to the truth to say

---

39. Auden, *For the Time Being,* p. 303.
40. Hughes, "The Fraying of America," p. 44.

that Herod is inclined to want the slaughter precisely because he is a liberal. Imprisoned by his own passion for order, lawfulness, and rationality, Herod cannot seek to do anything but exterminate a threat to all he holds most dear. "Naturally this cannot be allowed to happen," he says of the chaos that Revelation would bring. Like Hitler exterminating the "vermin" of the Jews, and like American bombers performing "surgical strikes" that decimated whole villages in Vietnam, Herod must call in the "professional tidiers" because "civilization must be saved." Herod does not shrink from the genocidal task in its conceptual form; he only wishes that he didn't have to be sullied by contact with it: "Why couldn't this wretched infant be born somewhere else? Why can't people be sensible? . . . How dare He allow me to decide? I've tried to be good. I brush my teeth every night. I haven't had sex for a month. I object. I'm a liberal. I want everyone to be happy. I wish I had never been born."[41]

In *Whose Justice? Which Rationality?* Alasdair MacIntyre argues that the last two hundred years of Western culture have witnessed a series of domestic disputes among members of the same family of liberal individualists. To MacIntyre, for example, the important truth about postmodernism is not its radical departure from modernist principles but the striking similarity of modernist and postmodernist assumptions about the nature of reality and the truth. If "post-Enlightenment relativism and perspectivism" constitute the "negative counterpart of the Enlightenment, its inverted mirror image," then the political atrocities of the twentieth century are directly descended from the revolutionary ideals of the Enlightenment and romanticism.

MacIntyre's insight is one that Auden had come upon almost half a century before him. Shortly after he had finished *For the Time Being* in 1942, the poet went to teach at Swarthmore College, where his course was entitled "Romanticism from Rousseau to Hitler." Because he was reading at the time such books as Charles Norris Cochrane's *Christianity and Classical Culture* and Reinhold Niebuhr's *The Nature and Destiny of Man*, Auden was much taken with the argument that only Christian faith could resolve the contradictions inherent in modernity and reverse the decline of Western civilization. In terms of the images of *For the Time Being*, for example, this line of thinking held that it would be fruitless to try to reconcile the values of the rational Herod with those of the irrational hordes by selecting the healthiest aspects of each approach to life and

41. Auden, *For the Time Being*, pp. 303-4.

combining them to produce a worldview with all of their virtues and none of their vices. Instead, Auden held that nothing less than a devoted recommitment to the neglected truth could save the individual soul or the culture as a whole.[42]

In the following chapters, I will be following the lead of the likes of Auden and MacIntyre in arguing that Christian belief presents distinct alternatives to Enlightenment rationalism and the pragmatic irrationality of postmodernity. In the last two decades, a series of challenges have been mounted by Christians against the Enlightenment paradigm; in each case, the challenges have attempted to demonstrate how one might remain committed to truth without being wedded to the foundationalism of Descartes or the rationalism and empiricism of the Enlightenment. One of these challenges has come from a Lutheran theologian from Germany; another has been made by a group of Reformed philosophers in America; yet another has been developed by a host of American church historians; and finally, in the work of MacIntyre and Charles Taylor, we have Catholic epistemologists and moral philosophers tackling the thorniest issues of modernity. Such work should encourage Christian students of contemporary culture and provide them with invaluable resources for a dialogue with postmodernity.

After all, the tumult in the universities is not an isolated phenomenon having to do with harmless, esoteric academic concerns. Rather, those disputes have to do with the most basic questions about the nature of truth, the possibility of transcendence, and the meaning of American culture. These are debates that the Christian critics of culture ought to listen to and then join. But the Christian who hopes to participate in that debate ought to have a solid historical perspective on the issues at stake and must maintain a strong awareness of the theological principles under contention. As Christians engage contemporary theories, they ought to do so critically, recognizing the need to renew their own vocabulary as well as to learn from the critiques offered by postmodern culture. If they do anything less than that, if they neglect their own heritage or view it solely as a source of corruption and oppression, Christians are in danger of selling their rich birthright — their saving vocabulary of sin and grace, judgment and forgiveness, death and resurrection — for a cold pottage of jargon and obscurity.

42. For Auden's reading and intellectual concerns at the time of his composition of *For the Time Being*, see Humphrey Carpenter, *W. H. Auden: A Biography* (Boston: Houghton Mifflin, 1982), pp. 321-30.

CHAPTER 2   *The Culture of Interpretation*

WHEN Bill Curry resigned as the head football coach at the University of Alabama in early 1990, his father spoke openly of his anger at those who had sought his son's dismissal. W. A. Curry believed that his son had never been accepted by fans who looked back to the days of the legendary Alabama coach Paul "Bear" Bryant. "The hardest thing for him [Bill] I think is to never really be accepted by the Alabama family, the influential alumni who never really got behind him," explained the elder Mr. Curry. The coach's father went on in that interview to blast the disloyal alumni in explicit biblical terms:

> It is amazing how many Judases and turncoats there are in the world. Bill's learned a hard lesson about people, I think. But Jesus Christ's advice in the Bible when you aren't welcomed is to dust your feet on the way out of town. Maybe that's what Bill needs to do.

Yet while Mr. Curry heard in the uproar over his son the echoes of biblical themes, a university trustee detected nothing more than a problem of perspective. That trustee, Aaron Aronov, admitted that Curry's support at Alabama had "been diluted," but he blamed this on the coach himself. In the words of the Associated Press story, Aronov charged that Curry had "created problems for himself with an inaccurate perception that he lacked support at Alabama." The story quoted the trustee as having said, "I think Coach Curry has been oversensitive to what he perceives as a lack of fan support."

This brief exchange provides a graphic illustration of the clash of two paradigms of interpretation. And in this conflict of interpretive models, we can trace the outline of critical changes that have taken place in modern theories of language and hermeneutics. The remarks of Bill Curry's father represent an understanding of language that has its roots in Christian tradition. For the father of the Alabama coach, personal conflicts are to be thought of as individual episodes in an epic spiritual drama. W. A. Curry envisions a world in which the ancient language of spiritual warfare corresponds, however roughly, to the very modern realities of vocational conflict and fame.

On the other hand, the University of Alabama trustee appears to hold to a distinctively postmodern understanding of the dilemmas faced by Bill Curry as a coach. Like the authors in *The Politics of Liberal Education*, Aaron Aronov turns to categories of interpretation and perspective to assess a conflict, rather than to the resources of moral and theological enquiry. For Aronov, the key to understanding Curry's dilemma might be better supplied by the wisdom of William Blake and his descendents than by the prophetic judgments of Jesus. "If the doors of perception were cleansed every thing would appear to man as it is, infinite," the English romantic poet Blake proclaimed in 1793; in turning the dispute into a problem of perception, the Alabama trustee was demonstrating his unwitting indebtedness to the romantic revolution in epistemology and to the triumph of perspectivism in contemporary theories of interpretation.[1]

Whether it is in everyday discourse or in the rarified vocabularies of critical theory, the language of perspective occupies a privileged place in

1. Blake, *The Marriage of Heaven and Hell,* in *The Poetry and Prose of William Blake,* ed. David V. Erdman (Garden City, NY: Doubleday, 1965), p. 39.

The Oxford English Dictionary Supplement defines *perspectivism* as "the theory that knowledge of a subject is inevitably partial and limited by the individual perspective from which it is viewed." The deficiency of this definition is that it gives little idea of the relativism at the heart of postmodern uses of the term *perspectivism.*

Robert Solomon describes perspectivism in the following manner: "This peculiar view, which sometimes parades under the title 'epistemological nihilism,' is in fact a form of relativism, or what Nietzsche calls his 'perspectivism' — the view that there are only truths for a certain sort of creature or a certain society, there is no truth as such" (*Continental Philosophy Since 1750: The Rise and Fall of the Self* [Oxford: Oxford University Press, 1988], p. 116). Solomon's description is an improvement upon the *OED* definition because it indicates the degree to which postmodern perspectivism denies the very possibility of truth.

the contemporary West, having assumed its position of prominence as a result of a series of events in intellectual and cultural history. At a time when confidence in epistemology has eroded significantly, perspectivism appears to afford an opportunity for the isolated self — which has been at the center of Western science, philosophy, and art for more than three centuries — to sustain its faith in its own powers. Even though we may no longer believe in the ability of the self to achieve moral perfection or to acquire indubitable knowledge, we are still able, through our contemporary theories of interpretation, to sustain faith in that self's ability to find satisfaction through the exercise of its creative powers. In postmodern America, we can observe this faith in "perspective" at work in everything from the self-help regimens promising easy wealth and psychic health to the fantastic visions of academic critics who see creative interpretation as a kind of explosive charge for blasting through the imprisoning walls of the metaphysical past.

Theory and Truth

If it is viewed superficially, the ascendancy of perspectivism in contemporary theories of interpretation might seem, even to some Christian critics, to be a happy sign of the triumph of literary values in Western culture. Since the romantic age, after all, it has been the goal of many defenders of literature and the arts to see such values — which have to do with the intangible realms of human feeling, desire, and spirit — established at the heart of Western societies. For a defender of literature such as the Victorian poet and critic Matthew Arnold, literary culture represented the last hope for a world in which science had supplanted religion as the organizing force. Arnold was convinced that if forced to choose between "humane letters" and "natural science," the "great majority of mankind . . . would do well . . . to choose to be educated in humane letters rather than in the natural sciences. Letters will call out their being at more points, will make them live more."[2] Because the "mass of mankind will never have any ardent zeal for seeing things as they are," it can only be through a "small circle [of disinterested critics] resolutely doing its own work that adequate ideas will ever get current at all." By undertaking "*a*

---

2. Arnold, "Literature and Science," in *Prose of the Victorian Period,* ed. William E. Buckler (Boston: Houghton Mifflin, 1958), p. 499.

disinterested endeavor to learn and propagate the best that is known and thought in the world," the critic will "help us for the future" and provide an answer to the question, "What will nourish us in growth towards perfection?"[3] Arnold had no doubts about the power of literature to play the key role in that "growth towards perfection."

Almost a hundred years after Matthew Arnold, the eminent literary critic Northrop Frye carried on the tradition of praising literature for its capacity to instill spiritual values in a culture dominated by empirical and pragmatic norms. Science may be adequate to the task of describing the world around us, the inhuman "environment" we inhabit; but only literature can create for us the satisfying images of the "home" we long to create in the midst of this environment. The poet's "job is not to describe nature, but to show you a world completely absorbed and possessed by the human mind."[4] Literature must be at the center of culture, because "in the imagination anything goes that can be imagined, and the limit of the imagination is a totally human world."[5]

Frye's formulations represent a modernist understanding of the relationship of science and philosophy to literature and the arts. That understanding was predicated upon an empiricist view of knowledge. For a very long time after the romantic period, that is, the promoters of literature were willing to concede large domains of knowledge and influence to science and its methods. As long as poetry and the other arts could hold on to their separate, affective provinces of experience, science was free to rule over the larger kingdoms of knowledge. But in recent decades, the theoretical confidence of Western culture in science has been shaken dramatically. Any number of factors — ranging from a general concern about the meaning and limits of technology to the specific influence of key books such as Thomas Kuhn's *The Structure of Scientific Revolutions,* Hans-Georg Gadamer's *Truth and Method,* and Jacques Derrida's *Of Grammatology* — have worked to bring about a dramatic questioning of science as a standard of epistemic certainty.[6] Into the vacuum

3. Arnold, "The Function of Criticism at the Present Time," in *Prose of the Victorian Period,* pp. 433, 440-41.

4. Frye, *The Educated Imagination* (Bloomington: Indiana University Press, 1964), pp. 32-33.

5. Frye, *The Educated Imagination,* p. 29.

6. Kuhn, *The Structure of Scientific Revolutions,* 2nd ed. (Chicago: University of Chicago Press, 1970); Gadamer, *Truth and Method,* 2nd rev. ed., trans. Joel Weinsheimer and Donald G. Marshall (New York: Crossroad, 1989); Derrida, *Of Grammatology,* trans. Gayatri Chakravorty Spivak (Baltimore: Johns Hopkins University Press, 1976).

created by the exhaustion of empiricism and logical positivism have rushed postmodern theories of literature and language, many of which celebrate the fictive quality of all knowledge and the imaginative nature of all supposed truth.

In contemporary literary and cultural theory, two examples of the triumph of perspectivism are the pragmatism of Richard Rorty, a speaker at the Duke University conference on "The Politics of Liberal Education" (discussed in Chapter 1), and the utopian radicalism of Frank Lentricchia, the editor of the journal in which the conference essays first appeared. After having begun his career as an analytic philosopher, Rorty later developed a strong interest in Continental philosophy, especially French poststructuralism and the German tradition of hermeneutical reflection. His "edifying" understanding of interpretation shows his special debt to the perspectivism of Friedrich Nietzsche. Like Nietzsche a century before him, Rorty has attempted, in his own words, "to undermine . . . confidence in 'the mind' as something about which one should have a 'philosophical' view, in 'knowledge' as something about which there ought to be a 'theory' and which has 'foundations,' and in 'philosophy' as it has been conceived since Kant."[7]

Rorty's first major work, *Philosophy and the Mirror of Nature*, set out to prove the bankruptcy of foundationalism, and each work of his since has taken that proof for granted. The collapse of the Enlightenment ethics and epistemology has left us with nothing but the consolations of hermeneutics. "Hermeneutics . . . is what we get when we are no longer epistemological." According to Rorty, the contemporary understanding of hermeneutics has happily served to promote that distinctively postmodern intellectual "attitude [which is] interested not so much in what is out there in the world, or in what happened in history, as in what we can get out of nature and history for our own uses." When we lose faith in the power of language to mirror the truth, that is, we acquire a newfound appreciation for its therapeutic capacity to help us get what we desire. To the "edifying" or therapeutic interpreter, "getting the facts right (about atoms and the void, or about the history of Europe) is merely propaedeutic to finding a new and more interesting way of expressing ourselves."[8]

That last phrase — "a new and more interesting way of expressing ourselves" — betrays Rorty's allegiance to romantic theories of language

7. Rorty, *Philosophy and the Mirror of Nature* (Princeton: Princeton University Press, 1979), p. 7.

8. Rorty, *Philosophy and the Mirror of Nature*, pp. 325, 359.

and the self. Rorty's elaboration of romanticism should give pause to any Christian student of culture who sees in the romantic movement a refuge for human spirituality and ethical values. In his later works *Consequences of Pragmatism* and *Contingency, Irony, and Solidarity,* Rorty presses the argument that postmodern culture should be thought of as a thoroughly romantic and literary culture. He asks that we let him "call 'romanticism' the thesis that what is most important for human life is not what propositions we believe but what vocabulary we use."[9] If we grant Rorty that premise, he will then tell us that our vocabularies cannot reveal the truth, in any conventional sense, about this world or any possible worlds. Instead, language can do no more than express human need and longing. Words are tools we use to get what we want, and "to say, with Nietzsche, that God is dead, is to say that we serve no higher purposes. . . . A sense of human history as the history of successive metaphors would let us see the poet, . . . the shaper of new languages, as the vanguard of the species."[10]

It is a measure of Rorty's influence that so many literary theorists, especially those with Marxist sympathies, have roundly criticized his work. Lentricchia, for example, complains that Rorty's vision of interpretation concedes too much to the oppressive capitalist orders of the West. According to Lentricchia and other critics with Marxist sympathies, Rorty's "edifying" philosophy seeks to use language for no other purpose than that of "coping" with all that is imponderable and oppressive in our experience. "Rorty's vision of culture is the leisured vision of liberalism: the free pursuit of personal growth anchored in material security," explains Lentricchia.[11] As a Marxist, he rejects Rorty's passive perspectival view of human understanding and calls instead for critics to adopt an aggressive approach to matters of interpretation and justice. "Since interpretation always makes a difference," Lentricchia believes that "a Marxist literary intellectual . . . should engage in . . . the activity of interpretation, an activity which does

---

9. Rorty, *Consequences of Pragmatism* (Minneapolis: University of Minnesota Press, 1982), p. 142. The essay from which this quotation is taken, "Nineteenth-Century Idealism and Twentieth-Century Textualism" (pp. 139-59), is a provocative exploration of the relationship between philosophical idealism and the postromantic theory and practice of literature.

10. Rorty, *Contingency, Irony, and Solidarity* (Cambridge: Cambridge University Press, 1989), p. 20.

11. Lentricchia, *Criticism and Social Change* (Chicago: University of Chicago Press, 1985), p. 19.

not passively 'see,' . . . but constructs a point of view in its engagement with textual events, and in so constructing produces an image of history as social struggle, of, say, class struggle."[12]

Though Lentricchia tries to distance himself from Rorty, the difference between them seems slight. They are debating about the pace and mechanisms of change, not about the goals of the process. As both extol the liberating power of interpretation to construct or transform the world, they are giving voice to what might be called our postmodern ideology of desire. In the secular eschatology of desire, the kingdom to come at the end of history is a realm in which expressive individuals enjoy expansive and flexible freedom. That freedom is put into the service of the self's quest for expression, acquisition, and satisfaction. Rorty and Lentricchia speak for an entire class of people in today's humanities departments, those who are members of what Roger Kimball has called "a new academic establishment, the establishment of tenured radicals."[13]

In whatever form it takes, the contemporary fascination with perspective and interpretation in academic study is grounded in a deeply embedded Western faith in the power of language and the individual will. Perhaps the most important recent source of postmodern theories of the centrality of interpretation is Nietzsche, whose views on language have exercised an extraordinary influence in the contemporary academic world. In a fragment written in 1873, Nietzsche asked, "What, then, is truth?" It is, he answered himself,

> a mobile army of metaphors, metonyms, and anthropomorphisms —
> in short, a sum of human relations, which have been enhanced, transposed, and embellished poetically and rhetorically, and which after long use seem firm, canonical, and obligatory to a people: truths are illusions about which one has forgotten that this is what they are; metaphors which are worn out and without sensuous power; coins which have lost their pictures and now matter only as metal, no longer as coins.
>
> . . . To be truthful means using the customary metaphors — in moral terms: the obligation to lie according to a fixed convention, to lie herd-like in a style obligatory for all.[14]

12. Lentricchia, *Criticism and Social Change*, p. 11.
13. Kimball, "The Humanities at Williams," *The New Criterion* 8 (Jan. 1990): 43.
14. Friedrich Nietzsche, "On Truth and Lie in an Extra-Moral Sense," in *The Portable Nietzsche*, ed. and trans. Walter Kaufmann (New York: Penguin Books, 1976), pp. 46-47.

For Nietzsche and his ideological descendents, all knowledge is a matter of perspective; that is, it is an issue of interpretation, and all interpretations are lies. It would be impossible for matters to be otherwise, Nietzsche would argue, because the only relationship of language to reality, of words to things, is that which has been established by acts of violence and power and through the agencies of habit and convention. If we deceive ourselves by believing in a "deep sense of how things are which it is the duty of philosophers to spell out in language," argues Rorty, an honest analysis will show us that what we call "common sense" is nothing more than a "disposition to use the language of our ancestors, to worship the corpses of their metaphors."[15] Metaphors originally gain their status as "truth" through acts of force and deception by those who promulgate them; those metaphors retain their power for succeeding generations only because of the predominance of sloth, ignorance, and forgetfulness in the human species. Since all uses of language involve deception, Nietzsche claims, one can do nothing more than seek to dissemble with power and effectiveness. According to Nietzsche, one lies for the purpose of satisfying one's desires or deepest needs:

> In this condition [of intoxication] one enriches everything out of one's own abundance: what one sees, what one desires, one sees swollen, pressing, strong, overladen with energy. The man in this condition transforms things until they mirror his power — until they are reflections of his perfection. This *compulsion* to transform into the perfect is — art.[16]

If Nietzsche is a most prominent recent source for contemporary theories of interpretation, we may track other influences — including, of course, those that helped to shape the thought of Nietzsche — back through several centuries. We can begin with the seventeenth century, at which time the outlines of a general theory of hermeneutics began to emerge even as a skeptical but influential minority in the Western world began to lose its faith in classical theism. In one sense, the decline of theism made inevitable the rise of what Robert Solomon has called our modern "transcendental pretence" of the self.[17] In another sense, however, the

---

15. Rorty, *Contingency, Irony, and Solidarity*, p. 21.

16. Nietzsche, *Twilight of the Idols*, trans. R. J. Hollingdale (London: Penguin Books, 1968), p. 72.

17. Solomon, *Continental Philosophy Since 1750*, pp. 3-7.

promotion of the transcendental self was itself one of the most powerful forces that quickened the pace at which a theistic understanding of transcendence lost its power as a unifying cultural force.

To claim that our contemporary passion for interpretive theory started to develop in earnest only in the seventeenth and eighteenth centuries is not to argue, of course, that hermeneutics is in any way a new subject.[18] In Greek mythology, Hermes was the messenger who shuttled back and forth between the conclaves of the gods and the world of mortals, conveying word of the divine judgments on human affairs. In Jewish and Christian history, hermeneutical activity flourished long before the name of Hermes ever became attached to a formal discipline in the eighteenth century. In both the classical and the Christian worlds, hermeneutics as a practice involved the effort to translate what was taken to be a divine, authoritative word into language that would have power and relevance for a particular community.

As interpreters began to reflect self-consciously about their practices in the early modern era, however, this long established view of interpretation underwent a dramatic transformation. With traditional texts and beliefs being questioned in revolutionary ways at that time, interpreters could no longer assume the reliability or authority of the documents and doctrines they were trying to understand. One consequence was that, by the time of the romantic movement, hermeneutics had come to be associated with the search for ways of making discredited texts relevant to skeptical readers, rather than with the task of explaining an authoritative word or command. Instead of assuming the authority of the text in question, the romantic interpreter had to prove that authority by demonstrating the text's power to provide a coherent explanation of the experience of its audience. In many ways, romanticism in literature and theology was a dramatic effort to snatch the ethical, aesthetic, and emotional relics of the Christian faith from its metaphysical house, which was being consumed by the flames of skepticism.

In Christian proclamation under the influence of romanticism, the new understanding of hermeneutics led to a preoccupation with the status of the audience to be addressed with the gospel. Pressured to demonstrate

---

18. Rorty claims that hermeneutics is the rightful heir to dethroned epistemology: "Hermeneutics does not need a new epistemological paradigm, any more than liberal political thought requires a new paradigm of sovereignty. Hermeneutics, rather, is what we get when we are no longer epistemological" (*Philosophy and the Mirror of Nature*, p. 325).

the relevance of Christian faith to its "cultured despisers" (Schleiermacher's memorable phrase), many Christian interpreters in the Enlightenment and romanticism pared the biblical narrative into an appealing shape in their attempts to appeal to an educated and often cynical audience. Whether they were promoting a rational or a romantic God, these early modern interpreters were often willing to spend the capital of Christian belief in exchange for earning high interest in the marketplace of intellectual currency.

From a philosophical standpoint the romantic movement had its origins in the Cartesian revolution of the early modern period. It was Cartesianism that had prompted Western thinkers to believe that the isolated, unaided self had the power to discover truth through its own ratiocination. This Cartesian confidence in turn served to promote the utopian visions of human progress and happiness that would figure so prominently in eighteenth-century thought. It was when this utopianism suffered dramatic setbacks at the hands of epistemological skepticism and the French Revolution that the romantic understanding of hermeneutics was born.[19]

In the intellectual world, the romantic age bequeathed to us a psychological and grammatical understanding of the hermeneutical process; and in the culture as a whole, romanticism has played a key role in bringing about "the triumph of the therapeutic."[20] A therapeutic culture seeks to

---

19. "When the historical tradition in its entirety up to the present moment moved into a position of remoteness, the problem of hermeneutics entered intrinsically into the philosophic awareness of problems. This took place in virtue of the great breach in tradition brought about by the French Revolution and as a result of which European civilization splintered into national cultures" (Hans-Georg Gadamer, *Reason in the Age of Science,* trans. Frederick G. Lawrence [Cambridge: MIT Press, 1981], p. 97).

In the past few years, several significant books have attempted to trace the complex history of contemporary theories of the self and interpretation. The most impressive is Charles Taylor, *Sources of the Self: The Making of the Modern Identity* (Cambridge: Harvard University Press, 1989).

20. Philip Rieff, *The Triumph of the Therapeutic: Uses of Faith After Freud* (New York: Harper & Row, 1966):

Having broken the outward forms, so as to liberate, allegedly, the inner meaning of the good, the beautiful, and the true, the spiritualizers, who set the pace of Western cultural life from just before the beginning to a short time after the end of the nineteenth century, have given way now to their logical and historical successors, the psychologizers, inheritors of that dualist tradition which pits human nature against social order. . . .

By this time men may have gone too far, beyond the old deception of good and

promote the efforts of the autonomous self to discover fulfillment independent of the restraints of precedent and community. "Ours is the first cultural revolution fought to no other purpose than greater amplitude and richness of living itself," Philip Rieff argues.[21] In that cultural revolution, the theory of interpretation has come to serve as a most useful tool in therapeutic hands. If Rorty is right when he celebrates the complete triumph of romanticism in Western culture — "About two hundred years ago, the idea that truth was made rather than found began to take hold of the imagination of Europe"[22] — then *construction* has come to replace *discovery* as the basic metaphor of the mind's activity. In a world where all truth is made rather than found, thought has no task except that of constructing interpretations that may help us live contentedly in a world where nothing is at stake beyond the therapist's "manipulatable sense of well-being."[23]

In short, in the postmodern West, we have inherited from romanticism an inveterate belief in the power of human language to transform the world, or at least to alter radically our perspectives on that world. It is this legacy that has bequeathed to the contemporary academic community its faith in what might be called *verbal fiat* — its faith in the power of the human word to transform "things until they mirror [human] power," as Nietzsche put it. We have come to the point, as Robert Hughes says, where we appear to "want to create a sort of linguistic Lourdes, where evil and misfortune are dispelled by a dip in the waters of euphemism."[24]

Even though the epistemological revolutions of the seventeenth and eighteenth centuries gave rise to dramatic conceptions of the self's

---

evil, to specialize at last, wittingly, in techniques that are to be called, in the present volume, "therapeutic," with nothing at stake beyond a manipulatable sense of well-being. This is the unreligion of the age, and its master science. (Pp. 3, 13)

For further discussion of the therapeutic model, see also Rieff, *Fellow Teachers/of Culture and Its Second Death* (Chicago: University of Chicago Press, 1985) and *The Feeling Intellect: Selected Writings,* ed. Jonathan B. Imber (Chicago: University of Chicago Press, 1990); Alasdair MacIntyre, *After Virtue,* 2nd ed. (Notre Dame: University of Notre Dame Press, 1984); and Robert Bellah et al., *Habits of the Heart: Individualism and Commitment in American Life* (Berkeley: University of California Press, 1985).

21. Rieff, *The Triumph of the Therapeutic,* p. 241.
22. Rorty, *Contingency, Irony, and Solidarity,* p. 3.
23. Rieff, *Triumph of the Therapeutic,* p. 13.
24. Hughes, "The Fraying of America," *Time,* 3 Feb. 1992, p. 45.

power, by the end of the eighteenth century the rationalism and empiricism that had done so much to build up the Enlightenment self had themselves succumbed to the pressures of skepticism. In the ensuing crisis, which served as the genesis of the romantic movement, epistemology was dethroned by hermeneutics, and the "culture of interpretation" was born.

The Rationalist Background

As René Descartes sat down before a fire in a room in Germany in the winter of 1619, he was embarking upon the paradigmatic intellectual journey of modernity. Hoping to discover a secure foundation for intellectual endeavors in general, he could have had little idea of the extent to which his experience would eventually shape Western thought about interpretation in particular.

Descartes began his most famous intellectual exercise in isolation:

> The onset of winter held me up in quarters in which, finding no company to distract me, and having, fortunately, no cares or passions to disturb me, I spent the whole day shut up in a room heated by an enclosed stove, where I had complete leisure to meditate on my own thoughts.[25]

Descartes claimed that he had long before noticed that in matters of morals and conduct it was necessary to follow "opinions one knows to be very unsure," but in the search for truth, "I thought I ought to do just the opposite, and reject as being absolutely false everything in which I could suppose the slightest reason for doubt, in order to see if there did not remain after that anything in my belief which was entirely indubitable." Descartes aimed to strip away all certainties — everything from the information provided by his senses and by the mathematical "reasonings I had hitherto accepted as proofs" to the most basic distinctions between waking and sleeping. Left with nothing but the thought "that everything was false," Descartes "immediately . . . became aware that, while I decided thus to think that everything was false, it followed that I who thought thus must be something; and observing that this truth: *I think, therefore I*

25. Descartes, *Discourse on Method and The Meditations,* trans. F. E. Sutcliffe (Harmondsworth: Penguin Books, 1968), p. 35.

am, was so certain and so evident that all the most extravagant suppositions of the skeptics were not capable of shaking it."[26]

By unearthing the foundational *Cogito, ergo sum,* Descartes believed that he had provided humanity with the secure foundation needed for the construction of a grand dwelling-place for knowledge. As an implacable foe of Aristotelianism and Scholastic obscurity, Descartes was looking for nothing less than a universal method for discovering truth. He sought to replace the messiness of tradition and authority with the cleanliness of method; in the search for indubitable truth, Descartes took the inner resources of the human mind to be adequate in ways that he believed institutions and traditions could not be.[27]

A generation after Descartes, Benedict de Spinoza would apply Cartesian principles to the study of the Bible. As a Jew whose parents had fled to Holland to avoid religious persecution, Spinoza was acutely sensitive to the power of interpretive disputes in human affairs:

---

26. Descartes, *The Meditations,* pp. 53-54.

27. "In place of a specific plurality of *human* sciences, . . . we have one single knowledge: science, Science with a capital 'S,' Science such as the modern world was to worship it; Science in the pure state, radiating from unique and unparalleled geometric clarity, and that Science is the human mind" (Jacques Maritain, *The Dream of Descartes,* trans. Mabelle L. Andison [New York: Philosophical Library, 1944], p. 168). Paul Hazard, Stanley Jaki, and Helmut Thielicke have expressed similar reservations about the implications of the Cartesian revolution. See Hazard, *The European Mind: 1680-1715,* trans. J. Lewis May (Cleveland: Meridian Books, 1963), pp. 119-54; Jaki, *Angels, Apes, and Men* (Peru, IL: Sherwood Sugden and Co., 1984), pp. 11-40; and Thielicke, *Modern Faith and Thought,* trans. Geoffrey W. Bromiley (Grand Rapids: Eerdmans, 1990), pp. 51-78.

Walter Ong, however, points out the "utter inadequacy of the view which regards interest in method as stemming from Bacon and Descartes. These late writers on method were great explosive forces indeed, but the reason was less the size of the bombs which they manufactured than the size of the ammunition dumps, stocked by whole centuries of scholasticism, on which the bombs were dropped" (Ong, *Ramus, Method, and the Decay of Dialogue* [Cambridge: Harvard University Press, 1983], p. 230).

Stephen Toulmin has also recently argued that though Descartes was enormously influential, his work was not an isolated intellectual phenomenon: "The shift within philosophy, away from practical issues to an exclusive concern with the theoretical — by which local, particular, timely, and oral issues surrendered their centrality to issues that were ubiquitous, universal, timeless, and written — was no quirk of Descartes. All the protagonists of modern philosophy promoted theory, devalued practice, and insisted equally on the need to find foundations for knowledge that were clear, distinct, and certain" (Toulmin, *Cosmopolis: The Hidden Agenda of Modernity* [New York: Free Press, 1990], pp. 69-70).

As I marked the fierce controversies of philosophers raging in Church and State, the source of bitter hatred and dissension, the ready instruments of sedition and other ills innumerable, I determined to examine the Bible afresh in a careful, impartial, and unfettered spirit, making no assumptions concerning it, and attributing to it no doctrines, which I do not find clearly therein set down.

After completing his examination of the Bible, Spinoza declared that "I found nothing taught expressly by Scripture, which does not agree with our understanding, or which is repugnant thereto." "Thoroughly convinced" that "the Bible leaves reason absolutely free," he concluded that "Revelation and Philosophy stand on totally different footings" and "that Revelation has obedience for its sole object." Therefore, "in purpose no less than in foundation and method, [Revelation] stands entirely aloof from ordinary knowledge; each has its separate province, neither can be called the handmaid of the other."[28]

In the eighteenth century, the wedge driven by Spinoza would serve as a most useful tool for those who wished to widen the gap between faith and reason. They could follow Spinoza's lead and affirm that the Bible is irrelevant to natural history, because "the meaning of Scripture should be gathered from its own history, and not from the history of nature in general, which is the basis of philosophy."[29] Since "nothing taught expressly by Scripture" contradicts human understanding, then Scripture has no significant knowledge to impart. The claims made by the Bible do "not aim at explaining things by their natural causes, but only at narrating what appeals to the popular imagination," and they do "so in the manner best calculated to excite wonder, and consequently to impress the minds of the masses with devotion."[30] According to Spinoza and others who followed him in the Enlightenment, the Bible uses poetry and stories only to beguile the naive minds

28. Spinoza, *Theologico-Political Treatise*, trans. R. H. M. Elwes (New York: Dover Publications, 1951), pp. 8-10.

29. Spinoza, *Theologico-Political Treatise*, p. 195. "The interpretation of nature, he [Spinoza] says in the *Theologico-Political Treatise*, is to inspire a new hermeneutics ruled by the principle of the interpretation of Scripture by itself. This step of Spinoza's . . . marks a curious rebound of the interpretatio naturae upon the interpretation of Scripture: the former scriptural model is now called into question, and the new model is henceforward the interpretatio naturae" (Paul Ricoeur, *Freud and Philosophy: An Essay on Interpretation*, trans. Denis Savage [New Haven: Yale University Press, 1970], p. 25).

30. Spinoza, *Theologico-Political Treatise*, p. 90.

and pliant wills of the unenlightened masses. The truly enlightened thinker has no need of such devices. For such a person, rational and mathematical rigor will suffice in the search for truth.[31]

Even though he believed that the scriptural text has no unique knowledge to reveal, Spinoza argued that we should nevertheless study it with the same rigorous standards we use in exploring nature. That is, first we must examine the "nature and properties" of biblical language; then we are to arrange the disparate materials of the scriptural texts under specific topics, leaving a special place for passages that are "ambiguous or obscure"; and finally, we should attempt to become "acquainted with the life, the conduct, and the pursuits of [the biblical] author" and learn "what was the occasion, the time, the age, in which each book was written."[32]

Robert Grant notes that Spinoza's techniques closely resemble those espoused by modern handbooks to the study of the Bible. Celebrating clarity and rationality above all else, Spinoza's methods sidestep the thorny disputes of scriptural interpretation. According to Spinoza, such skirting of controversy is appropriate in matters of biblical interpretation, "for scripture has no authority over the interpreter's mind. It may govern his actions, but only if he is somewhat unintelligent. If he is truly rational, reason alone will guide his whole life."[33]

Spinoza thought that there was little chance that the right to absolute individual freedom would come to conflict with the need for civil order. "I conclude," Spinoza explained near the end of the preface to *A Theologico-Political Treatise,* "that everyone should be free to choose for himself the foundations of his creed . . . ; each would then obey God freely with his whole heart, while nothing would be publicly honoured save justice and charity."[34] Harboring no doubts that "the true aim of government is

---

31. "Convinced, as Descartes was, that human controversies and confusions are, in essence, a matter of failed communication, of definitions not made or adhered to with sufficient rigor, Spinoza aimed at a grammar of truth. Where we define our terms closely, where we relate these terms in consistent propositions, we shall be able to put questions to which God — or his echoing aggregate which is the World — will give valid reply" (George Steiner, *Extraterritorial: Papers on Literature and the Language Revolution* [New York: Atheneum, 1976], pp. 75-76).

32. Spinoza, *Theologico-Political Treatise,* p. 103.

33. Grant, *A Short History of the Interpretation of the Bible,* rev. ed. (New York: Macmillan, 1963), p. 150.

34. Spinoza, *Theologico-Political Treatise,* p. 10.

liberty," Spinoza was confident that in a "post-dogmatic" age, rationality would rule over human affairs and bring humanity a degree of happiness it had never before experienced.

As intellectual histories commonly point out, the flowering of rationalism in the decades after Descartes and Spinoza coincided with a decline in the authority of Christian belief for an educated minority. On many fronts, orthodoxy seemed to be threatened: Newtonian physics made conventional notions of miracle look implausible; the sufficiency of reason made revelation appear superfluous; and faith in universal, rational truth made the historical particularity of the gospel offensive. A hundred years or so after Spinoza, for example, only the slightest traces of Trinitarian theism seem to remain in the enlightened deism espoused by Voltaire:

> United in this principle [i.e., of divine Providence] with the rest of the universe he [the theist] embraces none of the sects which all contradict each other. His religion is the most ancient and the most widespread: for the simple adoration of a God has preceded all the systems of the world. He speaks a language which all peoples understand. . . . He believes that religion consists neither in the opinions of an unintelligible metaphysics, nor in vain appearances, but in worship and justice. To do good, that is his cult; to submit to God, that is his doctrine.[35]

In most instances in the eighteenth century, skepticism about Christian doctrine only served to strengthen the confidence that enlightened individuals placed in the rational or emotive self.[36] As Immanuel Kant argued in a

35. Voltaire, quoted in Franklin L. Baumer, *Modern European Thought: Continuity and Change in Ideas, 1600-1950* (New York: Macmillan, 1977), p. 195; see also pp. 140-255 in Baumer's book. In addition, see Karl Barth's wide-ranging, exuberant study of the period in his essay "Man in the Eighteenth Century," which serves as the opening chapter in his *Protestant Thought: From Rousseau to Ritschl,* trans. Brian Cozens (New York: Simon and Schuster, 1969), pp. 11-57.

36. "Eighteenth-century man was the man who could no longer remain ignorant of the significance of the fact that Copernicus and Galileo were right, that this vast and rich earth of his, the theatre of his deeds was not the centre of the universe, but a grain of dust amid countless others in this universe. . . . What did this really apocalyptic revolution in his picture of the universe mean for man? An unprecedented and boundless humiliation of man? No, said the man of the eighteenth century . . . ; no, man is all the greater for this, man is in the centre of all things, in a quite different sense, too, for he was able to discover this revolutionary truth by his own resources and to think it abstractly. . . . It is paradoxical and yet it is a fact that the answer to his humiliation was those philosophical systems of rationalism, empiricism and scepticism which made men even more

very influential essay, the Enlightenment made possible the establishment of that intellectual autonomy which was essential to the unfolding drama of culture. By releasing the self from slavish deference to transcendent authority, skepticism freed that self to draw from the fathomless well of its own untapped resources. According to Kant, the free and critical thinker is the person best suited to tap humankind's natural powers and prerogatives. "Enlightenment is man's leaving his self-caused immaturity," he wrote in 1784. "Immaturity is the incapacity to use one's intelligence without the guidance of another. . . . *Sapere Aude!* Have the courage to use your own intelligence! is therefore the motto of the enlightenment." A "man may postpone for himself" his inevitable enlightenment, but only for a short time. "To resign from such enlightenment altogether," however, is "to violate and to trample underfoot the sacred rights of mankind."[37]

The claims for liberty made by Spinoza, Kant, and others were like a tributary feeding into the stream of Protestant individualism, and the confluence of these sources produced a torrent of changes in Western views of interpretation. Hans Frei correctly observes that although very little of Protestant orthodoxy survived in rationalist religion, "one thing surely did: the antitraditionalism in scriptural interpretation of the one bolstered the antiauthoritarian stance in matters of religious meaning and truth of the other."[38] In other words, as orthodox Protestants fought to affirm the perspicuity of Scripture and the priesthood of all believers, they ironically found themselves allied with rationalists who decried the obscurity of allegorical interpretation. In a strange and strained alliance, those who strove on behalf of biblical faith were allied with those who promoted autonomous rationality; for both, the enemy was authority. For almost all biblical Protestants, it was not authority as a principle against which they rebelled but the unjust and unwise exercise of authority; for the rationalists, however, it was the very idea of an authority external to men and women that was offensive.

Under the twin influences of Protestantism and rationalism, "the direct reading of the 'plain' text" became the "common ground among all the differing hermeneutical schools" in the eighteenth century. "Indeed,"

---

self-confident. The geocentric picture of the universe was replaced as a matter of course by the anthropocentric" (Barth, *Protestant Thought*, pp. 15-16).

37. Kant, "What is Enlightenment?" trans. Carl J. Friedrich, in *The Philosophy of Kant*, ed. Carl J. Friedrich (New York: Modern Library, 1949), pp. 132, 137.

38. Frei, *The Eclipse of Biblical Narrative: A Study in Eighteenth and Nineteenth Century Hermeneutics* (New Haven: Yale University Press, 1974), p. 55.

according to Frei, "it was this common position that made *general* hermeneutics possible. No matter what the privileged, singular truth of the Bible, the meaning of the texts as such could be understood by following the rules of interpretation common to all written documents." In searching for a general hermeneutic, critics in the eighteenth century were hoping to discover methods of textual analysis that would yield the single, plain meaning of any work to which these methods were applied. The desire for a method of this kind became so strong that belief in multiple meanings for the same text — literal, figural, moral, and spiritual — "virtually disappeared as a major force."[39]

Throughout the eighteenth century, rationalist interpreters searched for the univocal meaning of the biblical text; given the spirit of that age, it is hardly surprising that a number of these interpreters discovered, of all things, that the Bible was a primer of rationalism and common sense. John Toland, for example, interpreted the Bible in precisely this manner in *Christianity Not Mysterious,* published in 1702. He argued that the clarity of the Bible's meaning confirms its truthfulness, for the gospel "affords the most illustrious Example of close and perspicuous Ratiocination conceivable. . . . What is revealed in Religion, as it is most useful and necessary, so it must and may be as easily comprehended, and found as consistent with our common Notions, as what we know of Wood or Stone, of Air, of Water, or the like."[40] We know the Bible is true because its meaning is plain to the simplest reader. In striving to make the mysterious comprehensible, Jesus taught nothing but pure morals and reasonable worship, a truth "stripp'd bare" of all symbolic and ceremonial excesses.

In a similar vein, almost three-quarters of a century after Toland, Hermann Samuel Reimarus was to argue that in the history of the church neither miracles nor mysteries had been important in establishing the unique authority of Jesus. Instead, Jesus won the hearts of men and women by appealing purely to "a reason which operates and has operated at all times so naturally, that we need no miracle to make everything comprehensible and clear. This is the real mighty wind that so quickly wafted all the people together. This is the true original language that performs the miracles."[41]

---

39. Frei, *The Eclipse of Biblical Narrative,* pp. 55-56.
40. Toland, quoted in Basil Willey, *The Eighteenth Century Background: Studies on the Idea of Nature in the Thought of the Period* (Boston: Beacon Press, 1961), p. 9.
41. Reimarus, *Fragments,* trans. Ralph S. Fraser, ed. Charles H. Talbert (Philadelphia: Fortress Press, 1970), p. 269.

The rational God of Toland and Reimarus relied upon innocent, benevolent humans to act as his earthly agents. With men and women proving to be such capable servants, God had little need of a sacrificial Jesus who would die for the sins of humankind. Indeed, because the Christ of the cross was an embarrassment for the enlightened temperament, individuals such as Thomas Jefferson labored to disentangle the simple Jesus ("the greatest of all the reformers of the depraved religion of his own country") from the web of Jewish superstition and Greek sophistry that had held him fast for centuries. "Abstracting what is really his [Jesus'] from the rubbish in which it is buried, easily distinguished by its lustre from the dross of his biographers, and as separable from that as the diamond from the dunghill," wrote Jefferson, "we have the outlines of a system of the most sublime morality which has ever fallen from the lips of man." Jefferson's hope was that the plain and rational sense of Jesus would "in time . . . effect a quiet euthanasia of the heresies of bigotry and fanaticism which have so long triumphed over human reason" and have wickedly afflicted humankind. "But this work is to be begun by winnowing the grain from the chaff of the historians of his life."[42] To that end, on two occasions Jefferson attempted to snatch "the diamond from the dunghill" by pulling out of the Gospels only those sayings of Jesus that he took to be consistent with a rational and benevolent understanding of that first-century Nazarene.

Farewell to Knowledge and Benevolence: Kant and the Theory of Art

Even as Jefferson was writing his letters lauding the rational self, the moral sense, and the harmless vestigial Christianity he embraced, some thinkers in western Europe could feel the tremors beginning to shake the Enlightenment ground of confidence in the self. And to be sure, by the end of the eighteenth century twin revolutions — the Kantian epistemological revolution and the French political revolution — had produced cracks in the pillars supporting the edifice of the Cartesian self.

From Kant and David Hume, the challenge to self-certainty came as an attack upon claims about the mind's ability to apprehend reality, the *thing-in-itself,* directly. The empiricists and rationalists had taken their

---

42. Jefferson to William Short, 31 October 1819, in *Thomas Jefferson: Writings,* ed. Merrill D. Peterson (New York: Library of America, 1984), p. 1431.

understanding of nature and the human mind to constitute indubitable knowledge of the primary structures of reality. With Kant especially, however, that confidence was shaken. *The Critique of Pure Reason* pressed a claim that has since become a commonplace of intellectual life; it is the argument that the self does not so much *discover* preexisting order in the world as it *projects* order creatively upon the world:

> Since . . . nature's conformity to law rests on the necessary linking of phenomena in experience, without which we could not know any object of the world of the senses, in other words, such conformity rests on the original laws of the intellect, it sounds strange at first, but it is none the less true when I say in respect of these laws of the intellect: *The intellect does not derive its laws (a priori) from nature but prescribes them to nature.*[43]

Though it disabled the rationalism and empiricism of the eighteenth century, the Kantian revolution did not cripple the self that had moved under the power of Enlightenment philosophy and science. After Kant, that self would soar with new wings — those of the recently discovered faculty of the imagination. It is important, however, to remember that, at least for Kant, this active, creative self was not an isolated "I" but the "transcendental ego" of humanity imposing its forms upon the random facts of experience. What is *given* to humanity is the random information of the senses; the transcendental ego must supply the ordered meaning missing in the facts. Although some of Kant's admirers took his thought in directions he would have found appalling, he had already cleared a path for them in his work. By placing the active, knowing self at the center of things, he paved the way for more radical views, which proclaimed the individual will's unbounded capacity to impress its desires upon reality. In the arts in particular, Kantianism led to the development of a dramatically new conception of the creative spirit. "It was not until Kant that the realm of aesthetics assumed its own right," Ernst Behler notes. "Romanticism brought about a new appreciation of artistic creation — a glorification of creative imagination — and made of the artist a spokesman for the godhead, an orphic seer, and prophetic priest."[44]

Kant's redefinition of art would prove to be extraordinarily influential. Even as he celebrated artistic experience, Kant remained clear about

43. Kant, "Prolegomena to Every Future Metaphysics That May Be Presented as a Science," trans. Carl J. Friedrich, in *The Philosophy of Kant*, p. 91.

44. Behler, in his foreword to *German Romantic Criticism*, ed. A. Leslie Willson (New York: Continuum, 1982), pp. viii-ix.

its limits. He held that when we produce works of art, we are creating alternate worlds in which we hope to discover the purpose and order missing in our "real" world. As much as we need the delights and consolations of art, honesty demands that we always keep its essential triviality in mind. The world projected in a work of art is nothing more and nothing less than the product of the human imagination, and as such, it can never be an accurate representation of reality.

Out of Kant's thinking developed the now familiar distinction between "fine art" and the "useful arts." In the useful arts, we employ works of art to assist in our various activities. We sing hymns to God; we create images of the saints to instill devotion in the hearts of believers; or we make attractive objects to hold and serve our daily food. In contrast to these tools that we use, however, works of fine art exist for no purpose beyond themselves. Like God or moral absolutes, the products of the fine arts are meant to be contemplated and admired in themselves and not as means to other ends. While human beings pursue all other objects for the purposes of mastery and use, they may create and appreciate art with no end in sight but that of unselfish delight. Works of art are to be celebrated, because they provide us with a very different *perspective* upon human experience than the one we acquire through our customary ways of seeing and using the world around us.

If Kant's views do not at first glance appear to be provocative, that is only because the Kantian understanding of epistemology and aesthetics has become so dominant as to seem commonsensical. The transformation of thought that took place at the end of the eighteenth century represents one of the most dramatic revolutions in the history of Western culture. It involved a change from the mimetic theory of art — which had held sway in Western culture for more than two millennia — to the romantic theory of art as expression. Rather than being a *mirror* held up to nature, art became a *lamp* illuminating an otherwise darkened world; instead of attempting to *re*-present reality, the artist now sought to *express* himself or herself — that is, to press out to the surface whatever was within the self.[45]

While the shift from a mimetic to an expressive theory of art was in itself revolutionary, the creation of the "fine arts" also represented a dramatic change in thinking about the nature and purpose of art. By stressing the *disinterested* nature of the creation and appreciation of art, Kant helped to transfer to works of art properties that formerly had belonged to God alone

45. The classic study of this change is M. H. Abrams, *The Mirror and the Lamp: Romantic Theory and the Critical Tradition* (London: Oxford University Press, 1953).

in Christian theism. A primary source in the Western tradition for Kant's distinctions was St. Augustine's *On Christian Doctrine.* In that work, Augustine made a clear distinction between those things that are to be *used* and those that are to be *enjoyed.* The things that are to be *enjoyed* "make us blessed," while those that are to be *used* are intended by God to "help and . . . sustain us as we move towards blessedness." Because "to enjoy something is to cling to it with love for its own sake," our mistake, Augustine alleges, is that we all too often enjoy those things that we should use.

To illustrate this difference, Augustine asks us to imagine ourselves as wanderers who are miserable because we have strayed from home. To return to the homeland we were created to *enjoy,* we would *use* "vehicles for land and sea." But if we came to delight in the amenities intended for our use, Augustine argues, we would become "entangled in a perverse sweetness" and thus would alienate ourselves from our true home and our true blessedness. For all of humanity, "the things which are to be enjoyed are the Father, the Son, and the Holy Spirit, a single Trinity, a certain supreme thing common to all who enjoy it."[46]

In his aesthetic theory Kant let works of art themselves assume the place assigned to God in Augustine's theism. By making works of art ends in themselves, things to be *enjoyed* in and of themselves rather than things to be *used,* Kant was instrumental in ushering in the distinctly modern era in which, for an educated elite, art would come to serve as a surrogate for religion. In the next chapter, we will see how poets, novelists, and theorists in the nineteenth century greatly expanded the beachhead secured by Kant as they attempted to capture the modern world on behalf of the arts.

As poets and artists of all kinds labored to create a world ruled by artistic activity, they were following the lead of Kant, who believed that in art he had found a refuge for enlightened persons wishing to satisfy their spiritual desires while retaining their philosophical integrity. Kant held that in aesthetic experience a person may acquire the benefits of skepticism while still receiving the satisfactions of spirituality. It would be difficult to overestimate the influence of Kant on Western thinking about morality and the arts in the nineteenth and twentieth centuries. In Kantian epistemology the foundations were laid for postmodern perspectivism, and in Kantian aesthetics the plans were drawn up for the temple that many would try to build for the arts in the modern world.

---

46. Augustine, *On Christian Doctrine,* trans. D. W. Robertson, Jr. (Indianapolis: Liberal Arts Press, 1958), pp. 9-10.

CHAPTER 3   *The Liberation of the Spirit:*
Art and the Inner Perspective

THE WORK OF Immanuel Kant anticipated the triumph of perspectivism by effecting a profound shift in the understanding of the nature of knowledge. For almost two centuries before Kant, the twin movements of rationalism and empiricism had sought to answer vexing questions about what the isolated self could know of the truth and how it could come to know it. Whether in the rationalism of Descartes or in the empiricism of Francis Bacon, the philosophical traditions of the early modern period depicted the self as a *discoverer* of truth. The truth was to be found either within the inner regions of the mind and spirit or in the vast phenomena of the natural world. In any case, the duty of the mind was to uncover and document truths already *out there* in the world. With his claim that the mind helps to construct and constitute the very truths in which it believes, Kant gave systematic expression to the insights of a small number of poets and philosophers of his day. And by expressing those insights in a compelling manner, he helped to give birth to perspectivism and the culture of interpretation.

If Kant almost single-handedly summarized Enlightenment epistemology and aesthetics and paved the way for modernity, the French Revolution had similar consequences in the realms of politics and morals. Like no other event of the period, that vast exercise in transformation, purification, and terror transfixed the people of western Europe. It especially riveted the attention of artists and philosophers. Writing more than two decades after the fact, an Englishman described the

53

astonishment that had filled the hearts of many who watched the Revolution unfold:

> Every faculty of the mind was awakened, every feeling raised to an intenseness of interest, every principle and passion called into super-human exertions. At one moment, all was hope and joy and rapture; the corruption and iniquity of ages seemed to vanish like a dream; the unclouded heavens seemed once more to ring with an exulting chorus of peace on earth and good-will to men; and the spirit of a mighty and puissant nation . . . seemed rising in native majesty to draw new in-spiration from the rejoicing heavens.[1]

Simon Schama explains that many sympathetic observers of the Revolution "were fascinated by seismic violence, by the great primordial eruptions which geologists now said were not part of a single Creation, but which happened periodically in geological time." The events of the Revolution proved to be, "to borrow from Burke, both sublime and terrible."[2] Out of this cataclysm, many poets and philosophers anticipated nothing less than the dramatic renewal of the human race. In the words of the poet Robert Southey, "Old things seemed passing away, and nothing was dreamt of but the regeneration of the human race."[3] Indeed, in one sense, the whole of nineteenth-century literature, both in England and on the Continent, reads like a commentary on the rise and fall of ideals inspired by the revolution in France.

In an attempt to understand the impact of the French Revolution, we might consider the case of a then obscure English artist, poet, and printer who became caught up in the tumultuous events of the day. In 1794, William Blake put out a collection of his own work, entitled *Songs of Innocence and of Experience*. This edition was a dramatically expanded version of his *Songs of Innocence*, which Blake had published five years before. In the new work, the "songs of experience" were clearly distinguished from their earlier counterparts by a tone of irony and indignation. While the poems of 1789 had celebrated simple joys and undiminished innocence, the later lyrics expressed deep anger at injustice and profound hopes for the future of the liberated human spirit.

---

1. Thomas Noon Taulford, quoted in M. H. Abrams, *Natural Supernaturalism: Tradition and Revolution in Romantic Literature* (New York: W. W. Norton, 1971), pp. 329-30.

2. Schama, *Citizens: A Chronicle of the French Revolution* (New York: Alfred A. Knopf, 1989), pp. 860-61.

3. Southey, quoted in Abrams, *Natural Supernaturalism*, p. 330.

Each set of songs — the "Songs of Innocence" and the "Songs of Experience" — has an introductory poem, and the contrast between the two poems is enlightening. In the introduction to the "Songs of Innocence," the poet is depicted as a happy fellow "piping down the valleys wild / Piping songs of pleasant glee," having learned to write "my happy songs / Every child may joy to hear." The poet is a pleasant minstrel freely dispensing his melodious joy. The introduction to the "Songs of Experience," however, has a sharper tone and offers a radically different view of the poet. The amiable piper of innocence has become the cynical bard of experience:

> Hear the voice of the Bard!
> Who Present, Past, & Future sees
> Whose ears have heard
> The Holy Word,
> That walk'd among the ancient trees.

For Blake, the bard calls the people to repentance and renewal. He shows them how to reclaim the power and potential that are rightfully theirs, and his vision is one in which earthly life has been awakened to its proper, restored grandeur:

> O Earth O Earth return!
> Arise from out the dewy grass;
> Night is worn,
> And the morn
> Rises from the slumberous mass.[4]

Although there is little conclusive evidence to explain the revolutionary change in tone between the *Songs of Innocence* (1789) and the *Songs of Innocence and of Experience* (1794), some things are clear. One is that in the five years separating the volumes, the dramatic events of the French Revolution had unfolded: the Bastille had been stormed, the Republic declared, and the king beheaded. These revolutionary events seem to have galvanized Blake as a radical, and throughout western Europe political realities seemed to have altered precipitously. For Blake, as for a number of other writers of his day, the American and French revolutions repre-

4. Blake, *Songs of Innocence and of Experience,* in *The Poetry and Prose of William Blake,* ed. David V. Erdman (Garden City, NY: Doubleday, 1965), pp. 7, 18.

sented the dawning of a radically new day in human history.[5] It appeared that the millennial period that had been anticipated for so long in Christian history was about to be ushered in through cunning acts of rebellion.

Between 1791 and 1793, Blake also wrote the verses and etched the plates for a long poem called *America,* which celebrated the transforming power of the American and French revolutions.[6] In lines resonating with the rhythms and images of the Bible, *America* proclaims the dawning of a new order:

> The morning comes, the night decays, the watchmen
>   leave their stations;
> The grave is burst, the spices shed, the linen wrapped up;
> The bones of death, the cov'ring clay, the sinews shrunk & dry'd.
> Reviving shake, inspiring move, breathing! awakening!
> Spring like redeemed captives when their bonds & bars are burst,
> Let the slave grinding at the mill, run out into the field:
> Let him look up into the heavens & laugh in the bright air;
> Let the inchained soul shut up in darkness and in sighing,
> Whose face has never seen a smile in thirty weary years;
> Rise and look out, his chains are loose, his dungeon doors are open.
> And let his wife and children return from the opressors scourge;
> They look behind at every step & believe it is a dream.
> Singing. The Sun has left his blackness, & has found
>   a fresher morning
> And the fair Moon rejoices in the clear & cloudless night;
> For Empire is no more, and now the Lion & Wolf shall cease.[7]

Perhaps the most memorable account of the days of the French Revolution was written by Blake's contemporary, William Wordsworth.

---

5. For a fuller explanation of the central importance of the American and French revolutions for romantic literature, see Harold Bloom, *The Visionary Company: A Reading of English Romantic Poetry,* rev. ed. (Ithaca: Cornell University Press, 1971), and Abrams, *Natural Supernaturalism.*

6. "Blake etched *America* in the years 1791-93, which encompassed the early period of the French Revolution when Blake, like Wordsworth, Coleridge, and other enthusiastic poets and intellectuals, interpreted the Revolution as initiating the millennium that had been prophesied in the apocalyptic books of the Bible" (*The Norton Anthology of English Literature,* 4th ed., ed. M. H. Abrams et al. [New York: W. W. Norton, 1979], vol. 2, p. 63).

7. Blake, *America,* in *The Poetry and Prose of William Blake,* p. 52.

In the eleventh book of his autobiographical masterpiece *The Prelude,* Wordsworth tells of the events of his journey to France in 1791-92 and describes the unbounded hope fostered by the radical political developments of that time:

> Bliss was it in that dawn to be alive,
> But to be young was very Heaven! O times,
> In which the meagre, stale, forbidding ways
> Of custom, law, and statute took at once
> The attraction of a country in romance!
> When Reason seemed the most to assert her rights
> When most intent on making of herself
> A prime enchanter — to assist the work,
> Which then was going forward, in her name!
> Not favoured spots alone, but the whole Earth,
> The beauty wore of promise — that which sets
> (To take an image which was felt, no doubt,
> Among the bowers of Paradise itself)
> The budding rose above the rose full blown.
> What temper at the prospect did not wake
> To happiness unthought of?[8]

As optimistic as this poem sounds, its confidence is entirely a matter of the past. That is, Wordsworth writes of a time when it *had been* bliss to be alive and to be young *had been* "very Heaven." In the years separating the events discussed in the poem (the early days of the French Revolution) and the time of its composition (more than a decade later), several developments had devastated Wordsworth and others who had had revolutionary hopes. The apocalyptic promises of the Revolution had given way to what Thomas Carlyle called the relentless *systole-diastole* of the guillotine in the Reign of Terror, and those excesses in turn led to reaction in England and to the rise of Napoleon on the Continent. In 1817, the poet Percy Bysshe Shelley surveyed the years since the early stages of the Revolution and described them as an "age of despair." The Revolution had aroused in "every bosom" such hopes "of unmingled good as it was impossible to realize," and disgust with the Revolution and with Napoleonic tyranny had caused a spirit of "gloom and melancholy" to have "tainted the literature of the age."

8. Wordsworth, *The Prelude,* ed. J. C. Maxwell (Baltimore: Penguin Books, 1971), p. 440.

It is an experiment on the temper of the public mind as how far a thirst for a happier condition of moral and political society survives among the enlightened and refined the tempests which have shaken the age in which we live.[9]

Shelley hoped to keep alive the revolutionary desire for "a happier condition of moral and political society" and to defend the role of poetry at a time of political disillusionment and technological advancement. With those two purposes in mind, he composed "A Defence of Poetry" in 1821. According to Shelley, poets are essential to the health and stability of societies because they "imagine and express" the "indestructible order" behind all things. Anyone can observe the disparities and diversity of life on the surface of things; only the poet, however, can discern the invisible order beneath all apparent realities:

But Poets, or those who imagine and express this indestructible order, are not only the authors of language and of music, of the dance, and architecture, and statuary and painting; they are the institutors of laws, and the founders of civil society and the inventors of the arts of life, and the teachers who draw into a certain propinquity with the beautiful and the true, that partial apprehension of the agencies of the invisible world which is called religion. . . . A Poet participates in the eternal, the infinite, and the one.[10]

Shelley claims that all knowledge can be traced back to its origins in the imaginative work of individuals who perceive the *ideal* order undergirding the *apparent* disorder of everyday experience. But unlike Blake's "bard," Shelley's poet is not a revolutionary activist leading the charge against the barricades; rather, the poet guides the course of events behind the scenes by creating and detecting the forms that all human endeavors require. "Poets are the hierophants of an unapprehended inspiration," Shelley writes at the very end of "A Defence of Poetry." They are the mirrors of the "gigantic shadows [of] futurity," the "trumpets" that sing to battle, and the "influence which is moved not, but moves." Though few men or women realize it, the influence of the poets is powerful and pervasive. "Poets are the unacknowledged legislators of the World."[11]

9. Shelley, quoted in Abrams, *Natural Supernaturalism,* p. 328.

10. Shelley, "A Defence of Poetry," in *Prose of the Romantic Period,* ed. Carl Woodring (Boston: Houghton Mifflin, 1961), p. 491.

11. Shelley, "A Defence of Poetry," p. 513.

Although Shelley made sweeping claims for the power and significance of poetry, his defense represented an unmistakable humbling of the
poet, especially in light of the dramatic claims of romanticism in its earliest
stages. Shelley's modesty about the immediate efficacy of literature, however, would come to characterize Western thinking about the arts in the
later decades of the nineteenth century. Whether they assumed a moral or
an aesthetic approach, after the collapse of the French Revolution romantic
and Victorian theorists would be diffident in making their claims about
the power of literature to alter the course of history.[12]

For example, we find the romantic poet and critic Samuel Taylor
Coleridge, chastened by the disintegration of revolutionary hopes, defining
poetry as "that species of composition, which is opposed to works of science,
by proposing for its *immediate* object pleasure, not truth."[13] Saddened by "the
detestable maxims and correspondent measures of the late French despotism,"
which he attributed to the "poison-tree" or "magic rod of fanaticism,"
Coleridge sought to salvage the imagination by providing it with a safe haven
where it could exercise its powers without endangering the peace of the world
through its violent excesses. In a famous definition, Coleridge wrote, "The
primary IMAGINATION I hold to be the living Power and prime Agent of
all human Perception, and as a repetition in the finite mind of the eternal act
of creation in the infinite I AM." The imagination "dissolves, diffuses,
dissipates, in order to re-create." It is "essentially *vital,* even as all objects (*as*
objects) are essentially fixed and dead." For Coleridge, the French Revolution
revealed the destructive potential of the imagination when human beings,
rather than the verbal elements of a poem, were the objects it was dissolving,
diffusing, and dissipating. Only when it stands apart from science and history
can the imagination work its magic without its terror.[14]

In what is the decisive strategic retreat of romantic theory, Coleridge
and others after him conceded the question of truth to philosophic and

12. "Faith in an apocalypse by revelation had been replaced by faith in an apocalypse
by revolution, and this now gave way to faith in an apocalypse by imagination or cognition.
In the ruling two-term frame of Romantic thought, the mind of man confronts the old
heaven and earth and possesses within itself the power, if it will but recognize and avail
itself of the power, to transform them into a new heaven and new earth, by means of a
total revolution of consciousness" (Abrams, *Natural Supernaturalism,* p. 334).

13. Coleridge, *The Collected Works of Samuel Taylor Coleridge,* vol. 7: *Biographia
Literaria,* ed. James Engell and W. Jackson Bate (Princeton: Princeton University Press,
1983), part 2, p. 13.

14. Coleridge, *Biographia Literaria,* part 1, pp. 199, 197, 304.

scientific discourse. They attempted to salvage the imagination by celebrating its power to induce pleasure; they promoted poetry as an alternative
to the ways of knowing and experiencing offered by reason and science.
As a result of this key concession, later artists and critics would struggle
to find a place for literature and the imagination in the very world from
which key Enlightenment and romantic thinkers had banished it. In one
sense, the defenders of literature have been struggling for two centuries to
make grand that which their tradition has already rendered trivial.

In keeping with this reduced view of the power of literature, the
Victorian poet and critic Matthew Arnold maintained a healthy skepticism
about the ability of literature or criticism to shape immediately the development of events in political, economic, or moral life. In "The Function of
Criticism at the Present Time," Arnold specifically faults the French Revolution for having drawn men of ideas out of the study and onto the
barricades. It is "a very remarkable thing," Arnold acknowledges, that in the
case of France at the time of the Revolution "a whole nation should have
been penetrated with an enthusiasm for pure reason, and with an ardent zeal
for making its prescriptions triumph." But however remarkable it was, the
French Revolution erred, and so did those writers who were swept along by
its passions. Arnold quotes Joseph Joubert, a French moralist — "Force and
right are the governors of this world; force till right is ready" — and argues
that the Revolution made "the grand error" of "quitting the intellectual
sphere and rushing furiously into the political sphere."[15] As a result, the
Revolution produced no lasting intellectual legacy. Indeed, in its excesses, it
made inevitable a violent intellectual reaction against itself and thus served
to set back the very work of reason it had sought so earnestly to advance.

From this failure, Arnold draws a clear lesson for literature and
criticism. If the world is not ready for the rule of right, then the rule of
force must be tolerated for a while, he argues. Yet even as force is being
tolerated, the work of reason will go on quietly and unobtrusively. Shunning specific political commitments and practical concerns, criticism will
pursue disinterestedness "by resolutely following the law of its own nature,
which is to be a free play of the mind on all subjects which it touches."
Arnold grants that by choosing a "very subtle and indirect action," criticism may seem to condemn "itself to a slow and obscure work." That is
how it must be, he says. Because "the mass of mankind will never have

15. Arnold, "The Function of Criticism at the Present Time," in *Prose of the Victorian
Period*, ed. William Buckler (Boston: Houghton Mifflin, 1958), pp. 425-26.

any ardent zeal for seeing things as they are," it is only by the "small circle [of disinterested critics] resolutely doing its own work that adequate ideas will ever get current at all." By undertaking *"a disinterested endeavor to learn and propagate the best that is known and thought in the world,"* the critic will "help us for the future" and provide an answer to the question, "What will nourish us in growth towards perfection?"[16]

Thus, instead of the apocalyptic transformation of everyday life anticipated at the height of romanticism and its attendant political revolutions, we find in Arnold the promise of a gradual amelioration of the human condition and the slow growth of the rule of reason in human affairs. As the critical mind studies the monuments of past culture, it will eventually discover in "the best that is known and thought" those prescriptions of reason that are "absolute, unchanging, of universal validity."[17] With due deliberation, the critic will then seek to translate the universal truths into terms that "the mass of mankind" can find intelligible and compelling. If for Shelley the poet is the unacknowledged legislator of the world, then for Arnold the critic is the unappreciated interpreter of all that the poets have said, the one whose task it is to train men and women in the ways of "right" so that history might leave "force" behind forever.

Though Arnold's critical humanism has had an undeniably strong influence upon the development of the study of literature and culture, it does not represent the only significant response to the collapse of romantic hope. While criticism in England remained concerned about the ethical possibilities of the study of literature, in France a significantly different emphasis began to emerge. Instead of seeking ways to help literature do its cultural work of revolution slowly and subtly, several French writers simply abandoned the goal of transforming history through the creation and criticism of literature.

For instance, Gustave Flaubert, the author of *Madame Bovary* and *The Sentimental Education,* argued that literature accomplishes nothing specific in human affairs. As he wrote in a letter in 1857, "no great genius has come to final conclusions; no great book ever does so, because humanity itself is forever on the march and can arrive at no goal." Blake and Wordsworth had anticipated nothing less than a millennial redemption of history; Shelley and Arnold foresaw a more gradual, yet inevitable, progress of reason. For Flaubert, however, all such dreams of historical progress,

16. Arnold, "The Function of Criticism," pp. 429, 433, 440-41.
17. Arnold, "The Function of Criticism," p. 425.

sudden or slow, seemed groundless. Referring to the "perpetual evolution of humanity," he wrote: "I abominate all those frames which men try to cram it into by main force, all the formulas by which they define it, and all the plans they devise for it. Democracy is no more man's last word than was slavery, or feudalism, or monarchy."[18]

Flaubert believed that in contrast to the random course of history, literature offered a unique experience of order and perfection. "What I should like to write," he explained in 1852, "is a book about nothing, a book dependent on nothing external, which would be held together by the strength of its style . . . ; a book which would have almost no subject." He claimed to be seeking in his art nothing less than the establishment of "the axiom that there is no such thing as subject, style in itself being an absolute manner of seeing things."[19]

Thus, as Flaubert envisions it, literature becomes a refuge for the person of sensitive longings and frustrated hopes. Literature uniquely embodies the beauty and form missing in nature and society, and because the well-crafted work of literature is impervious to the passage of time, it can impart the comforting illusion of immutability. Artists are godlike in their powers, and their work is the good creation in which enlightened individuals are privileged to live. In Flaubert's own words, "an artist must be in his work like God in creation, invisible and all-powerful; he should be everywhere felt, but nowhere seen."[20]

The theories elaborated by Coleridge, Arnold, and Flaubert have set the course for the study of literature over the past century. Those who have been committed to the Flaubertian position have tended to be politically conservative. Many of the masters of modernism — including T. S. Eliot, Ezra Pound, and William Butler Yeats — were to varying degrees attracted to fascism, for it seemed to embody in the political realm the modernist ideals for poetry as a stabilizing, conserving force in the midst of what Eliot termed "the immense panorama of futility and anarchy which is contemporary history."[21] And in America, the participants in the Southern Agrarian movement — such as Cleanth Brooks, Allen Tate, and Robert

18. Flaubert to Mlle. Leroyer de Chantepie (1857), in *The Modern Tradition: Backgrounds of Modern Literature,* ed. Richard Ellmann and Charles Feidelson, Jr. (New York: Oxford University Press, 1965), pp. 72-73.

19. Flaubert to Louise Colet (1852), in *The Modern Tradition,* pp. 126-27.

20. Flaubert to Mlle. Leroyer de Chantepie (1857), in *The Modern Tradition,* p. 132.

21. Eliot, "Ulysses, Order, and Myth," in *Selected Poetry and Prose of T. S. Eliot,* ed. Frank Kermode (London: Faber & Faber, 1975), p. 177.

Penn Warren — offered in the New Criticism a way of interpreting literature that yielded brilliant insights into the complexities of the human spirit yet issued few challenges to the established political order.

Those who have sided with the views of Matthew Arnold, on the other hand, have been more prone to see literature as a means of transforming culture and society. By extending the reach and rule of reason, those of the Arnoldian temper claim that literature may eventually bring about the rule of *right* in place of *force*. To this tradition belong many of the great Victorian novelists, such as Charles Dickens, George Eliot, and Anthony Trollope, and twentieth-century critics of the likes of F. R. Leavis and Lionel Trilling. While those in the school of Flaubert had grudgingly concluded that "force" will forever be the "governor of this world," because "right" will never be obvious enough or powerful enough to be "ready" to govern, Arnold and others strove to maintain a faith in the power of the human will to redeem the course of human history.

"The history of the world is none other than the progress of the consciousness of freedom," G. W. F. Hegel proclaimed in the introduction to his *Philosophy of History*.[22] When he made that claim in the early nineteenth century, Hegel was living in the shadow of the French and American political revolutions and the romantic revolution in literature and philosophy. As we have seen, many shifts of emphasis took place in the course of two centuries within the overall paradigm of the artist and critic as combatants in the battle for human liberation. In our survey of this period, we have moved from the image of the poet as prophet (Blake, Wordsworth) proclaiming the demise of the present order and the coming of paradise, through the muted optimism of Shelley's claim that poets are "the unacknowledged legislators of the World," and finally to the options represented by Arnold and Flaubert in the second half of the last century — the belief that the criticism of literature may yet humanize culture ever so gradually, and finally the abandonment of the idea of progress altogether.

The Stream of Inwardness

The dramatic changes taking place in politics, philosophy, and literature in eighteenth- and nineteenth-century Europe coincided with major

22. Hegel, quoted in Peter Singer, *Hegel* (Oxford: Oxford University Press, 1983), p. 11.

changes in biblical interpretation. Indeed, in many ways radical seventeenth-century hermeneutical practices helped to prepare the way for the romantic revolution in literature and philosophy. Long before Wordsworth, Blake, or Emerson began to tout the virtues of imaginative inwardness, Protestant radicals had eagerly championed the Christ who dwells exclusively within the human heart.

By emphasizing the allegorical significance of Christian language for the inner life, the radical Protestant interpreters of the seventeenth century in their own way helped to bring about what Hans Frei has called "the great reversal" in hermeneutics as much as Spinoza did with his rationalist analysis of biblical truth. As the Puritan revolutionaries and Pietists were redefining the Bible as a primer of human inwardness, skeptical interpreters were following the earlier lead of Spinoza in abandoning their faith in the power of biblical narrative to comprehend human experience and to serve as "the adequate depiction of the common and inclusive world." By the end of the eighteenth century, "the great reversal had taken place; interpretation [had become] a matter of fitting the biblical story into another world with another story rather than incorporating that world into the biblical story."[23]

In Protestant England and New England, the typological interpretation of the Scriptures played a particularly crucial role in bringing about the "great reversal" and the romantic revolution. Typological exegesis stresses the manner in which a person or event in the sacred past prophetically anticipates a present reality and imparts to that reality a special spiritual significance. This kind of reading is crucial to the development of a narrative of sacred history. To be sure, typological interpretation was hardly new in the seventeenth century, for it was rooted in the very earliest practices of the Christian church. The Bible itself makes extensive use of typology in those Gospels and Epistles that view the Old Testament saints and the nation of Israel as prophetic forerunners of God's full revelation in Christ. In the history of the church, many *types* have been seen as pointers to Christ, the *antitype* who stands "at the center of history, casting His shadow forward to the end of time as well as backward across the Old Testament."[24]

23. Frei, *The Eclipse of Biblical Narrative: A Study in Eighteenth and Nineteenth Century Hermeneutics* (New Haven: Yale University Press, 1974), pp. 3, 130.
24. Sacvan Bercovitch, *The Puritan Origins of the American Self* (New Haven: Yale University Press, 1975), p. 36.

Through the Middle Ages, typology was largely kept in check through the exercise of the interpretive authority of the church. There were, however, forces at work within the church that would undermine that authority while unwittingly preparing the way for the Protestant and romantic movements of later centuries. One of the most important revolutionary figures in medieval Catholicism proved to be a monk, Joachim of Flora, who lived in the last half of the twelfth century. In his interpretation of the Bible and history, Joachim particularly favored those passages that seemed to promise a coming new age for humankind. He saw secular history, the history of salvation, and the trinitarian nature of God as parts of a single process. The "Age of the Father" extended from Adam to Christ, the "Age of the Son" from the time of Christ to the triumph of the universal Catholic Church in the Middle Ages; and according to Joachim, the "Age of the Spirit" was about to dawn in the thirteenth century. While the "Age of the Father" had been ruled by patriarchal values and the "Age of the Son" had been governed by priests and clerics, the coming "Age of the Spirit" was to witness the democratic transformation of "authority and status . . . within communities of men and women who consider themselves equals." Instead of looking back to a lost Eden or dwelling upon the present kingdom-perfection of the church, Joachimite interpretation anticipated the glorious *antitype* that would fulfill the promise of the shadowy types of the biblical record and the history of the church. "For Joachim, the best was always still to be."[25]

Joachim's interpretation of history favored innovation at the expense of precedent; and in its anticipation of a grand historical fulfillment *about to be,* the Joachimite interpretation itself prefigured later developments in Protestant and romantic hermeneutics.[26] Influence of that kind is clear in the typological practices of certain seventeenth-century Protestants in England and the New World; the practices of these Christians were unusual in the degree to which they read their own experiences as signs of eschato-

25. Steven Ozment, *The Age of Reform 1250-1550: An Intellectual and Religious History of Late Medieval and Reformation Europe* (New Haven: Yale University Press, 1980), pp. 104, 107.

26. By the end of the eighteenth century, writes M. H. Abrams, it had become possible to assume "that there is in human nature an inherent teleology of educational progression, which will lead inevitably to a 'time of perfection' when man 'will do the good because it is the good' — 'the time of a *new everlasting Gospel,*' or 'third age of the world' which, Lessing says, had been prematurely glimpsed by 'certain visionaries of the thirteenth and fourteenth centuries'; . . . that is, in the theory of an earthly millennium which had been proclaimed by Joachim of Flora and his followers" (*Natural Supernaturalism,* p. 202).

logical fulfillment. That is, they saw their particular activities as climactic events in the history of salvation.[27] Typologies always involve seeing similarities — Oliver Cromwell is seen to be like Moses, John Winthrop like Nehemiah. But for some of these sectarian Protestants, the analogies came to seem like identities; and once the two parties in an analogy become identical, the first party is rendered superfluous. If to be *like Christ* means to *become a Christ*, then the person of Jesus himself becomes redundant.

The career of the English Puritan Gerrard Winstanley illustrates well the radical implications of this kind of typological reading. As Christopher Hill explains, for Winstanley

> the Virgin Birth was an allegory; so was the resurrection. "Christ lying in his grave, like a corn of wheat buried under the clods of earth for a time, and Christ rising up from the powers of your flesh, above that corruption and above those clouds, treading the curse under his feet, is to be seen within"; Winstanley appears to reject any other resurrection or ascension. The resurrection of the dead occurs during our lives on earth: the day of judgment has already begun and some are already living in the kingdom of heaven. The casting out of covetousness and the establishment of a classless society will be "a new heaven and a new earth." Even more remarkably, all the prophecies of the Old and New Testaments regarding the calling of the Jews and the restoration of Israel refer to "this work of making the earth a common treasury." Salvation is liberty and peace. The second coming is "the rising up of Christ in sons and daughters"; the worship of any other Christ but the Christ within man must then cease.[28]

Though only a small number of Protestants may have engaged in such interpretive practices, this method of scriptural interpretation nevertheless provided a clear stimulus to romanticism in late eighteenth-century England and early nineteenth-century America.[29] Daring typo-

---

27. Perry Miller did pioneering work on this topic. See his *Errand into the Wilderness* (Cambridge: Harvard University Press, 1956). For a fuller examination of the revolutionary potential of scriptural reading in seventeenth-century England, see Christopher Hill, *The World Turned Upside Down: Radical Ideas During the English Revolution* (Harmondsworth: Peregrine Books, 1984); and for a treatment of early New England, see Bercovitch, *The Puritan Origins of the American Self.*

28. Hill, *The World Turned Upside Down,* pp. 144-45.

29. For the influence of Puritan radicalism on English romanticism, the classic study is Abrams, *Natural Supernaturalism.* See also Bloom, *The Visionary Company.* The influence

logical readings enabled interpreters of the Scriptures to appropriate spiritual satisfaction from the Bible without being obligated to regard seriously its historical and cosmological claims. For the radical typologist, the Bible was a storehouse of images with mystic or inspirational power, rather than a narrative comprising an "adequate depiction of the common and inclusive world." The story of human liberation became primary in this reading of the Scriptures, and the Bible was seen as fitting "into another world with another story rather than incorporating that world into the biblical story."[30] With their descriptive power and narrative authority significantly weakened, the Scriptures would increasingly be left with the primary task of feeding the self's insatiable appetite for metaphors and meaning.

Romanticism and the Therapeutic Culture

While these radical interpretive practices may have been unusual in the seventeenth and eighteenth centuries, with the advent of romanticism in the late eighteenth century they became the dogma of a new cultural orthodoxy. First expounded by such figures as the English poet William Wordsworth, the German theologian Friedrich Schleiermacher, and the American essayist Ralph Waldo Emerson, this romantic orthodoxy still governs as the central ideology of modernity in the West.

By reconstituting the self as an intuitive source of beauty and values, the romantics sought to sustain the inherited beliefs of their culture by providing them with a new source. In the words of M. H. Abrams, "the Romantic enterprise was an attempt to sustain the inherited cultural order against what to many writers seemed the imminence of chaos; and the resolve to give up what one was convinced one had to give up of the dogmatic understructure of Christianity, yet to save what one could save of its experiential relevance and values" seems to Abrams to have been an act "of integrity and of courage."[31]

---

of Puritan typological interpretation on American romanticism is documented in Bercovitch, *The Puritan Origins of the American Self*, pp. 136-86. In the past several decades, many works have documented and analyzed the role of millennial interpretation in American political, religious, and social life. A particularly comprehensive account is given in Ernest Lee Tuveson, *Redeemer Nation: The Idea of America's Millennial Role* (Chicago: University of Chicago Press, 1968).

30. Frei, *The Eclipse of Biblical Narrative*, p. 130.

31. Abrams, *Natural Supernaturalism*, p. 68.

For theologians of the romantic period, the struggle to salvage Christianity while celebrating the self involved an effort to maintain the "principle of autonomy" and "at the same time to account for and justify the place of religion in human life. . . . The question for many was thus whether religion in any form, traditional or deistic, could meet the Promethean ambitions which in Western Europe were firing the imaginations of the educated young as they entered upon" the nineteenth century.[32] Those efforts to promote the cause of human autonomy while preserving some place for religion led the romantics to create a refuge for the religious impulse within the confines of the self.

Schleiermacher explored that refuge in his speeches to the "cultured despisers" of religion. In the first of those speeches, he acknowledges that in the "ornamented dwellings" of nineteenth-century Europe, "the only sacred things to be met with are the sage maxims of our wise men, and the splendid compositions of our poets." Over the course of the previous two centuries, the physical sciences, politics, and philosophy had shown religious belief to be unnecessary as an explanatory device. And now, at the end of the Enlightenment, Schleiermacher has to admit that the culturally astute people of his own day do not even need religion to provide them with happiness. "Suavity and sociability, art and science have so fully taken possession" of their minds that they have no room for thoughts of the "holy Being." "I know how well," Schleiermacher tells the cultured despisers, "you have succeeded in making your earthly life so rich and varied, that you no longer stand in need of an eternity."[33]

Though he has expressed his sympathy for their disdain of the doctrinal "habitations and nurseries of the dead letter," Schleiermacher nonetheless urges his listeners to "turn from everything usually reckoned religion, and fix your regard on the inward emotions and dispositions, as all utterances and acts of inspired men direct."[34] Only by moving inward to the fluid source of all frozen systems may the enlightened soul be carried to the wellsprings of religion and be refreshed by the source of all sublimity:

> I maintain that in all better souls piety springs necessarily by itself; that a province of its own in the mind belongs to it, in which it has unlimited

---

32. Bernard M. G. Reardon, *Religion in the Age of Romanticism: Studies in Early Nineteenth Century Thought* (Cambridge: Cambridge University Press, 1985), pp. 32-33.

33. Schleiermacher, *On Religion: Speeches to Its Cultured Despisers,* trans. John Oman (New York: Harper & Row, 1958), pp. 1-2.

34. Schleiermacher, *On Religion,* pp. 16, 18.

sway; that it is worthy to animate most profoundly the noblest and best and to be fully accepted and known by them.[35]

In his later masterpiece *The Christian Faith*, Schleiermacher endeavored to develop a systematic theology out of his insights concerning the nature of the unique inner life of religion. "All propositions which the system of Christian doctrine has to establish," he argued, "can be regarded either as descriptions of human states, or as conceptions of divine attributes and modes of action, or as utterances regarding the constitution of the world."[36] Yet in spite of the fact that he had just affirmed the essential doctrinal equality of "descriptions of human states of mind, . . . utterances regarding the constitution of the world," and "conceptions of divine modes of action," Schleiermacher went on in *The Christian Faith* to "declare the description of human states of mind to be the fundamental dogmatic form." Statements about the nature of the world and the action of God, on the other hand, "are permissible only in so far as they can be developed out of propositions" stemming from the experience of inwardness.[37]

Schleiermacher's redefinition of the nature of faith profoundly influenced Christian doctrine and hermeneutics. Helmut Thielicke has observed that the effect of Schleiermacher's romantic reconstitution of religion was to conflate the separate disciplines of "anthropology (human conditions), theology (divine qualities and modes of action), and cosmology (the nature of the world)." Faced with the fact that Schleiermacher was willing to deny "theological rank" to any theological proposition that could not be translated into anthropological language "without any loss of value," Thielicke asks rhetorically, "Does not this pave the way for the normativity of the anthropological analysis of existence?"[38]

For the theory of interpretation, the anthropological revolution guaranteed that primacy would be given to human subjectivity and to the process of appropriation. For the romantic mind of Schleiermacher, the hermeneutical enterprise was no longer a search for ways of translating divine demands or imparting revelatory knowledge to an eager audience.

35. Schleiermacher, *On Religion*, p. 21.

36. In *Friedrich Schleiermacher: Pioneer of Modern Theology*, ed. Keith W. Clements (London: Collins, 1987), p. 140.

37. Clements, ed., *Schleiermacher*, p. 141.

38. Thielicke, *The Evangelical Faith*, vol. 1: *Prolegomena: The Relation of Theology to Modern Thought Forms*, trans. and ed. Geoffrey W. Bromiley (Grand Rapids: Eerdmans, 1974), p. 45.

Ethics, physics, and biology tell us all that we need to know about the nature of human action and the created order. For that reason, revelation can only serve as an adornment to the body of secular knowledge already developed by autonomous individuals.

This scheme of things leaves the interpreter of Christian texts with the task of translating them into language that an enlightened individual can understand without having to take offense. In Schleiermacher's view of hermeneutics, writes Karl Barth, "nothing remained of the belief that the Word or statement is as such the bearer, bringer, and proclaimer of truth, that there might be such a thing as the Word of God." Schleiermacher's understanding of the *kerygma* is of "a kerygma that only *depicts* and does not *bring*, that only *states* or *expresses* and does not *declare*. Truth does not come in the spoken Word; it comes in speaking feeling."[39]

At the very time that Schleiermacher was concluding his brilliant and revolutionary career, the American Ralph Waldo Emerson was entering upon his vocation as a romantic poet and essayist. And while there is no evidence of the specific influence of Schleiermacher upon Emerson, there are remarkable similarities in their convictions about the nature of religious experience and human understanding. In a pivotal early work, "The Divinity School Address," Emerson gave full expression to his romantic conception of Christian truth. The true source of revelation, Emerson told the students of the Harvard Divinity School in the summer of 1838, is not a transcendent God who spoke definitively in the life of an ancient race and a first-century carpenter. No, revelation has its source in the inspired self filled with the "sentiment of virtue." Jesus Christ is important for what he can tell us about that soul, not for what he might be able to impart to it: "Jesus Christ belonged to the true race of prophets. He saw with open eye the mystery of the soul. . . . He saw that God incarnates himself in man, and evermore goes forth anew to take possession of his world."[40]

Because truth "is an intuition" and "cannot be received at second hand," Emerson claimed that the students he was addressing had to go forth as "newborn bard[s] of the Holy Ghost," preaching "a faith like

---

39. Barth, *The Theology of Schleiermacher,* ed. Dietrich Ritschl, trans. Geoffrey W. Bromiley (Grand Rapids: Eerdmans, 1982), p. 210.

40. Emerson, "The Divinity School Address," in *Emerson: Essays and Lectures,* ed. Joel Porte (New York: Library of America, 1983), pp. 75-76, 80.

41. Emerson, "The Divinity School Address," pp. 79, 89, 88.

Christ's in the infinitude of man."[41] Men and women may "have come to speak of the revelation as somewhat long ago given and done, as if God were dead," but the inspired self knows to heed the call of "new revelation": "In the soul, then, let the redemption be sought. Wherever a man comes, there comes revolution. . . . [O]ne soul, and their soul, is wiser than the whole world."[42]

For Emerson and other romantics the truth discovered within the self was a mirror image of the truth hidden within nature. When we study nature and history, Emerson explains in "The American Scholar," we are simply classifying a multitude of facts. And "what is classification but the perceiving that these objects are not chaotic, and are not foreign, but have a law which is also a law of the human mind?" The mind finds itself "tyrannized over by its own unifying instinct," and so it "goes on tying things together, diminishing anomalies, discovering roots running under ground, whereby contrary and remote things cohere, and flower out from one stem." The end of this process is the discovery that the same moral and spiritual laws are at work within nature and within the human mind: "And, in fine, the ancient precept, 'Know thyself,' and the modern precept, 'Study nature,' become at last one maxim."[43]

By linking human consciousness to God and nature by means of human feeling, the romantics were able to sustain the Cartesian tradition's faith in the self's ability to discover the truth. For Emerson, Schleier-macher, and others of the age, what *coheres* within the self also *corresponds* in some way to the truth permeating nature and the divine consciousness. That truth within nature, however, is hidden in hieroglyphic form and is in desperate need of interpretation. Hence, the poet in romanticism takes the place of the preacher or the pope in the hermeneutical process:

> For, as it is dislocation and detachment from the life of God, that makes things ugly, the poet, who re-attaches things to nature and the Whole, — re-attaching even artificial things, and violations of nature, to nature, by a deeper insight, — disposes very easily of the most disagreeable facts.[44]

In Emerson's world, all of us are potential poets capable of recogniz-ing "in every work of genius . . . our own rejected thoughts" coming "back

42. Emerson, "The Divinity School Address," pp. 83, 88.
43. Emerson, "The American Scholar," in *Emerson: Essays and Lectures*, pp. 55-56.
44. Emerson, "The Poet," in *Emerson: Essays and Lectures*, p. 455.

to us with a certain alienated majesty."[45] What those rejected thoughts tell us is that each of us has the power to manipulate reality for our own well-being: "As the world was plastic and fluid in the hands of God, so it is ever to so much of his attributes as we bring to it. . . . [I]n proportion as a man has any thing in him divine, the firmament flows before him and takes his signet and form. Not he is great who can alter matter, but he who can alter my state of mind."[46]

Emerson and Schleiermacher represent the triumph of inwardness in the development of the Western theory of interpretation. In their work and in that of others of the romantic period, we witness the demise of efforts to find a correspondence between the biblical narrative and the book of nature or the events of history. In the world of romantic inwardness, hermeneutics became the art of reconciling the antiquated language of the Scriptures to the realities of the expansive, intuitive self. Writers such as Emerson effected that reconciliation by making the Bible an illustration of the drama of human inwardness. In what Hans Frei might consider the absolute "eclipse of biblical narrative," Emerson wrote in "Self-Reliance":

> Time and space are but physiological colors which the eye makes, but the soul is light; where it is, is day; where it was, is night; and history is an impertinence and an injury, if it be anything more than a cheerful apologue or parable of my being and becoming.[47]

*   *   *

The following chapters will attempt to fill in some of the outline of the development of romantic thought from the time of Emerson and Schleiermacher to the postmodern age. We will explore the complicated developments that led from the epistemological confidence of romanticism to the interpretive skepticism of postmodernism. In the key shifts that have led from romanticism to the world of contemporary theory, a constant factor has been the steady erosion of belief in the correspondence of the self's spiritual aspirations to the natural and historical realities. Charles Taylor calls this erosion a process of "disenchantment" by means of which the

---

45. Emerson, "Self-Reliance," in *Emerson: Essays and Lectures,* p. 259.
46. Emerson, "The American Scholar," p. 65.
47. Emerson, "Self-Reliance," p. 270.

"ontic logos" has gradually disappeared as a unifying belief for modern men and women. In the world of Cartesian philosophy and Newtonian mechanism, "theories of ontic logos cease to be meaningful for us. . . . The world consists of a domain of objects to which we can respond in varying ways." One consequence of the "disengagement from cosmic order" was that "the human agent was no longer to be understood as an element in a larger, meaningful order. His paradigm purposes are to be discovered within."[48]

To be sure, the changes wrought in Western thinking at the beginning of the modern era were hardly due to the influence of ideas alone. The period we have been discussing was one in which vast changes were taking place in the understanding of economics and society. Indeed, many of the developments we have observed to this point were hastened along by the explosive growth of market capitalism (in the seventeenth and eighteenth centuries in England and from the eighteenth century on in America). Making use of the social contract theories of Thomas Hobbes and John Locke, capitalist practices and theories helped to revolutionize Western conceptions of selfhood, history, and community. As difficult as it may be to determine whether ideas shaped the process or whether the process determined the ideas that would rationalize and justify it, it is clear that the new economic order emerging at the dawn of the modern era reinforced the understandings of selfhood and society being developed by the likes of Descartes and Kant.

Capitalism focused unprecedented attention upon the individual as an entity of production and consumption. In doing so, it preached an implicit gospel of radical egalitarianism; in the marketplace, matters of gender, class, and race were, in theory, irrelevant. The power of the market economy did as much as any belief about the self or truth to subvert the customary hierarchies of social and spiritual life and to isolate the self. Traditional theories of the self, Joyce Appleby explains, "begin with the person as a member of society born into a complex of obligations and identities"; on the other hand, the liberal individualism that both shaped and grew out of the development of capitalism "starts with the individual who possesses a common set of needs."[49] The desiring and acquiring self

---

48. Taylor, *Sources of the Self: The Making of the Modern Identity* (Cambridge: Harvard University Press, 1989), pp. 187, 193.

49. Appleby, *Capitalism and a New Social Order: The Republican Vision of the 1790s* (New York: New York University Press, 1984), p. 36.

of postmodern cultural theory bears more than a casual resemblance to the unit of consumption at the center of market economies and democratic societies.

From the vantage point of later history, romanticism appears as a transitional movement, a stage on the way from the magical and sacramental world of the late Middle Ages to the desacralized world of modernity. Language may still express human desire for the postmodernist, as it did for the romantics, but that desire is no longer seen to correspond to any realities outside the self. As Richard Rorty puts it: "To say that truth is not out there is simply to say that where there are no sentences there is no truth, that sentences are elements of human languages, and that human languages are human creations."[50] Though it has lost its ancestors' faith in the correspondence of the self to nature, the ironic, therapeutic self of the postmodernists is nevertheless the direct spiritual descendent of the willful, imaginative self of the romantics.

What the romantics did, after all, was to try to provide a different foundation for the intellectual and cultural enterprises undertaken at the beginning of the modern era. Romantic poets may have represented themselves as having spurned the rationalism and empiricism of the Enlightenment, but they were really challenging the means that the Enlightenment chose to pursue its ends. The romantics had little quarrel with the premises and goals of the Enlightenment project. Like their forebears, the romantic poets and philosophers assumed the validity of the Cartesian and Baconian understanding of the self and its relationship to nature, authority, and tradition. They also took it for granted that the fundamental problems of human life were problems of epistemology, rather than problems of the will. They assumed that truth was the product of the unimpeded interaction of the human subject with nature or of the complex play of the human mind or spirit within itself.

Over the past one hundred and fifty years the romantic self has been subjected to a number of assaults. Its claims to innocence and its confidence in its own powers have been questioned sharply by events of history and powerful new schools of thought. The brutal terrors of modern political and military history mock enlightened and romantic assertions of a fundamental human goodness, while modern understandings of the subconscious and the body make earlier claims about the powers of conscious-

---

50. Rorty, *Contingency, Irony, and Solidarity* (Cambridge: Cambridge University Press, 1989), p. 5.

ness appear hopelessly naive. There is no way for the contemporary thinker to recapture with integrity the confidence of a William Wordsworth or Walt Whitman. Like many others, those poets thought that by exploring their own inner regions and by observing the world about them they could discover universal moral and spiritual truths; they were confident that in speaking of their own experience they were speaking to the conditions and needs of all men and women.

Yet for many in our own century, the loss of the original utopian hopes of romanticism has not led to an abandonment of the romantic understanding of the self. The postmodernist is in every way a child of the romantics, one who stands alone in nature, defying demands upon the self and searching for that which will satisfy. The difference is that the postmodern self no longer harbors hopes of discovering truth or secure principles. Instead, driven by the ideals of therapy and consumption, it seeks, by whatever means will work, to provide satisfactions for the unencumbered self; it strives to reduce all individual moral actions to matters of choice for which there are no authoritative guidelines or binding principles. In the culture of therapy and interpretation, there is nothing to direct the self except its preferences. There is no goal for the actions of the self save the fulfillment of its desires.

CHAPTER 4   *Postmodern Gnostics*

AN ESSAY ABOUT Joe DiMaggio's remarkable 56-game hitting streak may seem at first to be an unlikely place to encounter a gnostic meditation, especially when the author of the essay is the eminent Harvard biologist Stephen Jay Gould, a renowned scholar in his specialty and an accomplished essayist with a wide audience outside his discipline. Yet the more one ponders the matter, the more sense it makes that a work by Gould — who is both a thoroughgoing naturalist and a keen moralist — might give evidence of gnostic influences. For the gnostics of the first centuries of the Christian era, the earthly life of men and women was cursed by an irreconcilable conflict between the sordid bodily world and the splendid heavenly realms. For modern naturalists such as Gould, the conflict can be just as dramatic — only now the split is between the bleak realities of matter in motion and the power of language to satisfy our longings and calm our fears.

In his essay, Gould complains that most of us cannot understand the "truly special character" of DiMaggio's record, because we are unable "to grasp the workings of random processes and patterning in nature." Because we "cannot bear" the "willy-nilly" workings of nature, we insist on concocting "comforting answers." In Gould's words, "our error lies not in the perception of pattern but in automatically imbuing pattern with meaning, especially with meaning that can bring us comfort, or dispel confusion." In ways that Gould considers both dishonest and cowardly, humans have persistently "tried to impose [the] 'heart's desire' upon the actual earth and its largely random patterns." To be intellectually rigorous, then, instead of distinguishing DiMaggio's streak "merely by quantity along a continuum of courage," we ought to see it "as a unique assault upon the otherwise unblemished record of Dame Probability." There is no deeper meaning than that in the streak.[1]

If that is the case, why do we continue to impose order upon randomness, when we ought to know better? Gould concludes that "our minds are not built (for whatever reason) to work by the rules of probability, though *these rules clearly govern our universe*" (emphasis mine). When confronted by the meaningless processes of natural life, our minds "match to type." That is, they extract what they take to be the essence of an entity and arrange all judgments about it "by their degree of similarity to this assumed type." Yet the problem is that that type exists nowhere except in the mind of the one who perceives it; the order we see when we "match to type" is one that we have imposed upon the realities we have examined. In short, in the world as Gould envisions it we are caught between the inexorable, unfeeling laws of matter and logic, on the one hand, and our instinctive need to fabricate meaning, on the other.[2]

Gould's argument represents a very sophisticated form of the ancient heresy of gnosticism. The term is derived from the Greek word for knowledge, *gnosis*. According to the gnostic sects in the early Christian era, the gospel is a special or secret form of knowledge that imparts salvation to those fortunate enough to have hold of it. Gnosticism posited a sharp dualism between matter and spirit and promised deliverance through knowledge of that dualism. In most cases, the redemption provided by *gnosis* was depicted as some form of release from the bondage of the body to the freedom of the spiritual realm. The gnostic considered embodiment, rather than sin, to be the primary cause of human suffering and frustration.

In the history of the church — a history that Stephen Jay Gould would clearly prefer to leave behind — no heresy has proved more stubbornly resilient than gnosticism. In the early centuries of the Christian age, gnosticism struggled with orthodoxy for the very soul of the faith. In later centuries, up through the modern age, the gnostic impulse has repeatedly resurfaced in church and culture. Although it has never been the official position of the church, the gnostic viewpoint has always posed a

---

1. Gould, *Bully for Brontosaurus: Reflections in Natural History* (New York: W. W. Norton, 1991), pp. 467-68.
2. Gould, *Bully for Brontosaurus*, p. 469.

threat and remained a temptation to orthodoxy. And in the past two hundred years, it has reemerged as a dominant intellectual and cultural force, even as the public influence of Christian faith has waned. When read in theological terms, the birth and flourishing of "the culture of interpretation" would appear to be one sign of a powerful resurgence of gnosticism in a particular contemporary guise.

The Gnostic Impulse

To speak of the rebirth of gnosticism in contemporary culture is one way of coming to theological terms with the moral and intellectual world of modernity and postmodernity. What are we to make of the history outlined in the first chapters of this book? Should the Christian who has a concern for justice and human dignity welcome the advance of secularity, the triumph of inwardness, and the celebration of human autonomy? Or should he or she condemn it as a sign of the triumph of godlessness? Is there a middle ground between a simple accommodation to the modern temperament and a thoughtless rejection of its claims?[3]

In one form or another, such questions have perplexed Christians increasingly in the centuries since the Reformation. In the nineteenth century, Friedrich Schleiermacher strove to define the Christian faith in ways that would allow educated persons to believe in God without being affronted by irrelevant doctrines of divine sovereignty and the implausible realm of the miraculous. In the next century, Schleiermacher's most brilliant theological critic and successor, Karl Barth, rejected the romantic theologian's apologetic approach to the gospel. Barth believed that Schleiermacher had conceded far too much to human nature and unregenerate culture; he charged that in the theology of Schleiermacher there remains

3. Paul Tillich devoted himself to the task of finding a middle ground. Consider, for instance, his answers to the question of the proper role of "*nomos* or the law of life": "Autonomy asserts that man as the bearer of universal reason is the source and measure of culture and religion — that he is his own law. Heteronomy asserts that man, being unable to act according to universal reason, must be subjected to a law, strange and superior to him. Theonomy asserts that the superior law is, at the same time, the innermost law of man himself, rooted in the divine ground which is man's own ground" (Tillich, *The Protestant Era,* trans. James Luther Adams [Chicago: University of Chicago Press, 1957], pp. 56-57). For all his efforts to reconcile authority and autonomy, however, Tillich ended up promoting a standard romantic argument about the relationship between the self and God.

no "ultimate opposition between God and man, between Christ and the Christian."[4] In turn, Dietrich Bonhoeffer, one of Barth's most brilliant theological heirs, faulted both Barth and Schleiermacher — Barth for having done too little to make revelation comprehensible to modern men and women, and Schleiermacher for having allowed the world to define the very gospel itself.

One way to resolve the question of the relationship of the church to culture is to think dialectically of the needs of the church at the present time. Given the direction of church and culture in the contemporary world, what word of reproof or challenge do they need to hear? It is difficult to avoid the conclusion that the needs of the late twentieth century are markedly different from those of the early nineteenth century, when Schleiermacher was at work. If the danger two centuries ago was that of a Christian faith become irrelevant, the present risk is that Christ may become so completely identified with the concerns of the present age that his person is rendered superfluous and his authority denied. When the eccentric exegetical practices of the radical Puritans have become the common habits of a therapeutic age, then the church and world need to hear something more than preaching about the "Christ within."

If, as Schleiermacher claims, the doctrines of the Christian faith are only "conceptions of states of mind of Christian piety, represented in speech," then when the human mind changes, those doctrines must change to be in accord with it. According to Barth, in Schleiermacher's view "theology, if only because it is merely the human word, . . . is free, capable of transformation, and relatively non-binding — not bound in respect to its subject."[5] At first glance, it may seem surprising that Schleiermacher's romantic view of Christian truth is remarkably like that of the poststructural pragmatist Richard Rorty. After all, Schleiermacher was a devout Christian who committed himself to proclaiming the person and work of Christ, while Richard Rorty is an avowed agnostic who finds nothing lasting or useful in the language of Christian belief. The longer one looks at these two figures, however, the more the line from Schleiermacher to Rorty appears to be simply yet another path wending its way from the heights of romantic inwardness to the valleys of pragmatic preference. Schleiermacher desperately wanted to make Christ relevant to the "cul-

---

4. Barth, *Protestant Thought: From Rousseau to Ritschl,* trans. Brian Cozens (New York: Simon and Schuster, 1969), p. 354.

5. Barth, *Protestant Thought,* p. 335.

tured despisers"; but as we have seen, for Richard Rorty a completely relevant Christ is a useless Christ, a needless verbal construct we would do well to discard once it no longer serves our purposes.

To understand the connections between postmodern pragmatism and ancient gnosticism, we need to realize that, although it would be false to claim that there has ever been a unified body of gnostic belief, there was even in the early years of the church a "common stock of ideas" behind the myriad forms of the gnostic heresy. Most gnostics were dualists who established "an infinite chasm between the spiritual world and the world of matter" and attributed the creation of the world to an inferior deity, rather than to the "God of light and goodness."[6] To the ancient gnostics it was *embodiment* that was the source of evil and affliction in human life, rather than *sin* or the waywardness of the will. In the gnostic view, the human spirit longs for release from the world of matter, and according to most forms of gnostic belief it gains that release by acquiring a secret knowledge or special revelation.

At least in part, many of the doctrinal developments in the early church may be seen as efforts to check the spread of gnostic influence. Through the doctrine of the Trinity, the early councils affirmed that God the Creator and God the Redeemer are one. In the consolidation of the canon, the church withstood gnostic attempts to divide the Scriptures, especially the attempts by Marcion to separate what he took to be the enlightened God of Jesus and the New Testament from the barbaric deity of Israel and the Old Testament. The doctrines of sin and grace, especially as they were elaborated by Augustine, undermined the gnostic explanations of evil and creation. And the public nature of Christian proclamation served to dissipate the power of gnostic claims to possess a secret, superior tradition.

Yet in spite of the official success of orthodoxy in its conflicts with gnosticism, the gnostic heresy has continued to trouble the church throughout its history. In its Manichean variety, for example, gnosticism has had considerable influence on Protestant sectarian movements, including fundamentalism. As we will see in a later chapter on Christianity and the arts, fundamentalists have historically emphasized the separation of Christ and his followers from the world. H. Richard Niebuhr explains that throughout history radical Christians have combined a "rejection of cul-

6. J. N. D. Kelly, *Early Christian Doctrines,* rev. ed. (New York: Harper & Row, 1978), p. 26.

ture . . . with a suspicion of nature and nature's God." They have been tempted to divide "the world into the material realm governed by a principle opposed to Christ and a spiritual realm guided by the spiritual God" and to equate redemption with release from the body.[7]

From the Montanists of the second century to modern fundamentalists, then, radical Christians have been prone to conceive of grace as the negation of nature and culture. In early Christian history, gnosticism led to the disparagement of the body, the Scriptures, and the life of the church. In the Western world since the Enlightenment, the gnostic impulse has prompted many to dismiss the idea of an order inherent in nature and to spurn that which has been given to men and women in their cultural and intellectual traditions.[8] It is not so much embodiment that contemporary gnostics take to be the source of evil as it is the embeddedness of the self within the limits of nature and the constrictions of society.

Gnosis and Enlightenment

While fundamentalism and perfectionistic sects have made strategic accommodations to gnosticism in the twentieth century, one modern cultural movement has been unabashed in its embrace of gnostic dualism. I am referring to the complex process of the *secularization of the spirit,* which is at the heart of both the Enlightenment and the romantic movement. In this process of secularization, "traditional Christian concepts" are retained, but they are "demythologized, conceptualized," and the individual "subject, mind, or spirit . . . [becomes] primary and takes over the initiative and functions which had once been the prerogatives of deity."[9] In earlier chapters we traced specific historical sources, particularly in philosophy, literature, and the theory of interpretation, in an effort to understand the origins of romanticism and the modern movements it has spawned. In considering gnosticism in this chapter, we are

7. Niebuhr, *Christ and Culture* (New York: Harper and Brothers, 1951), p. 81.

8. On the subject of the relevance of gnosticism for an understanding of the modern world, see two very different works: Hans Jonas, *The Gnostic Religion,* 2nd ed., revised (Boston: Beacon Press, 1963), pp. 320-40; and Philip J. Lee, *Against the Protestant Gnostics* (New York: Oxford University Press, 1987).

9. M. H. Abrams, *Natural Supernaturalism: Tradition and Revolution in Romantic Literature* (New York: W. W. Norton, 1971), p. 91.

looking at a form of thought that both is a perennial source of temptation to the Christian and forms a particular challenge for the Christian student of contemporary culture.

In the introductory chapter of his survey of nineteenth-century Protestant theology, Karl Barth provides an insightful analysis of this process of the secularization of the spirit that originates in the Enlightenment.[10] As he concludes his survey of eighteenth-century intellectual life, Barth discusses the thought and character of Leibniz. Barth considers this German philosopher and mathematician to represent the essence of Enlightenment humanism. Leibniz's philosophy of the *monad* is for Barth the epitome of the eighteenth century's view of the place of the self in the universe. "This simple and utterly individual, indeed unique spiritual substance is the fountain-head of all reality." In the world of the monad — as in the lofty worlds of Enlightenment rationalism and romantic intuitionism — it was "as if only God and the soul existed" and "the physical and the moral evil in the world which [man] imagines to be actively opposed to him contain in truth nothing positive, but are, so to speak, only a shadow fleeing before the light."[11]

To the person of the Enlightenment, scientific discoveries had disclosed that the natural universe is more physically complex and less morally purposeful than the universe had been conceived to be in the ancient world and Middle Ages. The earth was no longer to be seen as the center of the universe but was instead a "grain of dust among countless others in the universe," as Barth puts it.[12] Some were saddened by this *disenchanting* of the world, this rendering of the universe into a virtual mechanism. For instance, the French philosopher and mathematician Blaise Pascal, a devout Christian, found himself deeply distressed as he pondered the mechanical universe of Cartesian science and Copernican astronomy. "The eternal silence of these infinite spaces frightens me," he wrote of the demystified heavens of early modern physics. To Pascal, the loss of a finite and animated universe was tragic because it left the yearning soul lonely in the midst of an indifferent natural order.

Pascal was lonely because he longed to encounter responsiveness and intelligibility in the natural world; but for those who sought power through the mastery of nature, the disenchanted universe of science offered un-

---

10. Barth, *Protestant Thought*, pp. 11-57.
11. Barth, *Protestant Thought*, pp. 56-57.
12. Barth, *Protestant Thought*, p. 15.

bounded opportunities for the exercise of their wills. Pascal may have been humbled and saddened by the discovery of the earth's astronomical insignificance, but many educated persons of the eighteenth century took these discoveries as heartening indications of the central place of humanity in the scheme of things. "No, man is all the greater for this," Barth writes, "for he was able to discover this revolutionary truth by his own resources and to think it abstractly." The irony of the Enlightenment and romanticism is that "the geocentric picture of the universe was replaced as a matter of course by the anthropocentric."[13]

The hero of the anthropocentric world became the free and powerful self. Under the program of the Enlightenment, and later in romanticism, that self sought to assume the authority once granted to God in historic theism. Typical of this revolution in thought is the dismissal of the gods near the end of Walt Whitman's epic of inwardness, *Song of Myself.* Whitman disparages "the old cautious hucksters" — including Jehovah, Zeus, and Allah — who "did the work of their days" but are now a hindrance: "They bore mites as for unfledg'd birds who have now to rise and fly and sing for themselves."[14] Having grown into their enlightened adulthood, men and women have come to recognize that the source of all divinity lies within. And thus, according to Whitman and countless other writers of the Enlightenment and romantic movements, if the natural order seems dead and void of purpose, then the rational mind or the imaginative human spirit must bring it to life; if history seems disordered and unjust, then reason and the will must alter the course of history and redeem the time.

The view of the self in the Enlightenment tradition was, in important respects, gnostic. To be sure, the dualism formulated at the beginning of the modern period did not oppose a spiritual God to an evil natural world; rather, it posited a vast chasm between the divine self and the oppressive lifelessness of nature and tradition. Whether in the rational faculties of the disciplined mind or in the intuitive powers of the creative spirit, the Enlightenment tradition honored the disembodied power of the self. As we saw in an earlier chapter, at the height of Western optimism — in the decades immediately surrounding the French Revolution — it seemed that nothing was beyond the power of this self as it worked its will upon the

13. Barth, *Protestant Thought,* pp. 15-16.

14. Whitman, *Song of Myself,* in *Whitman: Complete Poetry and Collected Prose,* ed. Justin Kaplan (New York: Library of America, 1982), p. 233.

world. In a strong statement of the romantic ideal, William Wordsworth gave voice to what had become the common hopes of his day for the untrammeled self:

> Paradise, and groves
> Elysian, Fortunate Fields — like those of old
> Sought in the Atlantic Main — why should they be
> A history only of departed things,
> Or a mere fiction of what never was?
> For the discerning intellect of Man,
> When wedded to this goodly universe
> In love and holy passion, shall find these
> A simple produce of the common day.[15]

Like the gnostics of the early Christian centuries, the philosophers of the Enlightenment and the poets of romanticism took offense at the historical particularity of Christian belief. "Accidental historical truths can never become proofs for necessary truths of reason," wrote Gotthold Lessing in the eighteenth century.[16] And in complaining to a group of divinity students in 1838, Emerson argued that "historical Christianity" had mistakenly preached "not the doctrine of the soul, but an exaggeration of the personal, the positive, the ritual." Instead of dwelling "with noxious exaggeration about the *person* of Jesus," Emerson said, the church should proclaim Christ's faith in the power of "every man to expand to the full circle of the universe."[17]

The Fall of the Enlightened Self

In any number of ways, the intellectual history of the past two centuries might be read as a record of the initial boundless expansion of the Enlightenment self and its later severe contraction. In recent decades, any number of works have sought to document the course of its decline. These works

15. Wordsworth, preface to *The Excursion,* in *Wordsworth: Poetical Works,* ed. Thomas Hutchinson, revised by Ernest de Selincourt (London: Oxford University Press, 1936), p. 755.

16. Lessing, quoted in Barth, *Protestant Thought,* p. 137.

17. Emerson, "The Divinity School Address," in *Emerson: Essays and Lectures,* ed. Joel Porte (New York: Library of America, 1983), pp. 80-81.

have come from individuals of widely divergent interests, training, and commitments. For instance, four distinctly different books, recently published within a year of each other, have taken direct aim upon the Enlightenment view of the self. While they have very different subjects, each lodges sharp complaints against the Enlightenment self and implicitly challenges the "gnostic tradition" of modernity. Taken together, they are representative of a major contemporary reappraisal of the Enlightenment and the romantic movement.[18]

In *Continental Philosophy Since 1750: The Rise and Fall of the Self*, for example, Robert Solomon attacks the Enlightenment self through the use of a relatively simple thesis. His argument is that the great discovery of the eighteenth century was the "transcendental self . . . whose nature and ambitions were unprecedentedly arrogant, presumptuously cosmic, and consequently mysterious." In trying to account for the appearance of this self in the Enlightenment, Solomon describes three general characteristics of the Enlightenment — "its humanism, rationality, and universalism." At its core, the Enlightenment held to a bedrock faith in the ability of the self to discover universal, binding truths of science, politics, and morality. Since it conceived of human nature as essentially rational, the Enlightenment could claim that every free individual would reach similar conclusions about the most crucial matters of civic, moral, and intellectual life. "Thus the belief in universal reason becomes coupled to a confidence in individual *autonomy* — the ability of every human being to come to the right conclusions."[19]

The serene Enlightenment faith in the power of the isolated individual is a subject that has been treated in depth by the moral philosopher Alasdair MacIntyre in several books written in the past decade. Although half of *Whose Justice? Which Rationality?* is given over to an often brilliant exploration of Homer, Aristotle, Augustine, and Aquinas, MacIntyre's primary concern is with what he terms the "Liberal tradition

18. One of these books, Robert Solomon's *Continental Philosophy Since 1750: The Rise and Fall of the Self* (Oxford: Oxford University Press, 1988), is a work in the history of philosophy; the second, Alasdair MacIntyre's *Whose Justice? Which Rationality?* (Notre Dame: University of Notre Dame Press, 1988), is an analysis of Western philosophical traditions and contemporary moral reasoning; the third book is a collection of essays by Wendell Berry entitled *Home Economics* (San Francisco: North Point Press, 1987); and the fourth book is Richard Wilbur's *New and Collected Poems* (New York: Harcourt Brace Jovanovich, 1988).

19. Solomon, *Continental Philosophy Since 1750*, pp. 4, 9, 11.

of the Enlightenment." According to MacIntyre, the major philosophers of the Scottish Enlightenment, like the eighteenth- and early nineteenth-century Continental philosophers whom Solomon discusses, held "that the appearance of variation and disagreement in moral judgment between different cultural and social orders is an illusion."[20] Beneath the superficial differences separating individuals and cultures, there is a common moral wisdom available to all who have been freed from the tyranny of particularity and circumstance. In typical Enlightenment fashion, the Scottish philosophers disparaged tradition and lauded instead acts of isolated moral reflection.

In seeking to explain the theological significance of the Enlightenment, H. Richard Niebuhr writes that in the central cultural developments of the eighteenth and nineteenth centuries what had long been "heresy became the new orthodoxy." In many different figures of the age, the distinctions between Christ and human culture were obscured or openly denied as these individuals embraced "Christ as a hero of manifold culture." Locke, Kant, Jefferson, and others sought to make the Christian faith a matter of perfect rationality and plausibility. Like gnostics in the early church, the rationalists, empiricists, and romantics of the age "sought to disentangle the Gospel from its involvement with barbaric and outmoded Jewish notions about God and history; to raise Christianity from the level of belief to that of intelligent knowledge, and so to increase its attractiveness and power."[21] The question of the deity of Jesus is irrelevant, Jefferson wrote in 1803, because what is important about him is that he promoted "universal philanthropy . . . to all mankind, gathering all into one family, under the bonds of love, charity, peace, common wants and common aids."[22]

The captains of the Enlightenment and romanticism believed that it would be possible to maintain the moral ballast of Christian practice while jettisoning the theological cargo of Christian belief. As MacIntyre puts it, they were eager to free the self "from the contingency and particularity of tradition" and confident of their ability to discover clear standards of truth and right action. As a pious German Lutheran, Immanuel Kant believed that, in order to discover the truth, he did not even need to leave his "provincial town of Koningsberg, insisting that in its busy port

20. MacIntyre, *Whose Justice? Which Rationality?* p. 330.
21. Niebuhr, *Christ and Culture*, pp. 91, 86.
22. Jefferson to Dr. Benjamin Rush, 21 April 1803, in *Thomas Jefferson: Writings*, ed. Merrill D. Peterson (New York: Library of America, 1984), p. 1125.

he had the opportunity to observe all of humanity."[23] After all, if the universal structures of knowledge are implanted in all minds, and if the deepest moral principles are self-evident, the rational person does not need to travel anywhere else — in time or in space — to discover the truth.

Over the past century and a half, the collapse of the Enlightenment program has been precipitous and all but complete. The events of history — including the brutal realities of the Napoleonic wars, slavery and civil war in America, the trauma of the Great War, and the unspeakable horrors of Auschwitz and Hiroshima — have helped to topple that imperial self from its throne. In the nineteenth century, Kierkegaard scorned the palatial pretense of faith in universal rationality and inevitable progress; Marx attacked what he took to be the oppressive rule of the bourgeois individual in the West; and Nietzsche mocked his culture for its having contrived to seek pleasure and peace at the right hand of the divine father whom, in effect, it had already slain.

If the realities of history and the radical critiques of philosophy have not completely enfeebled the imperial self, Solomon claims, then recent developments in theories of knowledge and interpretation provide further compelling proof of the bankruptcy of the Enlightenment ideal. In the final chapter of *Continental Philosophy Since 1750*, for example, Solomon describes the work of Michel Foucault and Jacques Derrida as a "wholesale rejection of the transcendental pretense . . . [and] its expansive sense of self, its confidence in our knowledge, its a priori assurance that all people everywhere are ultimately like us." For Solomon, poststructuralism may be either the first hint of a new brand of philosophy, which would be post-Christian and post-Enlightenment, or "'just more of the same,' a final, negative expression of the old transcendental pretense." In either case, the poststructuralist critique of modern thought provides strong evidence of the fact "that the intellect is prone to self-aggrandizement, and that intellectual arrogance will always take a fall."[24]

Unlike Solomon, MacIntyre does not employ poststructuralist arguments to press his points about the demise of the Enlightenment self. Instead, he argues that the Enlightenment program may be judged to have failed by its own standards. If the appeal "to genuinely universal, tradition-independent norms . . . was and is the project of modern liberal, individualist society," he writes, then

23. Solomon, *Continental Philosophy Since 1750*, p. 7.
24. Solomon, *Continental Philosophy Since 1750*, pp. 194, 196, 202.

the most cogent reasons that we have for believing that the hope of a tradition-independent rational universality is an illusion derive from the history of that project. For in the course of that history liberalism, which began as an appeal to alleged principles of shared rationality against what was felt to be the tyranny of tradition, has itself been transformed into a tradition whose continuities are partly defined by the interminability of the debate over such principles.[25]

Liberal individualism, the child of the Enlightenment, has become a tradition of disparaging the value of tradition. Yet having claimed that it would uncover universal standards for truth, that tradition has become mired in endless disputes about the very ideals it initially set out to identify, clarify, and elaborate. The self that was to break out of the imprisoning confines of prejudice and discover universal truth now finds itself trapped within the cells of individual perception. With its epistemological and ethical claims discredited, that Enlightenment self seems to have before it a limited number of options. It may attempt to justify the dismissal of truth by celebrating the centrality of preference and the primacy of desire, or it may attempt to restore confidence in nature and revelation as sources of truth.

After the Fall

If the Enlightenment and romantic self has been dramatically weakened, how does one respond to that fact? That question seems to preoccupy Solomon and MacIntyre. Does one try to prop up the transcendent self so that it can do further work in the culture, or does one accept its demise and improvise solutions for use in a world in which final questions can no longer be answered? Or, perhaps, is it possible to find something profoundly constructive in the very fact that the self is situated in nature and history? As vital as such questions are for anyone in the culture of the West, they are especially pertinent to Christians in America. Because of the pervasive influence of the Enlightenment upon American culture and the specific importance of romanticism to nineteenth-century American evangelicalism, contemporary Christians have much at stake in the debate about the Enlightenment self.

25. MacIntyre, *Whose Justice? Which Rationality?* p. 335.

88

For his part, Robert Solomon prescribes as an antidote to the overdose of self represented by the "transcendental pretence" a large dose of pragmatism of the kind produced by the likes of William James, John Dewey, and Richard Rorty. In the final paragraph of *Continental Philosophy Since 1750,* Solomon calls for a "perfectly modest sense of self." In his words, "the lesson of the transcendental pretence is that in order to be human we do not need to be more than human."[26] Solomon's suggestions resemble those of Rorty and others who are inclined to view intellectual life not as a quest for truth but as a means of escaping boredom and catastrophe through unending "conversation." In the postmodern philosophy that Solomon promotes, gnosticism survives in a sophisticated form. Unlike the heretics of the early church, Solomon's postmodern theorist neither offers access to the secret truths of the world of pure spirit nor promotes the romantic vision of the self's power to transform history and the natural order. Instead, he or she preaches the gospel of language; its saving message is that language does not lead us to any secret truths or havens of beauty and power but rather is itself the only place of safety and delight in a hostile world. In contemporary theory, the ironic, playful consolations of language are the postmodern equivalent of a gnostic heaven in which weary souls may find rest.

To the postmodern pragmatism espoused by Solomon, Rorty, and others, MacIntyre offers a sharp rejoinder. He holds that the power of their highly subjective perspectivism derives from the "inversion of certain central Enlightenment positions concerning truth and rationality." The proponents of "post-Enlightenment relativism and perspectivism claim that if the Enlightenment conceptions of truth and rationality cannot be sustained, theirs is the only possible alternative."[27] Faced with the demise of the quest for certainty, they cannot entertain the thought of truth as something other than indubitable knowledge acquired by a reasoning self. Like their enlightened ancestors, the contemporary pragmatic conversationalists cannot conceive of "the kind of rationality possessed by traditions," MacIntyre argues. Because they are tied implicitly to a view of history as progress, the pragmatic poststructuralists reject the idea that truth might reside in traditions that have been repressed, neglected, or forgotten and that stand in need of recuperation.[28]

26. Solomon, *Continental Philosophy Since 1750,* p. 202.
27. MacIntyre, *Whose Justice? Which Rationality?* p. 353.
28. Such efforts at recuperation are decidedly different from the goals of Heidegger, who does not seek to recuperate the authority of the Bible or the life of the church but

Each in his own way, Wendell Berry and Richard Wilbur celebrate order in nature and seek to bring dormant tradition to life. Their essays and poetry show an abiding concern with the fate of the self in the contemporary world. In addition, their work gives evidence of strong sympathy for Christian understanding, if not an explicit commitment to Christian belief. Like MacIntyre, Berry and Wilbur discover grace in the givens of life and reject the gnostic detachment of the self from the traditions of the past, the communities of the present, and the mysteries of the creation.

Though there are significant differences between them on a number of points, MacIntyre, Berry, and Wilbur desire to imagine how Western men and women might regain the ability to conceive of the given worlds of nature and moral history as signs of grace rather than as threats of bondage. They are aware of the reluctance of postmodern theorists to respond favorably to orders that they discover rather than impose; furthermore, to MacIntyre, Berry, and Wilbur, that unwillingness is as much an ethical dilemma as it is an epistemological problem. Might it not be a tragic pride in our own godlike powers, they ask, that makes us reluctant to acknowledge that truth is imparted to us as well as constructed by us?

Berry addresses directly the relationship between pride and knowledge in a "Letter to Wes Jackson," which serves as the introductory chapter of *Home Economics*. He begins the chapter by quoting another writer describing the passage of raindrops through trees into the soil of a forest. The drops "pass in random fashion through an imaginary plane above the forest canopy," the quoted essay explains, are intercepted by the leaves and branches and sent to the ground in "distinctive . . . patterns," and filter into the soil, eventually leaving the ecosystem as they "entered it, in randomized fashion."[29]

Berry questions the use of the word *random* in this context. Does it mean "a verifiable condition or a limit of perception?" That is, can we prove that order does not exist, or is our failure to detect it a sign of our creaturely limitations? Berry concludes that *random* indicates a limit of perception, for "pattern is verifiable by limited information, whereas the information required to verify randomness is unlimited." For the sake of accuracy, then, the passage "should have said that rainwater moves from

---

desires instead to recover "the question of Being." To Heidegger, the history of Christian theology is part of the larger history of the error that is Western metaphysics.

29. Berry, *Home Economics*, p. 3.

mystery through pattern back into mystery." When we call the mystery of life " 'randomness' or 'chance' or a 'fluke,' " asserts Berry, we are taking "charge of it on behalf of those who do not respect pattern. To call the unknown 'random' is to plant the flag by which to colonize and exploit the known."[30]

Indeed, for many writers since the romantic age, the claim of randomness in nature has been not a cause for despair but a call to action. The greater the disorder in nature and history, the greater is the power of artists as they create beauty and pattern where none existed before. Through the possibilities inherent in the vocabulary of any language, artists may create both the appearance of chaos and the illusion of their power to impose order. It is a heroic tale that has been told countless times in the Western world since the romantic period — the saga of the bankrupt state of creation being replenished with surplus funds from the rich vaults of the artist's spirit. As Nietzsche put it, "One enriches everything out of one's own abundance." The creative person "transforms things until they mirror his power — until they are reflections of his perfection. This *compulsion* to transform into the perfect is — art."[31]

In *Standing By Words,* Berry quotes a poet who maintains that the fear of chaos originates with "people who get up every morning at eight o'clock, teach an Aesthetic Theory class at 10, get the department mail at twelve o'clock, give a graduate student exam in the afternoon, go home and have two drinks before dinner." To this, Berry responds: "Maybe so. But it seems to me more likely that the *praise* of chaos must come from people whose lives are so safely organized."[32] Like St. George slaying the dragon, the academic poets mount an assault upon chaos to prove their heroic worth. Unable to find any stories of epic stature in a disenchanted world, the artists make their own activity the heroic drama, as their art risks all to slay the dragon of the void.

If it is randomness that we encounter in nature, Berry argues, then we do indeed need the power of knowledge to bring order out of chaos. But if it is mystery that we confront, "then knowledge is relatively small, and the ancient program is the right one: Act on the basis of ignorance."

30. Berry, *Home Economics,* pp. 3-4.

31. Nietzsche, *Twilight of the Idols,* trans. R. J. Hollingdale (London: Penguin Books, 1968), p. 72.

32. Wendell Berry, *Standing By Words* (San Francisco: North Point Press, 1983), p. 12.

To act in this manner is to recognize that failure and error are lively possibilities and that "second chances are desirable." On the other hand, a cultural activity that is "knowledge-based and up against randomness . . . conforms exactly to what the ancient[s] . . . understood as evil or hubris. Both the Greeks and the Hebrews told us to watch out for humans who assume that *they* make all the patterns."[33]

The temptation to hubris is particularly great for those who use language with grace and force and whose sense of power grows as they play with words detached from particular contexts and specific commitments. In the last half of the nineteenth century, several poets and fiction writers began a search for an absolute language, for a way of writing in which there would be, as Gustave Flaubert put it, no subject but only style. For a master of language, no freedom could be greater than that afforded by words that serve the will without imposing any obligating constraints upon it. The nineteenth-century quest that Flaubert and others undertook in searching for an absolute language was, in turn, an ancestor of the various formalist and structuralist systems of literary theory so popular in the modern world. In these systems, we witness sophisticated efforts to turn the structure of language itself into the primary or exclusive object of study. "The triumph of the structural point of view," writes Paul Ricoeur in *The Conflict of Interpretations,* "is at the same time a triumph of the scientific enterprise."[34]

In *Home Economics* Berry questions this modern tendency to study language by detaching it from objects and human actions. In what he labels the "specialist approach" to language, Berry says that we encounter the study of language "within itself. It echoes within itself, reverberating endlessly like a voice echoing within a cave." Such examination of language as an object in itself yields surprising insights, but it leads to a severely limited understanding of nature and history. To think of language solely as a system of signifiers referring to each other is to ignore the rich relationships between words and deeds and things. It is the essence of language "to turn outward to the world, to strike its worldly objects cleanly and cease to echo — to achieve a kind of rest and silence in them."[35] Or

33. Berry, *Home Economics,* pp. 4-5.

34. Ricoeur, "Structure, Word, Event," trans. Robert Sweeney, in Ricoeur, *The Conflict of Interpretations: Essays in Hermeneutics,* ed. Don Ihde (Evanston: Northwestern University Press, 1974), p. 83.

35. Berry, *Home Economics,* p. 79.

as Ricoeur explains: "The structural point of view also excludes . . . the primary intention of language, which is to say something about something."[36]

Facts and words must be verified by being "carried back to the things they stand for," Berry explains. When words are not brought back to their corresponding things, they rattle around in the echo chamber of language like so many disembodied spirits in a gnostic heaven. "This carrying back is not specialist work but an act generally human, though only properly humbled and quieted humans can do it." When we use the word *tree,* for example, we are not manipulating an empty cipher or a simple fact. Instead, we

> are at once in the company of the tree itself and surrounded by the ancestral voices calling out to us all that trees have been and meant. This is simply the condition of being human in the world, and there is nothing that art and science can do about it, except get used to it.[37]

For more than four decades, Richard Wilbur has tried to bring words back to things in his poetry. Although acknowledged as one of the finest technical masters of contemporary poetry, Wilbur has consistently resisted any temptation to think of language as a haven from reality or of verbal dexterity as an end in itself. Wilbur is "one whose Way in his dealings with the body of this world is not the Way of Rejection but rather the way of Affirmation," explains Nathan A. Scott, Jr.[38] For instance, in "Love Calls Us to the Things of this World," Wilbur imagines himself in the uncertain world between sleep and waking, between dream and fact. In

36. Ricoeur, "Structure, Word, Event," p. 84.

37. Berry, *Home Economics,* p. 80. The Russian theoretician Mikhail Bakhtin makes this same point more abstractly: "When discourse is torn from reality, it is fatal for the word itself as well: words grow sickly, lose semantic depth and flexibility, the capacity to expand and renew their meanings in new living contexts — they essentially die as discourse, for the signifying word lives beyond itself, that is, it lives by means of directing its purposiveness outward" (Bakhtin, *The Dialogic Imagination: Four Essays,* ed. Michael Holquist, trans. Caryl Emerson and Michael Holquist [Austin: University of Texas Press, 1981], pp. 353-54).

38. Scott, "The Poetry of Richard Wilbur — 'The Splendor of Mere Being,'" *Christianity and Literature* 39, 1 (Autumn 1989): 8. "His [Wilbur's] is the vigilance of one upon whom the natural order of common things is pressing all the time, and he wants to translate into the images and meters of poetry not the light that never was on land or sea but, rather, the light of ordinary day, for, above all else, he is convinced that it is in the order of common things that, as Charles Williams puts it in his great book on Dante, 'the great diagrams are perceived; [that it is] from them [that] the great myths open; [and that it is] by them [that we understand] the final end.'"

the poem, the soul whose "eyes open to a cry of pulleys" is "astounded."
Hanging for a moment "bodiless and simple," the

> soul shrinks
> From all that it is about to remember,
> From the punctual rape of every blessed day.[39]

The Neoplatonic image of the waking soul, with which Wilbur is
working in this poem, is a rich one in the romantic tradition. In several of his
most famous works, William Wordsworth depicted the awakened soul as one
that had been saddened and that sought through poetry the wonder it had
lost upon entering the world of time. In "Ode: Intimations of Immortality,"
for instance, Wordsworth wrote that "our birth is but a sleep and a forgetting";
the soul within us "hath had elsewhere its setting, / And cometh from afar":

> Not in entire forgetfulness,
> And not in utter nakedness,
> But trailing clouds of glory do we come
> From God, who is our home.[40]

The goal of adult life, according to Wordsworth's poem, is to recapture
childhood through memory, to recall the time when the soul was as close
to eternity as the waking mind is to the dreams from which it has just
emerged. In "Love Calls Us to the Things of this World," however, Wilbur
has the waking soul renounce the desire to retreat from the dawning world:

> The soul descends once more in bitter love
> To accept the waking body, saying now
> In a changed voice as the man yawns and rises,
>   "Bring them down from their ruddy gallows;
> Let there be clean linen for the backs of thieves;
> Let lovers go fresh and sweet to be undone,
> And the heaviest nuns walk in a pure floating
> Of dark habits,
>   keeping their difficult balance."[41]

---

39. Wilbur, "Love Calls Us to the Things of this World," in *New and Collected Poems*, p. 233.

40. Wordsworth, "Ode: Intimations of Immortality," in *The Norton Anthology of English Literature*, 5th ed., ed. M. H. Abrams et al. (New York: W. W. Norton, 1986), vol. 2, p. 211.

41. Wilbur, "Love Calls Us to the Things of this World," pp. 233-34.

Desire allures us with its promises of purity of spirit and language, but love calls us incessantly back to the things of this world.

While many poets and critics since the romantic age have conceived of poetic skill as a means of apprehending the wonders of imaginary worlds, Wilbur thinks of it as a way of striking a delicate balance between the desires of the heart and the constraints of creation. In a longer poem entitled "Walking to Sleep," he addresses a person trying to drift into unconsciousness. Wilbur first advises the person to "step off assuredly into the blank of your mind." But he also gives the following warning:

> Try to remember this: what you project
> Is what you will perceive; what you perceive
> With any passion, be it love or terror,
> May take on whims and powers of its own.

"What you hope for" at the end of the "pointless journey" of the mind through its own labyrinths is that,

> when you least expect it,
> Right in the middle of your stride, like that,
> So neatly that you never feel a thing,
> The kind assassin Sleep will draw a bead
> And blow your brains out.[42]

In the second half of the poem, when the aimless drift of the mind has failed to lead the person into sleep, Wilbur offers contrary advice:

> What, are you still awake?
> Then you must risk another tack and footing.
> Forget what I have said. Open your eyes
> To the good blackness not of your room alone
> But of the sky you trust is over it,
> Whose stars, though foundering in the time to come,
> Bequeath us constantly a jetsam beauty.

In this second journey, "if you are in luck, you may be granted . . . / A moment's perfect carelessness" and then

42. Wilbur, "Walking to Sleep," in *New and Collected Poems*, pp. 158, 160.

> sink to sleep
> In the same clearing where, in the old story,
> A holy man discovered Vishnu sleeping,
> Wrapped in his maya, dreaming by a pool
> On whose calm face all images whatever
> Lay clear, unfathomed, taken as they came.[43]

If there is in the heritage of the Enlightenment an implicit gnostic desire to spurn the created order — to shun nature in favor of a self-generated grace — then there is in Wilbur's poetry a tendency to blur the distinctions between the self and the created order, that is, to turn nature into grace. In most cases, however, irony keeps Wilbur from succumbing to that temptation. As one of his witty short poems realizes, the self and nature cannot be in perfect harmony precisely because human transgression has "loosened the grammar" of God's world:

> Shall I love God for causing me to be?
> I was mere utterance: shall these words love me?
>
> Yet when I caused his work to jar and stammer,
> And one free subject loosened all his grammar,
>
> I love him that he did not in a rage
> Once and forever rule me off the page,
>
> But, thinking I might come to please him yet,
> Crossed out *delete* and wrote his patient *stet.*[44]

Latin for "let it stand," *stet* is a proofreader's mark indicating that a passage marked to be changed or deleted from a text should be allowed to remain instead. In a world that is both bountiful and cursed, nothing less than the patience of God is required to keep the self from ruin.

In a recent poem called "Lying," Wilbur ponders the way we respond to the *given* world. Its opening lines describe a lie:

> To claim, at a dead party, to have spotted a grackle,
> When in fact you haven't of late, can do no harm.

---

43. Wilbur, "Walking to Sleep," pp. 160-61.
44. Wilbur, "The Proof," in *New and Collected Poems*, p. 152.

To say that you have seen this most common of birds will neither damage "your reputation for saying things of interest" nor rupture "the delicate web of human trust." Later, however,

> You may enjoy a chill of severance, hearing
> Above your head the shrug of unreal wings.

Why do we lie, then? The world is not "tiresome" in itself, but "boredom,"

> a dull
> Impatience or a fierce velleity,
> A champing wish, stalled by our lassitude,

makes it seem tiresome. Yet no matter how much we fantasize about our power to create and to redeem, the fact remains that

> In the strict sense, of course,
> We invent nothing, merely bearing witness
> To what each morning brings again to light:
> Gold crosses, cornices, astonishment
> Of panes, the turbine-vent which natural law
> Spins on the grill-end of the diner's roof,
> Then grass and grackles . . .
> . . . .

> All these things
> Are there before us; there before we look
> Or fail to look.

And the fact that "all these things / Are there before us"

> is what galled the arch-negator, sprung
> From Hell to probe with intellectual sight
> The cells and heavens of a given world
> Which he could take as but another prison.

Satan, the "arch-negator," was considered a heroic figure by some romantic poets because he refused to accept the limitations placed upon him by his creator. In refusing to accept them, he turned to the joyful pretense of creating by destroying. The first true gnostic, Satan was able to find in the "given world" nothing but "another prison."[45]

Like Satan reacting to the created order, modern thinkers often seem doomed to choose between two extremes as they respond to nature and the past. MacIntyre argues that the Enlightenment bequeathed to us an unworkable dichotomy between the uncritical adherence to tradition and the categorical rejection of it. If these stark options appear to us to be the only possible alternatives, MacIntyre argues, it is because since the eighteenth century we in the West have made a fundamental error in our conception of tradition. MacIntyre asserts that a genuine tradition is not marked by unreflective rigidity but is distinguished by its very ability to respond to legitimate challenges; in meeting such challenges, the tradition may expand or modify itself in previously unimagined ways. MacIntyre himself is an Aristotelian, but his Aristotelianism has passed through Augustine and Aquinas, and his Thomism, in turn, has had to respond to the challenges of the Cartesian and empiricist traditions. Thus his particular tradition is marked, as are all lively traditions, by continuity and by change.

As MacIntyre argues that moral reasoning arises out of given traditions and is compelled to adapt those traditions to changing demands and new realities, so Wendell Berry claims that the self is in a state of dynamic tension with nature. According to Berry, it is a mistake to assume that there is a "divisibility between nature and humanity," but it is also wrong to claim that there is "no difference between the natural and the human." Life would be far easier than it is, Berry says, if nature and the self could be divided (as the gnostic tradition seeks to do) or if there were no difference at all between the human and the natural. "Our problem, exactly, is that the human and the natural are indivisible, and yet are different."[46]

Because modern gnosticism eliminates the dynamic tension between the self and nature, Christian faith must take issue with it, especially at those points where it conflicts with a Christian understanding of creation and the incarnation. For instance, like their Enlightenment forebears, many skeptical postmodernists see nature as an amoral realm subject to the dominion of the human will. What the German sociologist Max Weber called the "disenchanting" of the world began in the earliest stages of modernity. "We could also call it neutralizing the cosmos," says Charles Taylor, "because the cosmos is no longer seen as the embodiment of meaningful order which can define

45. Wilbur, "Lying," in *New and Collected Poems*, pp. 9-10.
46. Berry, *Home Economics*, p. 139.

the good for us." Instead, we have come to see the world as a mechanism so that it no longer contains mysteries that speak to us of the *ends* for which our lives are intended but becomes a "domain of possible means."[47]

In *King Lear,* written almost four hundred years ago, Shakespeare created in one character, Edmund, a prototype of the modern aspiring self that sees nature exclusively as a means to private ends. As the illegitimate second son of an earl, Edmund stands to inherit nothing upon his father's death. He turns to nature because she has no scruples about that accident of birth for which custom has consigned him to an inferior position:

> Thou, Nature, art my goddess; to thy law
> My services are bound. Wherefore should I
> Stand in the plague of custom, and permit
> The curiosity of nations to deprive me,
> For that I am some twelve or fourteen moonshines
> Lag of a brother? Why bastard? . . .
> . . . .
>
> . . . . Fine word, "legitimate."
> Well, my legitimate, . . .
> . . . . Edmund the base
> Shall top th' legitimate. I grow, I prosper.
> Now, gods, stand up for bastards.[48]

Like the gnostic self imagined in contemporary theories of language and culture, Edmund wishes to owe nothing to custom or to nature's God. He worships nature because he sees her as a force sanctioning his fantastic desires.

Edmund appears to be wedded to a view of the world much like that embraced by Richard Rorty and by a European thinker highly prized by Rorty, Hans Blumenberg. In *The Legitimacy of the Modern Age,* Blumenberg agrees with those who claim "that there is a connection between the modern age and Gnosticism." But unlike the critics of modernity who see a decadent form of gnostic belief governing contemporary life, Blumenberg claims that the "modern age is the second overcoming of Gnosticism." The truly gnostic moment in modernity, Blumenberg asserts, occurred in the late Middle Ages, when the nominalist attack on universals

---

47. Taylor, *Sources of the Self: The Making of the Modern Identity* (Cambridge: Harvard University Press, 1989), pp. 148-49.

48. *King Lear,* act 1, scene 2, ll. 1-6, 18-19, 20-22, in *William Shakespeare: The Complete Works,* rev. ed., ed. Alfred Harbage (New York: Penguin, 1969), pp. 1068-69.

proved to be so thorough and successful that "a disappearance of order" took place. With a sovereign, arbitrary, and "hidden" God ensconced within his own transcendent mystery, nominalist Christians could "no longer [perceive] in given states of affairs the binding character of the ancient and medieval cosmos." The "disappearance of order" led to a "new concept of human freedom" at the dawn of the modern world, and it eventuated in the last century in Nietzsche's celebration of "the triumph of man awakened to himself from the cosmic illusion" and to the assurance of "his power over his future. The man who conceives not only of nature but also of himself as a fact at his disposal has traversed only the first stage of his self-enhancement and self-surpassing."[49]

In effect, Blumenberg's argument is that men and women in the Western world were wise and perfectly within their rights at the beginning of the modern age to turn their backs upon a God whose transcendence rendered him irrelevant and to focus instead upon their own technological and pragmatic powers. Edmund questions the authority of "legitimacy" — "fine word, 'legitimate'" — and resolves to consider himself and his world as facts at his own disposal and not as links in some great chain of being. Similarly, Blumenberg sees the modern world not as a child to be blamed for having strayed from its parents' course but as an orphan free to celebrate the creative opportunities occasioned by its abandonment.

The "disenchanted" view of nature espoused by Edmund — and established at the center of Blumenberg's thought — contrasts sharply with the understanding of creation put forth by John Calvin in his *Institutes*. To Calvin, of course, it was the child's act of rebellion, rather than the parent's abandonment of the child, that served as the key metaphor for the human condition. For those who have been adopted through Christ into the family of God, nature is far more than a fact at humanity's disposal. Heaven and earth are wonderfully adorned "with as unlimited abundance, variety, and beauty of all things as could possibly be, quite like a spacious and splendid house, provided and filled with the most exquisite and . . . abundant furnishings."[50] In the face of the unfathomable complexity and order of the universe, we ought not to be "ashamed," but rather should take "delight in the works of God open and manifest in this most beautiful

49. Blumenberg, *The Legitimacy of the Modern Age*, trans. Robert W. Wallace (Cambridge: MIT Press, 1983), pp. 126, 137, 139.

50. Calvin, *Institutes of the Christian Religion*, 2 vols., ed. John T. McNeill, trans. Ford Lewis Battles, The Library of Christian Classics, vols. 20 and 21 (Philadelphia: Westminster Press, 1960), vol. 1, p. 180.

theater."[51] As Calvinism developed in the seventeenth century, the doctrines of creation and providence made it possible to affirm divine sovereignty without having recourse to a medieval, magical view of nature.[52]

The doctrine of the incarnation also challenges the modern gnostic view of selfhood. To bring life to the mechanical, disenchanted world of post-Newtonian science, romantic poets and philosophers promoted the power of the imaginative spirit. In a poem written at the very beginning of the nineteenth century, Samuel Taylor Coleridge laments the "dull pain," the "grief without a pang, void, dark, and drear" that he feels while gazing at a beautiful western sky. The problem is that the beauty is one he can "see, not feel." He does not resolve his crisis of despondency until he realizes that he has been mistaken in looking to "outward forms" for "the passion and the life, whose fountains are within." In our encounters with nature,

> we receive but what we give,
> And in our life alone does Nature live:
> Ours is her wedding garment, ours her shroud!
> And would we aught behold, of higher worth,
> Than that inanimate cold world allowed
> To the poor loveless ever-anxious crowd,

51. Calvin, *Institutes*, vol. 1, p. 179. Statements such as these represent what William J. Bouwsma calls the "philosophical" side of Calvin. This was Calvin as "a philosopher, a rationalist and a schoolman in the high Scholastic tradition represented by Thomas Aquinas, a man of fixed principles, and a conservative. This philosophical Calvin craved desperately for intelligibility, order, certainty." But the "other Calvin was a rhetorician and humanist, a skeptical fideist in the manner of the followers of William of Ockham, flexible to the point of opportunism, and a revolutionary in spite of himself. This Calvin did not seek, because he neither trusted nor needed, what passes on earth for intelligibility and order; instead, he was inclined to celebrate the paradoxes and mystery at the heart of existence" (Bouwsma, *John Calvin: A Sixteenth-Century Portrait* [New York: Oxford University Press, 1988], pp. 230-31).

52. In *Religion and the Decline of Magic* (New York: Charles Scribner's Sons, 1971), Keith Thomas examines the complex relationship between Protestantism and the anti-sacramental bias of modern science. He writes of the Reformation's "onslaught on the central Catholic doctrine of the Mass. . . . The Papists, wrote Calvin, 'pretend there is a magical force in the sacraments, independent of efficacious faith.' . . . In place of the miraculous transubstantiation of the consecrated elements was substituted a simple commemorative rite, and the reservation of the sacrament was discontinued. It went without saying that none of the Protestant reformers would countenance any of the old notions concerning the temporal benefits which might spring from communicating or from contemplating the consecrated elements" (p. 53).

> Ah! from the soul itself must issue forth
> A light, a glory, a fair luminous cloud
> Enveloping the Earth.[53]

As long as Coleridge and the romantic poets believed that the spirit at work within their separate selves was the same as the divine spirit at work in all creation, this praise of the imagination was tempered by humility about its meaning and ultimate source. The imagination was only seeking those spiritual and moral truths the pursuit of which science had forsaken.

With the breaking of the bond between the self and truth in the late nineteenth century, however, the postromantic poet was left with no justifications for imaginative activity beyond those of preference and desire. With the loss of a belief in the spiritual and ethical significance of creation and the human body, the contemporary aesthetic temperament has found an easy justification for license. If nature and the human body are essentially amoral mechanisms to be used as means to whatever private ends we have, then the human will is free to do with them what it will, confident that any activity may be sanctified as a legitimate manifestation of desire.

The doctrine of the incarnation challenges the amoral and utilitarian orientation of the modern gnostic self. It affirms that nature and the body are significant, not because they are the useful tools of imaginative, willful human activity, but because God has taken on human form and dwelt among us. Because "the Word became flesh," Christians may affirm the significance of creation and wait in hope for its transformation. The incarnation of Christ, in the words of Langdon Gilkey, "was of such a character that it established a new relation between eternity and time which . . . flattened the cycles of time out to become the linear stage of God's purposes."[54]

In the work of theology, as in all cultural labor, it is essential to maintain a difficult balance — a balance between the demands of the present and the claims of the past and between the power of the human will and the ordered limits of creation. In Western culture since Descartes, there have been more than enough weighty forces siding with the mind against the body, with the creative power of the intellect against nature, and with the promises of the future against the authority of the past. The

---

53. Coleridge, "Dejection: An Ode," in *The Norton Anthology of English Literature*, vol. 2, p. 376.

54. Gilkey, *Maker of Heaven and Earth: The Christian Doctrine of Creation in the Light of Modern Knowledge* (Garden City, NY: Anchor Books, 1965), p. 302.

works by MacIntyre, Berry, and Wilbur are part of a growing minority tradition in contemporary intellectual life. Contrary to Coleridge and the poets and theorists who followed in his wake, these authors tell us that we do indeed receive far more than we give. For that very reason, these minority voices need to be heard as they seek to strike a balance by speaking of what is, in actuality, a gift — a gift of grace in the given.

Without question, there are many elements in the given world that constitute burdens to be discarded, wounds to be healed, and wrongs to be righted. But there are also in that world gifts to be received. As we will see in the following chapter on Ralph Waldo Emerson, one of the most powerful of romantic voices, those who cannot discern grace in the given are unable to express gratitude for what they have received. This ingratitude, and its attendant resentment, are distinguishing attributes of much of contemporary literary and cultural theory.

CHAPTER 5   *Emerson and the*
             Spirit of Theory

Perhaps only in America could a major cultural figure such as Ralph Waldo Emerson become a spokesman for a popular brand of athletic shoes. During a summer campaign in the late 1980s, Reebok International put the clipped, gnomic sentences of "Self-Reliance" to work selling designer sneakers. In one spot from the twenty million dollar promotion, a fairy godmother, briefcase in hand, spouted Emersonian wisdom: "Insist on yourself. Never imitate. To be great is to be misunderstood." Whether it featured triplets on tree swings or twins cavorting in front of a diner, each segment quoted "Self-Reliance" and closed with the same message: "Reeboks let U.B.U."

There were ample ironies in this use of Emerson. The American prophet of spontaneity, individualism, and originality was pressed into the service of a sophisticated campaign to manipulate consumer tastes for profit in a mass market. When Emerson left the ministry of the Christian church in the 1830s, he looked forward to the flowering of joyous individual freedom in America, anticipating that liberated citizens would usher in an era of spiritual glory and moral refinement. In dreaming of the grandeurs of liberty, he had something far different in mind than the right to choose the color of one's sneakers.

Viewed in another way, however, the conscription of Emerson to sell running shoes may make a certain kind of sense. Emerson and fellow romantics plumbed the self, expecting to discover within its depths nothing less than universal truths for moral and communal life. Those truths were to reconcile mysteriously the demands of the expansive, imperial self with the realities of other selves. "If the single man plant himself indomitably on his instincts, and there abide," Emerson could proclaim with genuine confidence in 1837, "the huge world will come round to him."[1] Or as Emerson's poetic disciple Walt Whitman blithely asserted in the preface to *Leaves of Grass:* "Did you suppose there could be only one Supreme? We affirm there can be unnumbered Supremes."[2]

In the early nineteenth century, Emerson could dream of the reconciliation of supreme egotism and community and have that dream seem plausible. He wrote for an age whose assumptions and expectations would seem fantastic today. As Quentin Anderson has written, "a denial of pain, terror, and death which complements Emerson's own must . . . have conditioned the exorbitant character of the demands on reality made by some of Emerson's contemporaries."[3] The realities of history, however, have blasted the hopes Emerson and his generation had for the imperial self. By the late twentieth century, his rhetoric might seem more appropriate as advertising copy to sway the groundless choices of consuming individuals than as a serious and convincing call to a new life.[4]

In many ways, the developments that have led to the use of Emerson's prose as a marketing device are emblematic of the fate of the Cartesian paradigm in American culture. With its emphasis upon the self-conscious "I" and the necessity of doubt, Cartesianism has had a special importance in American life and possesses great explanatory power for the American experience. This is the case even though the actual works of Descartes have had only marginal influence on the course of American culture. "Descartes's epochal change in philosophy was very much a move toward subjectivity and the self," claims Robert Solomon. "Indeed, there is no

1. Emerson, "The American Scholar," in *Emerson: Essays and Lectures,* ed. Joel Porte (New York: Library of America, 1983), p. 70.

2. Whitman, *Leaves of Grass,* in *Whitman: Poetry and Prose,* ed. Justin Kaplan (New York: Library of America, 1982), p. 14.

3. Anderson, *The Imperial Self: An Essay in American Literary and Cultural History* (New York: Vintage Books, 1971), p. 56.

4. For the relationship of romantic themes to contemporary consumerism and the preoccupation with fame, see Daniel Boorstin, *The Image: A Guide to Pseudo-Events in America* (New York: Atheneum, 1987), pp. 239-61; and Leo Braudy, *The Frenzy of Renown: Fame and Its History* (New York: Oxford University Press, 1986), pp. 445-583.

question but that Descartes . . . was also the founder of the modern philosophical obsession with the self."[5]

In cultivating an Emersonian obsession with the self, American culture has embraced, however unwittingly, the foundational premises of Cartesianism. If an understanding of gnosticism provides invaluable insight into the ethical and theological implications of modern thought, then a knowledge of Emerson might serve equally well to make sense of the atomistic individualism that is the locus of contemporary gnostic belief. In the life and work of Emerson we have a paradigm of the modern ideal of the self-defined, self-reliant individual.

In effect, when Emerson forsook the ministry of the Christian church in 1832 he was announcing his discovery of Cartesian first principles. The letters and journal entries from his years as a pastor, as well as his decisive sermon on the Lord's Supper, show him on the brink of discovering the infinite self whose wonders he would promote for the rest of his life. In proclaiming the unprecedented powers of the uncharted self, Emerson did much to chart the future course of American literary theory and practice; in bequeathing to his cultural descendents an abhorrence of intellectual and moral bequests, he helped to secure the Cartesian legacy in American culture.[6]

We can detect that legacy in the difficulties that contemporary theories of language have in conceiving of possible grounds for human gratitude — in trying, that is, to conceive of the conditions under which the human spirit might be grateful for the power of the past. In many contemporary theories of language and interpretation, one can detect a Cartesian skepticism about tradition and an Emersonian antipathy toward the power of the Other, whether that Other is another self, God, or the past.[7] Such

---

5. Solomon, *Continental Philosophy Since 1750: The Rise and Fall of the Self* (Oxford: Oxford University Press, 1988), p. 5.

6. "There is a distinct and clearly influential climate of Cartesianism in the humanities at the present time. It has been growing ever since World War II. . . . Neither scholarship nor its indispensable ways of working and thinking have the appeal and strength today in the humanities that they had up until the war. More and more the Cartesian adjuration to banish everything from the mind ever learned, and then think intuitively and geometrically by oneself, is the sacred writ of our time" (Robert Nisbet, *The Present Age: Progress and Anarchy in Modern America* [New York: Harper & Row, 1988], p. 129).

7. Richard Grusin has shown how Emerson worked to turn the tables on God, to "put God in his debt": "Emerson's injunction [in "Compensation"] 'Put God in your debt' not only reverses the traditional Christian relation of lender and debtor but insists that in

skepticism and antipathy have been displayed in the passion of theorists for the themes of oppression and liberation and in their penchant for telling stories in which the past becomes exclusively a scene of bondage and injustice, from which the demystified perception of the present alone has the power to free us. In many recent works, interpretation theorists appear to present themselves as exorcists who jet from conference to conference, casting out the demons of ideology with the latest theoretical incantations.

The ungrounded freedom celebrated in much contemporary literary theory is a variation upon a central theme in the history of romanticism. As we have seen, in the decades following the American and French revolutions many poets and critics envisioned themselves as soldiers in the vanguard of the forces of liberation. Of course, for more than a century after the advent of romanticism, the literary tradition was seen as an ally in that battle against intellectual and political despotism. As we have seen, Matthew Arnold had argued in the nineteenth century that, by undertaking a *"disinterested endeavor to learn and propagate the best that is known and thought in the world,"* the literary critic was supposed to further the inevitable progress of *"right* over *force* in the world."* Yet in the past few decades, those very examples of "the best that is known and thought in the world" have frequently been accused of serving as collaborators in the sorry Western history of imperialism and oppression. Hence, the idea of the *classic* itself must be subjected to the distancing, dismantling scrutiny of the critical self.[8]

---

the economy of the soul it is expenditure, not trade, that constitutes the human exchange with God" (Grusin, " 'Put God in Your Debt': Emerson's Economy of Expenditure," *PMLA* 103, 1 [Jan. 1988]: 37).

8. Arnold, "Literature and Science," in *Prose of the Victorian Period,* ed. William E. Buckler (Boston: Houghton Mifflin, 1958), pp. 440-41. Consider, for example, the following comments at the end of an essay on John Milton by Christine Froula:

> We can, through strategies of rereading that expose the deeper structures of authority and through interplay with texts of a different stamp, pursue a kind of collective psychoanalysis, transforming 'bogeys' that hide invisible power into investments both visible and alterable. In doing so, we approach traditional texts not as the mystifying (and self-limiting) 'best' that has been thought and said in the world but as a *visible* past against which we can teach our students to imagine a different future. Because its skeptical regard of the past is informed by responsibility to that future, feminist theory is a powerful tool with which to replace Arnold's outworn dictum. . . . We . . . will undo the invisible power of the literary tradition and make for a richer world." (Froula, "When Eve Reads Milton: Undoing the Canonical

American Descartes

"Of all the countries in the world, America is the one in which the precepts of Descartes are least studied and best followed," observed Alexis de Tocqueville as he analyzed "the philosophical approach of the Americans" in *Democracy in America*. "The Americans never read Descartes's works because their state of society distracts them from speculative inquiries, and they follow his precepts because this same state of society naturally leads them to adopt them." As Tocqueville saw them, Americans were Cartesian in most significant ways:

> To escape from imposed systems, the yoke of habit, family maxims, class prejudices, and to a certain extent national prejudices as well; to treat tradition as valuable for information only and to accept existing facts as no more than a useful sketch to show how things could be done differently and better; to seek by themselves and in themselves for the only reason for things, looking to results without getting entangled in the means toward them and looking through forms to the basis of things — such are the principal characteristics of what I would call the American philosophical method.[9]

Tocqueville, of course, recognized the irony in speaking of the "philosophical approach" of Americans, for he found the inhabitants of the new nation to be less reflective than the citizens of "any other country of the world." With a wild continent to subdue, they had little time to hack their way through the thickets of Continental thought. Even G. W. F. Hegel, proprietor of one of Europe's densest forests of the mind, described America as "the land of desire for all those who are weary of the historical lumber-room of Europe. . . . It is for America to abandon the ground on which hitherto the History of the World has unfolded itself."[10] If weariness caused those in the New World to discard such things as the huge, rough

---

Economy," in *Canons*, ed. Robert von Hallberg [Chicago: University of Chicago Press, 1984], pp. 171-72)

For a powerful counterargument, see Joel Weinsheimer, *Philosophical Hermeneutics and Literary Theory* (New Haven: Yale University Press, 1991), pp. 124-57.

9. Tocqueville, *Democracy in America*, ed. J. P. Mayer, trans. George Lawrence (Garden City, NY: Anchor Books, 1969), p. 429.

10. Hegel, quoted in Robert Spiller et al., *Literary History of the United States*, 4th ed., rev. (New York: Macmillan, 1974), p. 214.

timbers hewn from Hegel's brain, most Americans were happy to do so for the sake of progress in their practical affairs.

Yet in spite of their disdain for philosophical discussion, the "people of the United States," Tocqueville was surprised to discover, "almost all have a uniform method and rules for the conduct of intellectual inquiries."[11] Though skeptical of speculation, nineteenth-century Americans were fond of rules and methods. Indeed, the dominant models of knowledge in early America, commonsense realism and Baconian empiricism, claimed to arrive at epistemological and moral certainty while bypassing the perplexities of ancient systems of belief.[12] What Tocqueville discovered in America was our national tradition of disavowing traditions; indeed, as he came to recognize, for many people of the New World, the only truth a study of the past could reveal was that the past has no binding truth to reveal.

According to Tocqueville, citizens of a democracy distrust the past because their relentless activity breaks the links between generations and causes each new generation to lose interest in the beliefs of its predecessors. As a result, the influence of "one man's mind over another's" is severely limited in America, where citizens "do not recognize any signs of incontestable greatness or superiority in any of their fellows." Unable to defer to the authority of others, Americans "are continually brought back to their own judgment as the most apparent and accessible test of truth." Unwilling to accept *anyone's* word as proof of *anything,* "each man is narrowly shut up in himself, and from that basis makes the pretension to judge the world."

> Being accustomed to rely on the witness of their own eyes, they like to see the object before them very clearly. They there free it, as far as they can, from its wrappings and move anything in the way and anything that hides their view of it, so as to get the closest view they can in broad daylight. This turn of mind soon leads them to a scorn of forms, which they take as useless, hampering veils put between them and truth.[13]

11. Tocqueville, *Democracy in America*, p. 429.

12. For discussions of the prominence of commonsense realism and Baconianism in nineteenth-century America, see D. H. Meyer, *The Instructed Conscience: The Shaping of the American National Ethic* (Philadelphia: University of Pennsylvania Press, 1972); and Theodore Dwight Bozeman, *Protestants in an Age of Science: The Baconian Ideal and Antebellum American Religious Thought* (Chapel Hill: University of North Carolina Press, 1977).

13. Tocqueville, *Democracy in America*, p. 430.

The reforming spirit espoused by Luther, Descartes, and Voltaire had become the dominant force of the Enlightenment in Europe, especially in France, whose people "were the first to generalize and call attention to a philosophic method by which all ancient things could be attacked and the way opened for everything new." Why have similar radical attitudes not provoked revolutionary turmoil in America? Tocqueville explains that in this culture zeal for the overthrow of established institutions is tempered by the mediating influence of the Christian faith. In the United States, "Christianity itself is an established and irresistible fact which no one seeks to attack or to defend." Its authority assures the transmission of a stabilizing set of moral values from generation to generation. By restraining thought and practice in a free society, such values counterbalance the radical first principles of American "philosophy."[14]

In short, the picture Tocqueville paints of America in 1831 is of a nation in which a potentially dangerous habit of mind — Cartesian skepticism — has been kept in check by conventional piety. Americans accept Christian dogma without question and "are bound to receive in like manner a great number of moral truths." Such willing faith "puts strict limits on the field of action left open to individual analysis and keeps out of this field many of the most important subjects about which men can have opinions."[15] Thus, with Christian spiritual and moral truth apparently exempt from the skeptical scrutiny given to other forms of knowledge and authority, America seemed to Tocqueville in 1831 to be securely within the boundaries of orthodox Christian belief.

Breaking the Bonds: Emerson and the Church

At the very time that Tocqueville was touring America and admiring it as a society built upon its unshakeable Christian foundations, Ralph Waldo Emerson felt himself to be trapped in a cellar of dogma with those very foundations collapsing upon him. In 1880 Emerson wrote of the period from 1820 to 1840 that "the ancient manners were giving way" as men and women were growing "reflective and intellectual" and discovering "a new consciousness." While traditions had long held that humans existed

14. Tocqueville, *Democracy in America*, pp. 431-32.
15. Tocqueville, *Democracy in America*, p. 432.

for the service of the state, "the modern mind believed that the nation existed for the individual; . . . the individual is the world."

> This perception [that 'the individual is the world'] is a sword such as was never drawn before. It divides and detaches bone and marrow, soul and body, yea, almost the man from himself. It is the age of severance, of dissociation, of freedom, of analysis, of detachment. Every man for himself. . . . People grow philosophical about native land and parents and relations. There is an universal resistance to ties and ligaments once supposed essential to civil society. The new race is stiff, heady and rebellious. . . . They rebel against theological as against political dogmas; against mediation, or saints, or any nobility in the unseen.[16]

In such an age, "authority falls" and "experiment is credible; antiquity is grown ridiculous." The social world dissolves and life becomes a matter of "every one for himself; driven to find all his resources, hopes, rewards, society and deity within himself."[17]

As he charted this history of "life and letters" in mid-nineteenth-century America, Emerson was effectively writing his autobiography for those years. As he had grown into manhood and rebelled against the thought of "any nobility in the unseen," antiquity increasingly had come to seem "ridiculous" to him. Like many young men in early New England, Emerson had entered into training for the ministry because his ancestors had done so for generations. Yet, in heeding the call of the "party of the Past," he had possessed little enthusiasm for his task and remained diffident about the ministry throughout his preparation and service. For example, shortly before he enrolled at Harvard Divinity School Emerson wrote of his vocation:

> It is my own humor to despise pedigree. I was educated to prize it. The kind Aunt . . . told me oft the virtues of her & mine ancestors. They have been clergymen for many generations & the piety of all & the eloquence of many is yet praised in the Churches. But the dead sleep in their moonless night; my business is with the living.[18]

---

16. Emerson, "Historic Notes of Life and Letters in New England," in *The Transcendentalists: An Anthology*, ed. Perry Miller (Cambridge: Harvard University Press, 1950), pp. 494-95.

17. Emerson, "Historic Notes," p. 496.

18. *Emerson in His Journals*, ed. Joel Porte (Cambridge: Harvard University Press, 1982), p. 54.

Throughout Emerson's journals and letters, the references to the ministry are typically ambivalent. In their timidity and detachment these references stand in remarkable contrast to Emerson's later proclamations about the power and mission of the artist. "In the wind of these great events," Emerson wrote, referring to the recent deaths of John Adams and Thomas Jefferson on July 4, 1826, "I am to assume my office, the meek ambassador of the Highest."[19] Or as he wrote in a poem at that time:

Days that come dancing on fraught with delights,
Dash our blown hopes as they limp heavily by,
But I the bantling of a country Muse,
Abandon all those toys with speed to obey
The King whose meek ambassador I go.[20]

In accepting the call of the Second Church of Boston in January 1829, Emerson continued to express reservations about his potential:

I come to you in weakness, and not in strength. In a short life, I have yet had abundant experience of the uncertainty of human hopes. I have learned the lesson of my utter dependency; and it is in a devout reliance upon other strength than my own, in a humble trust on God to sustain me, that I put forth my hand to his great work.[21]

Emerson served for more than three years as pastor of the Second Church. He was well received by his parishioners and by all accounts fulfilled his ministerial duties in the manner expected of him. Though his sermons contained scattered hints of a radical rethinking of Christian commitment, they did not shock his listeners at the time; their titles give evidence of a standard Unitarian emphasis upon moral improvement: "The Best Part of Life Is Unseen," "Religion Is Doing One's Duty," "The Love of Virtue Is Innate," and "Man Is Improvable." Early in his ministry, Emerson courted and married Ellen Tucker. In private love and in public life, Emerson seemed orthodox and content.

In his biography of Emerson, however, Gay Wilson Allen cautions against reading too much into the apparent orthodoxy of Emerson's years in

19. *The Letters of Ralph Waldo Emerson*, vol. 1, ed. Ralph L. Rusk (New York: Columbia University Press, 1939), p. 54.

20. Emerson, quoted in Gay Wilson Allen, *Waldo Emerson* (New York: Viking Press, 1981), p. 81.

21. *The Letters of Ralph Waldo Emerson*, vol. 1, p. 261.

the pastorate: "Some of Emerson's ideas about God and religion at the time of his first marriage," writes Allen, "might lead one to think he was more orthodox than he actually was."[22] Even as he preached conventional sermons, Emerson was reading widely in unconventional sources, such as Coleridge's *Aids to Reflection* and *The Friend* and selected pre-Socratic philosophers. The idealism Emerson discovered in these sources only deepened the trust in intuition that he had acquired early in his training, especially through his encounters with Common Sense Realism as a student at Harvard. And the more he read and reflected, the more he found himself in conflict with the professions of his church. As Emerson privately became convinced of innate human goodness and power, he remained saddled in his public role with dogmas that spoke of sin, repentance, and revelation.

While Emerson's dissatisfaction with the ministry may be traced in part to new ideas he acquired through his reading, it may also have grown out of a profound antipathy to authority, the origins of which were in the dark, intricate regions of his spirit and memory. Allen begins his biography by telling how in 1850 Emerson received a request for a memoir of his father, Reverend William Emerson. While pondering his response to this request, Waldo complained to his brother William:

> But I have no recollections of him that can serve me. I . . . only remember a somewhat social gentleman, but severe to us children, who twice or thrice put me in mortal terror by forcing me into the salt water off some wharf or bathing house, and I still recall the fright with which, after some of this salt experience, I heard his voice one day, (as Adam that of the Lord God in the garden,) summoning us to a new bath, and I vainly endeavouring to hide myself.[23]

Even in the memory of his earliest years Emerson found authority, shame, and autonomy linked in a terrible complexity.

Several journal entries written during his time as minister of the Second Church register Emerson's increasing specific disdain for authority in matters of the intellect and spirit. For example, in September of 1830 Emerson wrote in his journal of his conviction that

> it is when a man does not listen to himself but to others, that he is depraved & misled. The great men of the world, the teachers of the

22. Allen, *Waldo Emerson*, p. 160.
23. Emerson, quoted in Allen, *Waldo Emerson*, p. 3.

race, moralists, Socrates, Bacon, Newton, Butler, & the like, were those who did not take their opinions on trust, but explored themselves and that is the way ethics & religion were got out.[24]

And in December of that year (less than two months before the death of Ellen), Emerson wrote of his growing sense that if the Christian truth were to survive in the modern world, it would have to rely upon the self-confirming testimony of the soul rather than the authority of historical record:

> Internal evidence outweighs all other to the inner man. If the whole history of the New Testament had perished & its teachings remained — the spirituality of Paul, the grave, considerate, unerring advice of James would take the same rank with me that now they do. I should say as now I say this certainly is the greatest height to which the religious principle of human nature has ever been carried.[25]

After the death of Ellen on February 8, 1831, the journal's "debate" with historic Christianity became more pointed and persistent. Emerson's grief seemed to crystallize his dissatisfaction and to precipitate the crisis leading to his separation from Second Church in September 1832. On June 20, 1831, he wrote that it is not wise to belong to any religious party, for "as fast as we use our own eyes, we quit these parties." In late July he complained, "suicidal is this distrust of reason; this fear to think; this doctrine that 'tis pious to believe on others' words, impious to trust entirely to yourself." He concluded this entry with a note of sarcastic resignation: "To think is to receive."[26]

Emerson's displeasure with the ministry is apparent in many entries from 1832. He argued on January 10 that "the best part of man . . . revolts

24. *Emerson in His Journals,* p. 71.

25. *Emerson in His Journals,* p. 74. Kenneth Cameron has located in Coleridge a passage that parallels what Emerson says in his journal about the primacy of the "inner man." "Coleridge's faith in God would remain steadfast even if Scriptures should prove to be forgeries — his inner reason is proof enough": this is the heading Cameron gives to the following passage from *Table Talk:* "Mr. Coleridge used very frequently to insist upon the distinction between belief and faith. He once told me, with very great earnestness, that if he were that moment convinced . . . that the New Testament was a forgery from beginning to end — wide as the desolation in his moral feeling would be, he should not abate one jot of his faith in God's power and mercy through some manifestation of his being towards man, either in time past or future, or in the hidden depths where time and space are not" (Cameron, *Emerson the Essayist,* vol. 1 [Hartford: Transcendental Books, 1972], n.p.).

26. *Emerson in His Journals,* pp. 77, 80.

most against his being the minister." The problem with orthodox Christianity and its offices "is that we do not make a world of our own but fall into institutions already made & have to accommodate ourselves to them to be useful at all." Though Calvinism suited Ptolemaism, he wrote in May, it was no longer relevant to the modern world. The Sermon on the Mount will be able to retain its authority because it is "true throughout all the space which the eye sees & the brain imagines but St. Paul's epistles, the Jewish Christianity, [are] unintelligible" in times and places other than the ones in which they were written.[27]

By June of 1832, Emerson was ready to resign the pulpit:

> I have sometimes thought that in order to be a good minister it was necessary to leave the ministry. The profession is antiquated. In an altered age, we worship in the dead forms of our forefathers. Were not a Socratic paganism better than an effete superannuated Christianity?[28]

In that same week in early June, Emerson apparently sent to his congregation a letter outlining his reservations about the Lord's Supper and his desire to be excused from administering it. A committee refused Emerson's request, in the hope that their report might "meet with your acquiescence, if not with your entire approbation."[29] But Emerson could not agree to their terms and drafted a letter of resignation. It was delivered on September 11, 1832, two days after he had preached his decisive sermon on the Lord's Supper.[30]

Emerson begins that sermon, which occupies a pivotal point in his development, by surveying the history of the church's differences over the meaning of communion. In the church, "no subject has been more fruitful of controversy than the Lord's Supper," and Emerson dismisses as "frivolous" most arguments over the doctrine in church history. It is difficult to take differences on this matter seriously, because "the questions

27. *Emerson in His Journals*, pp. 81, 82-83.
28. *Emerson in His Journals*, p. 83.
29. Emerson, quoted in Ralph Rusk, *The Life of Ralph Waldo Emerson* (New York: Charles Scribner's Sons, 1949), p. 161.
30. Eight years earlier, Emerson's brother William had faced a similar dilemma. While studying theology in Germany, William suffered anxiety about "returning to New England to preach doctrines he no longer believed." He sought the advice of Goethe on the subject. "Goethe advised him to be practical, to keep his doubts to himself, and his parishioners would be none the worse for the harmless deception" (Allen, *Waldo Emerson*, p. 79).

have been settled differently in every church, who should be admitted to the feast, and how often it should be prepared." Since the practice of the Lord's Supper has hardly been "a tradition in which men are fully agreed, there has always been the widest room for difference of opinion upon this particular."[31]

Emerson knew, of course, that for two centuries the sacrament of the Lord's Supper had been at the center of controversy in New England churches.[32] As obscure as they may seem to modern observers, these debates about the nature of the church and the privilege of communion were the first crucial arguments by European settlers about the meaning of American identity. These Puritans were the first immigrant group, but by no means the last, to agonize over the perils and promises of ideological and ethnic purity, on the one hand, and of assimilation on the other.[33]

Very early in the experience of the settlement in Massachusetts, disputes had arisen about the right to receive the broken bread of the communion table. In the Old World, the Catholic and Anglican churches depended upon civil authority to compel church membership; in European cultures, with few exceptions, the Eucharist was open to all citizens and the church left questions of purity and sincerity to God. The New England Puritans, on the other hand, believed that a church should be made up of "visible saints" alone. Only by limiting membership to the clearly regenerate did the Puritans believe they could maintain crucial distinctions between the church and the world, between the elect and the reprobate.

Distinctions were especially important for the corporate identity of the early settlers of the Massachusetts Bay Colony. They were led by John

---

31. Emerson, "The Lord's Supper," in *Emerson: Essays and Lectures,* pp. 1129-30.

32. The classic text on communion and communal identity in early New England is Edmund Morgan, *Visible Saints: The History of a Puritan Idea* (Ithaca: Cornell University Press, 1965).

33. David Hackett Fischer has written extensively on the enduring influence of early English settlements on American culture. The argument he offers at the beginning of *Albion's Seed* would seem to support my assertion about the importance of the early Massachusetts debates about the Lord's Supper: "Today less than 20 percent of the American population have any British ancestors at all. But in a cultural sense most Americans are Albion's seed, no matter who their own forebears may have been. . . . The legacy of four British folkways in early America remains the most powerful determinant of a voluntary society in the United States today" (Fischer, *Albion's Seed: Four British Folkways in America* [New York: Oxford University Press, 1989], pp. 6-7).

Winthrop, whose shipboard sermon in 1630, "A Model of Christian Charity," has provided American culture with several enduring images of its ideals. Winthrop reminded his fellow pilgrims that they had "entered into covenant" with God for a special work in the New World. They were to be a community "knit together . . . in brotherly affection," upholding a "familiar commerce together in all meekness, gentleness, patience and liberality." They had come to New England so that they might serve as a compelling example of reform to the churches of their native land: "We shall find that the God of Israel is among us, . . . when He shall make us a praise and glory that men shall say of succeeding plantations, 'the lord make it like that of NEW ENGLAND.' For we must consider that we shall be as a city upon a hill. The eyes of all people are upon us, so that if we shall deal falsely with our God in this work we have undertaken . . . we shall be made a story and a by-word through the world."[34]

Winthrop's "city upon a hill," however, did not include the sum of all the people who lived in the New World. The "city upon a hill" was the church triumphant and pure, perched on the highest peak as a beacon to catch the eye of other New World plantations and corrupt Old World cultures. With the redemptive city planted upon the hill, the backsliders, opportunists, and outright pagans of the larger community were left to spread out in the valleys and backwaters below.

To assure the purity of the church, Winthrop's fellow Puritans came up with a series of innovations during the first decades of their settlement. With no established churches around them, they created "gathered" con-gregations of repentant sinners who were able to testify to the saving grace of God in their lives. By means of the narrative of conversion alone could churches guarantee that their communicant members belonged to the elect in the kingdom of God. Only the narrative of conversion made it possible to maintain the distinction between the community of the regenerate and the unrepentant multitudes. And without that distinction clearly estab-lished, how could Christians of the New World shine forth as the "city upon a hill"?

The stringent demand for narrative evidence of the grace of God kept many New Englanders out of the church, even though in the Old World these same men and women would have been welcomed into fellowship at birth. But while such standards could help the Puritans to

34. Winthrop, "A Model of Christian Charity," in *The Norton Anthology of American Literature*, 3rd ed., ed. Nina Baym et al. (New York: Norton, 1989), vol. 1, pp. 40-41.

keep their churches pure, they also threatened to empty the pews. Edmund Morgan describes the inevitable effects of immigration upon the church, even in the first decade of its life in the New World:

> For ten years the human flood swept into Massachusetts, pushing up the rivers, swarming over the champion lands, some twenty thousand souls, and every soul was checked off as saved or damned. The effect on those who failed to make the grade is difficult to calculate. . . . Whoever they were they made surprisingly few complaints about exclusion from the privileges of church membership.[35]

The effect of this process on the saints within the church was easier to calculate, however. As the human tide swarmed over the land, those saints had to come to terms with the decline in membership and influence that their stringency seemed to make inevitable. To meet these challenges, the New England church leaders made key compromises after a few decades. The most famous of these, dubbed the "Half-Way Covenant" by those opposed to it, allowed the children of church members to be baptized and to join the church; until they could provide a narrative of conversion, however, such "half-way" members could not vote in church elections, nor could they participate in the Lord's Supper.

For more than a century, then, the privileges of the communion table were debated heatedly in New England churches. At first, almost all the churches held to the restrictions of the Half-Way Covenant. But over the course of several decades, the tide turned against those who favored strict tests for full membership and communion. One of the proponents of change was Solomon Stoddard, the grandfather of Jonathan Edwards and a powerful pastor in the Connecticut River valley. Stoddard vigorously promoted an open communion for all Christians, whether or not they could provide compelling narrative evidence of the grace of God in their lives. To him, "a church was a territorial unity that embraced all professing Christians within it, whether regenerate or unregenerate."[36] Increasingly, as the church rooted itself in the New World, Stoddard's associates and contemporaries came to share his view of the communion experience as a converting ordinance, a means of broadening the appeal of the gospel in the world.

35. Morgan, *The Puritan Dilemma: The Story of John Winthrop* (Boston: Little, Brown, 1958), p. 79.
36. Morgan, *Visible Saints*, p. 149.

The controversies over the Lord's Supper dealt with fundamental problems of identity in the New World. While there was in fact a limited social hierarchy in New England, in theory the only distinction that ultimately mattered was not one of race, class, gender, or ability but the distinction between heaven and hell, salvation and damnation. By stressing the need for personal narratives, church leaders sought to make clear the difference between the covenantal community of Christ and the larger culture of the New World.[37]

Ralph Waldo Emerson was to spend his entire career as an essayist denying the validity of that distinction. When he came to preach on the Lord's Supper, though he understood the dispute between those who sought to limit participation in the sacrament and those who pressed for a broad administration of it, he did not wish to take the argument seriously. By charging that the debates had been frivolous and by turning the history of doctrine into a saga of groundless controversy, Emerson sought to clear a space for his own blunt "opinion":

> Having recently given particular attention to this subject, I was led to the conclusion that Jesus did not intend to establish an institution for perpetual observance when he ate the Passover with his disciples; and further, to the opinion, that it is not expedient to celebrate it as we do.[38]

In addressing in his sermon the question of Jesus' intentions for the Last Supper, Emerson focuses upon what the New Testament does not say. Matthew and John were present at the Last Supper, but neither recorded in his Gospel the words of Jesus, "This do in remembrance of me." Furthermore, neither of them "drops the slightest intimation of any intention on the part of Jesus" to establish a permanent ritual in his name. Emerson asks whether a solemn institution, which God intended to be practiced to the end of the age, could "have been established in this slight manner."[39]

37. Egalitarianism was more than a theoretical matter in Puritan Massachusetts. Though they could not be called modern democrats, the Massachusetts Bay Puritans significantly modified some of the authoritarian patterns of their English heritage. As Fischer explains in *Albion's Seed,* "Unlike the rulers of other European colonies," the authorities of Massachusetts Bay "deliberately excluded an aristocracy from their ranking system" (p. 178). In addition, "the laws of Massachusetts gave women many protections. . . . Custom as well as law in the Bay Colony required husbands to treat their wives not only with decency, but respect" (pp. 84-85).

38. Emerson, "The Lord's Supper," p. 1130.

39. Emerson, "The Lord's Supper," pp. 1130-31.

But a reader of the New Testament might ask, What are we to make of the actual recorded statements of Jesus? Did he not command his disciples to continue to observe the Supper? Emerson's conclusion is that when Jesus said in Luke's Gospel, "This do in remembrance of me," he was using "a prophetic and an affectionate expression," speaking as "a friend to his friends." He had no desire to "impose a memorial feast upon the whole world," but only hoped to be recalled by members of the "living generation." As for Jesus' explicit commands, Emerson has the following explanation: "'This is my body which is broken for you. Take; eat. This is my blood which is shed for you. Drink it.' — . . . they are not extraordinary expressions from him." Like so many of the things Jesus said, they are tropes, for "he always taught by parables and symbols" and was always ready "to spiritualize every occurrence."[40]

In distinguishing between the beautiful Nazarene and those who have sunk foundations for weighty dogmatic structures into the sands of his simple life, Emerson adumbrates a very important argument of several of his major essays and addresses. According to the "Divinity School Address," the error that "historical Christianity" has fallen into is that "it has dwelt, it dwells, with noxious exaggeration about the *person* of Jesus. The soul knows no persons." The gospel that Jesus preached was a simple one, "a faith . . . in the infinitude of man," but his followers distorted his message beyond recognition.[41] "In the Divinity School *Address*," Barbara Packer explains, "Emerson suggests that the real crucifixion was inflicted on Jesus not by the Romans but by his own followers, by the Christians who take the 'high chant' from the prophet's lips and render it into squalid and murderous dogma: 'This was Jehovah come down out of heaven. I will kill you, if you say he was a man.'"[42]

Jesus' followers destroyed him by calcifying as dogma what had flowed from him as poetry. Throughout his essays, Emerson argues that in democratic America truth must well up from the depths of the individual and that all claims to truth must remain fluid and not fixed. In a well-known passage from "The Poet," he compares the free-flowing course of the poet with the icy rigidity of the orthodox believer:

40. Emerson, "The Lord's Supper," pp. 1130-31.
41. Emerson, "The Divinity School Address," in *Emerson: Essays and Lectures*, pp. 81, 88.
42. Packer, "Origin and Authority: Emerson and the Higher Criticism," in *Reconstructing American Literary History*, ed. Sacvan Bercovitch (Cambridge: Harvard University Press, 1986), p. 69.

Here is the difference betwixt the poet and the mystic, that the last nails a symbol to one sense, which was a true sense for a moment, but soon becomes old and false. For all symbols are fluxional; all language is vehicular and transitive, and is good, as ferries and horses are, for conveyance, not as farms and houses are, for homestead. . . . The history of hierarchies seems to show, that all religious error consisted in making the symbol too stark and solid, and, at last, nothing but an excess of the organ of language.[43]

The arbitrary decisions made by the early Christians about the Lord's Supper, then, do "not settle the question for us." Because they were bound to their "Jewish prejudices," the first Christian leaders failed to have "the influence of Christ . . . enlarge their views." Blinded by their prejudices, they sought to impose their peculiar will upon later generations. Spiritual sanity calls for us to rebel against their dogmas, Emerson argues. If we are to commune directly with God, we must abolish the lifeless forms of the past and make our own lively present judgments, which will be "more in accordance with the spirit of Christianity than was the practice of the early ages."[44]

The second half of Emerson's argument has to do with "the question of expediency." Setting aside the matter of authority, Emerson presses the argument that the Lord's Supper "tends to produce confusion in our views of the relation of the soul to God." By focusing upon Christ, the ritual puts a "second God" between us and God. If Jesus is to mediate our experience of God, then he should do so "in that only sense in which possibly any being can mediate between God and man — that is an Instructor of man. He teaches us how to become like God."[45] Such a claim boldly anticipates the theme of self-deification that was soon to become a touchstone of Emerson's philosophy. In 1838 Emerson would tell the students of the Harvard Divinity School that "alone in history, [Jesus Christ] estimated the greatness of man. . . . He saw that God incarnates himself in man, and evermore goes forth anew to take possession of his world."[46]

Even if it were not a matter of confusing "the relation of the soul to God," Emerson tells his congregation that a simple distaste for the Lord's

---

43. Emerson, "The Poet," in *Emerson: Essays and Lectures,* pp. 463-64.
44. Emerson, "The Lord's Supper," p. 1136.
45. Emerson, "The Lord's Supper," pp. 1136-37.
46. Emerson, "The Divinity School Address," p. 80.

Supper may justify him in refusing to participate in it. "This mode of commemorating Christ is not suitable to me. That is reason enough why I should abandon it." He will choose some other way to show his appreciation for his "glorified friend," Jesus, hoping to avoid the error that other Christians have made in giving an importance to communion "which never can belong to any form." Emerson admits that "forms are as essential as bodies; but . . . to adhere to one form a moment after it is out-grown, is unreasonable, and it is alien to the spirit of Christ." Thus Emerson here anticipates his later claims about the plasticity of aesthetic form and the minimal authority of genres, and in emphasizing taste as a deciding criterion he shows how crucial intuitive preference was to him in matters of the spirit.[47]

For Emerson, as for many romantics, the linchpin of moral truth was the conviction that the self's innocence assured that the preferences of the individual would correspond to the demands of the community. Emerson devoutly believed that to pursue the deepest desires of the heart was to choose universal truth: "To believe your own thought, to believe that what is true for you in your private heart is true for all men, — that is genius."[48] There were times in his career, as in the essay "Experience," when Emerson peered through the grates of preference and saw nothing but an abyss of solipsism below. But even when he wrote of the terror of the self's plunge into meaninglessness, he always seemed able to summon up assurance, as at the end of "Experience": "Never mind the ridicule, never mind the defeat: up again, old heart! . . . there is victory yet for all justice; and the true romance which the world exists to realize, will be the transformation of genius into practical power."[49]

Whatever questions he was to have later, however, Emerson had no doubts as he left the ministry about his ability to span the chasm between the self and truth. Indeed, the explicit claim of "The Lord's Supper" and other essays is that timeless principles known intuitively by the self — rather than time-bound truths revealed to the self — provide the only secure bridge for Christian faith in the modern world. Emerson's own generation had failed to bridge the gap because it had built with the materials and methods of its ancestors, rather than in ways of its own devising. All that the self can legitimately seek to receive from the past,

47. Emerson, "The Lord's Supper," p. 1138.
48. Emerson, "Self-Reliance," in *Emerson: Essays and Lectures*, p. 259.
49. Emerson, "Experience," in *Emerson: Essays and Lectures*, p. 492.

the "Divinity School Address" makes clear, is assurance of its own infinitude and divinity. According to Emerson, we must not look back to the cross of Christ for the forgiveness of sins. Instead, that cross must symbolize our inalienable freedom, which we foolishly sacrifice when we submit to fixed forms or authorities. In the words of "The Lord's Supper,"

> That for which Paul lived and died so gloriously; that for which Jesus gave himself to be crucified; the end that animated the thousand martyrs and heroes who have followed his steps, was to redeem us from a formal religion, and teach us to seek our well-being in the formation of the soul.[50]

Emerson concludes his sermon by announcing his readiness to resign his pastorate. He would be willing to continue in his duties, he tells the members of his congregation, if they would be willing to excuse him from administering the Lord's Supper. He does not object to the participation of others in the rite: "I am only stating my want of sympathy with it. . . . That is the end of my opposition, that I am not interested in it." Though saddened by the prospect of resigning the office of pastor, Emerson can find one comfort in leaving the ministry: "I am consoled by the hope that no time and no change can deprive me of the satisfaction of pursuing and exercising its highest functions."[51]

In severing his ties to the church and to orthodoxy, Emerson did not think he was abandoning his work as a preacher. As he became the prophet of the expressive self, he exchanged his pulpit for a podium and the form of the sermon for the essay and public address. Indeed, he believed that his departure from the church would allow him to pursue his spiritual goals with greater power and integrity. In the case of the issue of communion, as we have seen, he was convinced that the historical particularity of the ritual was a stumbling block.

To Emerson, the premise of the American experiment was Jesus' own assumption — that the way into the kingdom of God was through the imagination alone. One can imagine how Emerson might have rewritten the parable of the wedding banquet in Matthew 22. In that parable, Jesus tells of the man who comes to the banquet without the proper wedding clothes. The King spies the man and has him bound and flung into the outer darkness, "the place of wailing and grinding of teeth" (Matt. 22:13,

---

50. Emerson, "The Lord's Supper," p. 1139.
51. Emerson, "The Lord's Supper," p. 1140.

REB). Commentaries typically surmise that the proper wedding clothes would be either good deeds and a pure heart or the gospel message of the forgiveness of sins. Either way, according to the logic of the parable — "many are called, but few are chosen" (v. 14, NRSV) — the garments are a gift from God. In the history of the church, the sacrament of the Lord's Supper has served as the central act of remembrance; it brings to mind the gift of the death and resurrection of Jesus and serves as a foretaste of the banquet of heaven. For Emerson, on the other hand, all who came to the wedding banquet in fabric woven by their own imaginations would be welcome. Only those who wore the garments of received faith would be cast into a private hell of unfulfilled potential.

Thus, although he was about to become a profane man by leaving the ministry, Emerson was convinced that he would continue more effectively in his sacred calling. He was ready to devote himself to the gospel of America as the kingdom of God. And he was eager to proclaim that the imagination had replaced the cross as the central symbol of spiritual experience.

The Emersonian Paradigm

In one sense, Emerson's conflict with the Unitarian church had little effect on American culture, for, as Stanley Cavell observes, it was the fate of Emerson and Thoreau to remain largely "unknown to the culture that they founded."[52] In the mid-nineteenth century, "average Americans warned as insistently, if not as eloquently, as did their recognized spokesmen Hawthorne and Melville against the unleashing of the self," Lewis Saum has written. Emerson's praise of unadulterated selfhood, his "ultimatums directed at father, mother, wife, and others within earshot would have defied all instincts and training, and would have seemed unadorned ventures into callousness."[53] In America at that time, the self as Emerson envisioned it was circumscribed by the fear of God and the love of others, by what Tocqueville had called the "established and irresistible fact" of Christianity.

52. Cavell, "In Quest of the Ordinary: Texts of Recovery," in *Romanticism and Contemporary Criticism,* ed. Morris Eaves and Michael Fischer (Ithaca: Cornell University Press, 1986), p. 236.

53. Saum, *The Popular Mood of Pre–Civil War America* (Westport, CT: Greenwood Press, 1980), pp. 108-9.

Nevertheless, Emerson's break with the Second Church is of more than casual significance in the history of American culture. Lawrence Buell correctly asserts in the opening sentence of a work on Emerson and his circle: "The outstanding symbolic event in the history of Transcendentalism is Emerson's resignation from his Boston pastorate in 1832 in order to become a scholar-at-large."[54] In rejecting the authority of the Bible, liturgical tradition, and the church, Emerson discovered his alternatives of aesthetic power and radical intellectual freedom. As a precedent, Emerson's break would inspire a small number of disaffected men and women to seek spiritual solace completely outside the boundaries of the church and orthodox doctrine. Furthermore, his dismissal of the claims of tradition and the church helped make it easier for later American writers to define themselves and their tasks independent of Christian belief.[55] In making the ordinance of the Lord's Supper the issue over which he broke with the pastorate and the Christian tradition, Emerson rejected all efforts aimed at sustaining the particularity and exclusivity of the gospel, and he made Christ, the romantic self, and America indistinguishable from one another.

As the debates over the Lord's Supper in the early history of New England indicate, from the earliest stages of the American experience citizens in the New World have wrestled with the tension between the self and authority. But until the time of Emerson, almost all attempts to resolve that struggle took place within the confines of orthodox Christian belief, however attenuated that orthodoxy might have become. In unbridling the expressive self, Emerson became a central figure in the drama of the secularization of the spirit in America. Like his counterparts in England and Germany, he was willing to give up what was necessary "of the dogmatic understructure of Christianity" — for Emerson, this constituted all of historic orthodoxy — in order to save whatever possible of Christianity's "experiential relevance and values." But whereas European writers were concerned "to sustain the inherited cultural order against what to many writers seemed the imminence of chaos," Emerson was eager to cast

---

54. Buell, *Literary Transcendentalism: Style and Vision in the American Renaissance* (Ithaca: Cornell University Press, 1973), p. 21.

55. James Turner has examined the crisis of belief in mid-nineteenth-century America in *Without God, Without Creed: The Origins of Unbelief in America* (Baltimore: Johns Hopkins University Press, 1985). Though his study only briefly discusses Emerson, it does offer a compelling explanation of the process by which the sentimental, expressive self supplanted Christian belief in nineteenth-century America.

off the burden of that order as he plumbed his soul and scanned the horizon of the future for its splendors.[56]

Thinking as Thanking

In casting off the shackles of dogmatic belief, Emerson believed that he was freeing the expansive self to do its innocent works of power. Yet, as we have seen, in the century and a half since Emerson began to promote the expressive self, his spiritual descendents have been able neither to discover the innocent self he sought nor to establish the redeemed society he anticipated. Robert Solomon gives the name "transcendental pretence" to romantic assumptions about the "innocence [and] remarkable inner richness and expanse of the self."[57] "Having been provoked to transcendental arrogance by Rousseau and Kant" and "expanded to cosmic proportions by Hegel and the other idealists" (including Emerson), that self has been battered by the intellectual discoveries and historical realities of the past century. "It looks as if the self, which had been raised to transcendental then cosmic status," Solomon concludes, "has now disintegrated into nothingness."[58]

Ironically, even with the self subjected to an unrelenting assault, contemporary literary theorists continue to find ways of reasserting its powers and prerogatives. They do so by abandoning Emerson's theological and epistemological claims for the self, while continuing to clutch at his confidence in the power of the will. That is, in their different forms, the recent theories have shown their indebtedness to an Emersonian conception of the self and its relationship to moral and intellectual legacies. In the voices clamoring to be heard in the conversation of the culture of interpretation, the echoes of Emerson reverberate.

This point could perhaps best be illustrated through brief citations from four books on literary theory published in the 1980s. With the exception of the first selection, each of the following passages serves as the concluding passage of the book from which it is taken:

---

56. M. H. Abrams, *Natural Supernaturalism: Tradition and Revolution in Romantic Literature* (New York: W. W. Norton, 1971), p. 68.

57. Solomon, *Continental Philosophy Since 1750*, p. 1.

58. Solomon, *Continental Philosophy Since 1750*, p. 126.

Let me call "romanticism" the thesis that what is most important for human life is not what propositions we believe but what vocabulary we use. . . .

Their contribution [that of William James and Nietzsche] was to replace romanticism by pragmatism. Instead of saying that the discovery of vocabularies could bring hidden secrets to light, they said that new ways of speaking could help get us what we want. Instead of hinting that literature might succeed philosophy as discoverer of ultimate reality, they gave up the notion of truth as a correspondence to reality.[59]

The fate of Marxism will be decided by the active involvement of individuals in the great struggle of persuasion. To say this about the fate of socialism, that it will be decided in rhetorical war, is to say nothing especially specific to its vision. The fate of all visions, or nightmares, as the case may be, of the good life, will be similarly decided.[60]

I shall end with an allegory. *We* know that the lion is stronger than the lion-tamer, and so does the lion-tamer. The problem is that the lion does not know it. It is not out of the question that the death of literature may help the lion to awaken.[61]

We care about texts for many reasons, not the least of which is that they bring us news that alters our way of interpreting things. If this were not the case, the Gospels and the teachings of Karl Marx would have fallen upon deaf ears. Textual power is ultimately power to change the world.[62]

Whether it is in the deconstructive pragmatism of Richard Rorty, the Marxism of Frank Lentricchia and Terry Eagleton, or the liberal humanism of Robert Scholes, the legacy of Emersonian romanticism is evident in these quotations. The self they envision is unable to *receive*

---

59. Richard Rorty, "Nineteenth-Century Idealism and Twentieth-Century Textualism," in *Consequences of Pragmatism* (Minneapolis: University of Minnesota Press, 1982), pp. 142, 150.

60. Frank Lentricchia, *Criticism and Social Change* (Chicago: University of Chicago Press, 1983), p. 163.

61. Terry Eagleton, *Literary Theory: An Introduction* (Minneapolis: University of Minnesota Press, 1983), p. 217.

62. Robert Scholes, *Textual Power: Literary Theory and the Teaching of English* (New Haven: Yale University Press, 1985), p. 165.

either truth from the past or the promise of a significant *telos*. Left to its own devices, that self is free to construct its own systems of belief, to find satisfactions for its own desires, and to conceive of whatever ends it can imagine for human life. This is the Emersonian self, stripped of its naive and buoyant optimism, yet resolute in its antagonism to the claims of the past and in its determination to employ language as an instrument of utility or power. "Freedom," as Emerson declared in his sermon on the Lord's Supper, must "be as flexible as the wants of men." So too must language and thought be flexible in the world of contemporary theory if they are to protect the self and procure its desires.

But is there no other viable way to think about *thinking* in the postmodern world? George Steiner has observed that Martin Heidegger was fond of the seventeenth-century Pietist phrase *Denken ist Danken,* "to think is to thank." Steiner concludes that to be able to conceive of *thinking* as *thanking* and to engage in "that highest act of mortal pride and celebration which is to give thanks" may well be "indispensable if we are to carry on as articulate and moral beings."[63] *"To think is to thank."* What could this mean in an intellectual world grounded in Descartes and Emerson and bounded at present by Jacques Derrida and Michel Foucault? In the spirit of contemporary theory, the conception of thought as an expression of gratitude — in anything but a self-congratulatory form — seems unfathomable. Emerson's "Self-Reliance" defines as well as anything the nature of gratitude in modernity: "In every work of genius we recognize our own rejected thoughts: they come back to us with a certain alienated

---

63. Steiner, *Martin Heidegger* (New York: Penguin Books, 1980), p. 15. In " 'Critic'/ 'Reader' " Steiner meditates upon the detachment of criticism and the immediacy of reading. In Steiner's terminology, Emerson is decidedly a "critic," as are most contemporary theorists. Of the attitude of the reader, Steiner writes:

He situates himself within, rather than traversing it with conventional concession and logical embarrassment, the supposition that the text, the work of art, the musical composition are *data* not in the "scientific" or realistically objectivized sense, but in the primary and archaic signification of "that which is given to us." That they are not "objects" even in a special "aesthetic" category, but "presences," "presentments" whose existential "thereness" (Heidegger's word) relates less to the organic, as it does in Aristotelian and Romantic poetics and theories of art, than it does to the "transubstantiational." . . . What is implicit is the notion and expression of "real presence." The reader proceeds *as if* the text was the housing of forces and meanings, of meanings of meaning, whose lodging within the executive verbal form was one of "incarnation." (*George Steiner: A Reader* [New York: Oxford University Press, 1984], p. 85)

majesty."[64] For several hundred years in Western intellectual life, the form of gratitude that has seemed superior to all others is that of the self thanking itself for whatever freedom it has attained or whatever satisfaction it has acquired.

In discussing W. H. Auden's struggles with the romantic heritage, Edward Mendelson argues that Auden's early poetry should be seen as the culmination of the romantic tradition in English poetry, just as "recent theories of poetic language are the culmination of romantic literary theory."[65] The burden of the romantic tradition has been one of incessant innovation, a need to surpass the literary accomplishments of the previous generation. For a century after the romantics, this competition from generation to generation was largely a concern of poets. "He most honors my style who learns under it to destroy the teacher," Walt Whitman announced in *Song of Myself,* and over the course of the last hundred years innovation has steadily grown in importance as a poetic ideal.[66] Since the early years of this century, fiction writers have become preoccupied with the matter of innovation; and in the decades since World War II, with the explosive growth of graduate education and its affiliated industries of literary criticism and theory, theorists of literature have also grown increasingly concerned to "make it new." But as Mendelson says, "efforts to extend the modernist revolution either in poetry or in criticism . . . lead to arid parodies of what came before."[67] Auden eventually discovered the futility of moving a step beyond the latest development; what was needed instead was a step that would move "in a different direction" entirely.

Because modern literary studies have been captive to romantic conceptions of the self and language, it has largely fallen to thinkers in other fields to search for a "different direction" than the one mapped by the Enlightenment and romanticism. One particularly fruitful avenue of in-

64. Emerson, "Self-Reliance," p. 259.

65. Mendelson, *Early Auden* (New York: Viking Press, 1981), p. 22. There are many studies of modern theory that point to the continuities of romantic and postromantic views of literature. See Robert Langbaum, *The Poetry of Experience: The Dramatic Monologue in Modern Literary Tradition* (New York: Random House, 1957); Geoffrey Hartman, *Beyond Formalism: Literary Essays 1958-1970* (New Haven: Yale University Press, 1970); Gerald Graff, *Literature Against Itself: Literary Ideas in Modern Society* (Chicago: University of Chicago Press, 1979); and Jerome McGann, *The Romantic Ideology: A Critical Investigation* (Chicago: University of Chicago Press, 1983).

66. Whitman, *Song of Myself,* in *Whitman: Poetry and Prose,* p. 242.

67. Mendelson, *Early Auden,* p. 22.

vestigation has been that of philosophical hermeneutics. Especially under the influence of Heidegger, prominent Continental thinkers have sought paths out of the maze of Cartesian self-consciousness. They have done so by attempting to describe the manner in which we actually go about the task of reading texts and experiences. In their views of tradition, language, and the self, these hermeneutic philosophers provide fruitful ways for the Christian to think about revelation, truth, and human finitude.

For instance, in *The Symbolism of Evil*, Ricoeur examines the language of fault and accusation and concludes that the Cartesian ideal of a free and indubitable starting point for knowledge is an impossibility: "it is necessary to renounce the chimera of a philosophy without presuppositions and begin from a *full* language."[68] Because it cannot hold every assumption in abeyance, skeptical thought must start "from speech that has already taken place, and in which everything has already been said in some fashion." Thus, Ricoeur concludes, all thought is grounded in the unconscious resources encoded in the history of language and human experience; for this reason, the moral past is alive in present speech. Ricoeur writes of "the *gift* of meaning from the symbol." In his words, "the symbol gives; but what it gives is occasion for thought, something to think about."[69] For philosophical hermeneutics, knowledge is a gift before it becomes a task; it must be received before it can be doubted.

For Emerson, however, knowledge always took the form of a task rather than a gift. After he left the ministry, he repeatedly argued that only self-reliant individuals could discover truth through their imaginative exertions. Preaching to students at Harvard Divinity School, he spoke of the "one stern condition" of truth: "this, namely; it is an intuition. It cannot be received at second hand. Truly speaking, it is not instruction, but provocation, that I can receive from another soul."[70] And in the opening paragraph of "Self-Reliance" Emerson argued that the highest merit of the likes of Moses, Plato, and Milton was that "they set at naught books and traditions, and spoke not what men but what they thought." According to "Self-Reliance," we cannot *receive* knowledge because when we learn something we are only uncovering what we already *possess* within us: "In every work of genius we recognize our own rejected thoughts: they come

68. Paul Ricoeur, *The Symbolism of Evil*, trans. Emerson Buchanan (Boston: Beacon Press, 1967), p. 19.

69. Ricoeur, *The Symbolism of Evil*, p. 348.

70. Emerson, "The Divinity School Address," p. 79.

back to us with a certain alienated majesty." As "Self-Reliance" concludes, "Nothing can bring you peace but yourself. Nothing can bring you peace but the triumph of principles."[71]

In pitting the isolated mind against external authority, Emerson proved himself a true child of Cartesianism and the Enlightenment. The Enlightenment "distorted the very concept of authority," Hans-Georg Gadamer explains. By depicting authority to be "diametrically opposed to reason and freedom: to be, in fact, blind obedience," and by establishing an absolute "antithesis between authority and reason," the Enlightenment set as its goal "the subjection of all authority to reason." Gadamer argues that authority has nothing to do with blind obedience, but is rather a matter of recognition and knowledge — "knowledge, namely, that the other is superior to oneself in judgment and insight."[72] It is impossible to acknowledge such authority in the romantic world of Emerson.

Admittedly, there are distinct differences between an Enlightenment conception of reason and Emerson's romantic stress upon intuition. The one emphasizes law and pattern, while the other stresses spontaneity and freedom; the one enshrines reason, while the other exalts the imagination. Yet in spite of their differences, Cartesian rationalism and Emersonian romanticism share a deep trust in the power of the self to unveil the truth and a deep distrust of tradition. For Descartes and Emerson and their theoretical descendents, tradition threatens knowledge. By clamping burdensome prejudices upon the mind and crippling restraints upon the spirit, it disables the self, leaving it enslaved to the power of others and powerless to heed the beckoning call of truth.

The truth always does call, Emerson affirmed repeatedly, but it does so from the depths and recesses of the self. In trying to resuscitate what he took to be the moribund spirituality of Unitarianism, Emerson urged the Harvard Divinity students "to go alone; to refuse the good models, even those which are sacred in the imagination of men, and dare to love God without mediator or veil."[73] All sacred texts, received opinions, and settled practices have the power to veil the truth. Emerson's fear of such mediating forces is what Tocqueville meant by the American "scorn of forms, which they take as useless, hampering veils put between them and truth."

71. Emerson, "Self-Reliance," pp. 259, 282.

72. Gadamer, *Truth and Method*, 2nd rev. ed., trans. Joel Weinsheimer and Donald G. Marshall (New York: Crossroad, 1989), pp. 279, 277-78.

73. Emerson, "The Divinity School Address," pp. 88-89.

To Heidegger, it is sheer folly to dream that one might tear the veil to gain an unobstructed view of truth. Contrary to the beliefs of the Cartesian tradition, all perception and reflection are enmeshed in language and its history. "Intuition" and "thinking" are both derivatives of understanding, for

> when we have to do with anything, the mere seeing of the Things which are closest to us bears in itself the structure of interpretation. . . . When we merely stare at something, our just-having-it-before-us lies before us *as a failure to understand it any more.*[74]

The self, that is, always has truth mediated for it by the traditions and communities in which it has developed and in which it lives. Through our participation in communities of language, we *receive* our very ability to comprehend anything at all. In this most fundamental sense, "Denken *ist* Danken," "thinking *is* thanking," for without the gift of language — and without the traditions of practice, interpretation, and belief that are embedded in language — the isolated self would be at a loss as to how to comprehend, let alone respond to, its world.

In an intriguing way, these insights from the hermeneutical reflections of Continental philosophers parallel the conclusions of several contemporary moral philosophers and social scientists. *Habits of the Heart,* for instance, voices the concerns of many observers about the destructive potential of American ideas of the self. Seeking a way out of the "dead end of radical individualism," Robert Bellah and his colleagues call for the recovery of an awareness of the self's profound indebtedness and dependence. Such an understanding contrasts with the "almost hegemonic" view of the self "in our universities and much of the middle class." That image of the untethered individual "is based on inadequate social science, impoverished philosophy, and vacuous theology," Bellah argues. Encumbered by Cartesian and Lockean notions of an unencumbered self, contemporary Americans cannot account for the fact that "there is much in our life that we do not control, that we are not even 'responsible' for, that we receive as grace or face as tragedy."[75] The "culture of separation," however, has not become dominant in American culture "because there are still oper-

---

74. Martin Heidegger, *Being and Time,* trans. John Macquarrie and Edward Robinson (New York: Harper and Brothers, 1962), p. 190.

75. Bellah et al., *Habits of the Heart: Individualism and Commitment in American Life* (Berkeley: University of California Press, 1985), pp. 81, 84.

ating among us, with whatever difficulties, [primarily biblical and republican] traditions that tell us about the nature of the world, about the nature of society, and about who we are as people."[76]

As we saw in the last chapter, Alasdair MacIntyre has reached similar conclusions by way of a critical study of Anglo-American moral philosophy. In *Whose Justice? Which Rationality?* he observes that "a central aspiration of the Enlightenment" was that "reason would displace authority and tradition." The Enlightenment sought "to provide . . . standards and methods of rational justification" to use in judging the worth of "alternative courses of action in every sphere of life." The hope was that reason could supplant tradition by providing principles that "no rational person could deny." Such principles would be free "of all those social and cultural particularities which the Enlightenment thinkers took to be the mere accidental clothing of reason in particular times and places."[77] Because it has been committed to the Enlightenment "prejudice against prejudice," liberal individualism has remained blind to the fact that all rational enquiry is "embodied in a tradition"; it has been unable to recognize that "to be outside all traditions is to be a stranger to enquiry; it is to be in a state of intellectual and moral destitution."[78]

MacIntyre's observations could serve as a telling judgment of Emerson's objectives. Emerson rejected historic Christianity because of his belief that spiritual truth is universal and must not be bound to doctrines, accidents of history, or liturgical practices. In the early and mid-nineteenth century, when political and cultural revolutions made a decisive break with the past appear desirable and possible, Emerson's optimism about the self may have possessed a degree of plausibility. As long as Emerson had the resources of tradition and the stability of a community to draw upon — even as he sought to draw away from them — his defiant proclamations made a certain sense. But what has become the fate of Emersonian individualism when the paradigm of the sovereign self has become exhausted? Because "nothing . . . about the essence of anything can be learned from the study (in Cartesian isolation) of the first person alone," we can no longer "begin our enquiries from the first person case and think that it gives us a paradigm of certainty," philosopher Roger Scruton argues. "For

---

76. Bellah et al., *Habits of the Heart*, pp. 281-82.

77. MacIntyre, *Whose Justice? Which Rationality?* (Notre Dame: University of Notre Dame Press, 1988), p. 6.

78. MacIntyre, *Whose Justice? Which Rationality?* p. 367.

taken in isolation, it gives us nothing at all."[79] Unable to provide moral or epistemological certainty, the Emersonian individual in the postmodern world appears fated to be a consumer of objects and experiences rather than a prophet of new revelation.

For the Christian critic of culture, W. H. Auden provides a constructive response to the collapse of the romantic self in postmodernism. Mendelson describes Auden's poetry of the 1930s as "the record of his passage from indifference to forgiveness." By 1939, after a decade of flirting with various promises of psychological, economic, and political salvation, Auden discovered that "it was the gift of charity that reconciled where all else failed."[80] In the following year, having made the connection between charity and Christian faith, Auden committed himself to the practice of that faith. In gratitude for forgiveness and with thanksgiving for the sheer givenness of things, Auden found a means of moving in a "different direction entirely," beyond the glory and the ignominy of the imperial self.

In his later poems and essays, Auden regularly explored the complex relationship between Protestantism and the romantic and modernist heritages against which he was struggling to define himself. In a 1960 review of Erik Erikson's *Young Man Luther,* Auden wrote of his conviction that the Protestant era — "that is to say, an era in which the dominant ideology was protestant (with a small p) and catholic ideology the restraining and critical opposition" — had come to an end and that Western culture had entered a new Catholic era. The change had come about "precisely because of the success of protestantism in all its forms. A solution to our difficulties cannot be found by protestant approach because it is protestantism which has caused them."[81]

Tracing the beginning of the Catholic era to the conversion of John Henry Newman in 1845, Auden argues for the need to recover a Catholic vision of the communal nature of the earthly and heavenly cities:

> Whether one considers oneself, one's friends and neighbors, or the history of the last hundred years, it seems clear that the principal threat to a sense of identity is our current lack of belief in and acceptance of the existence of others. Hence the grisly success of various totalitarian

79. Scruton, *From Descartes to Wittgenstein: A Short History of Modern Philosophy* (New York: Harper & Row, 1982), pp. 282-84.

80. Mendelson, *Early Auden,* p. 365.

81. Auden, *Forewords and Afterwords* (New York: Vintage Books, 1974), pp. 86-87.

movements, for the Evil One can only seduce us because he offers bogus solutions to real needs, one of which is the need for personal authority both to obey and to command (force is impersonal and altogether evil). The function of protestantism today is not to solve our problems but to warn against and oppose all solutions that are speciously, not authentically, catholic, to point out that the catholic community can only be realized by the will of each lutheran individual to create it.[82]

To a significant extent, the confusion of modern theories of language and the self is rooted in the attempt of romanticism, as exemplified in the case of Emerson, to ground spiritual and moral values in the transcendent self. With the collapse of that self in the postmodern world, the efforts to continue in this vein have taken on an increasingly desperate air. To some observers, such efforts appear doomed because they attempt to discover in critical detachment itself a sufficient foundation for the moral, spiritual, and communal life of humanity. If Emerson is to have authority for us in coming years, it may indeed be necessary to conclude of him what Auden suggested about the Protestant principle in general. The isolated detachment of the Emersonian individual will be useful "not to solve our problems but to warn against and oppose all solutions that are speciously, not authentically, catholic."

In a poem addressed to his senses entitled "Precious Five," Auden issues a command to each organ of sense — "Be patient," "Be modest," "Be civil," "Look," and "Praise" — and he implores his senses to "be happy" and do as they "are told." He also tells them that if he were

> To face the sky and roar
> In anger and despair
> At what is going on,

the response he would get would be

> That singular command
> I do not understand,
> *Bless what there is for being,*
> Which has to be obeyed, for
> What else am I made for,
> Agreeing or disagreeing?[83]

82. Auden, *Forewords and Afterwords,* p. 87.

83. Auden, "Precious Five," in *Collected Poems,* ed. Edward Mendelson (New York: Random House, 1976), pp. 447-50.

To those students of literary culture who have acquired the habit of Narcissus, of seeing in nature only their own reflected glories, and who hear in the voices of the past only their "own rejected thoughts" coming back to them "with a certain alienated majesty," the call to "bless what there is for being" may make little sense at all. But to those who feel the pinch of the poverty of Emersonian theories of language and the self, such commands may take on the character of promises. Those who look with care for more than their own reflections may catch a glimpse of a splendor that is as yet unrevealed. For those who have ears for more than the echo of their own speech, there may indeed be much to hear.

CHAPTER 6 *Hawthorne, History,*
and the Heart

EMERSON DETESTED the hold of the past and struggled to be free of it. "History is an impertinence and an injury," he said, "if it be anything more than a cheerful apologue or parable of my being and becoming."[1] In the middle of the nineteenth century, it was still possible for Emerson to argue convincingly about the moral possibilities of the self freed from constraint. Inspired by the Enlightenment attack upon prejudice, Emerson was confident that the romantic intuitional self would be able to accomplish what the enlightened rational self could not do in its struggle against the past. In one sense, Emerson's romanticism represents one of the last grand efforts of the Cartesian tradition to discover indubitable truth through the exertions of the isolated self freed from custom and external authority.

Emerson's confidence in the self pitted against history may have appeared plausible at the height of romanticism in America, but it seems awkwardly out of place in the modern world. We now realize, in the words of Hans-Georg Gadamer, that "history does not belong to us; we belong to it. Long before we understand ourselves through the process of self-examination, we understand ourselves in a self-evident way in the family, society and state in which we live." The possibilities of our cultural and spiritual life are shaped by the language and traditions we inherit, and not

---

1. Emerson, "Self-Reliance," in *Emerson: Essays and Lectures,* ed. Joel Porte (New York: Library of America, 1983), p. 270.

just by the choices that we make. *"That is why the prejudices of the individual, far more than his judgments, constitute the historical reality of his being."* [2]

Most contemporary schools of theory acknowledge the power of the past to shape language and the self. It has become a truism of contemporary thinking that we always speak as selves dramatically circumscribed by the meanings of the words we employ, and not as totally free selves choosing words and meanings at will. Every word that we use carries a history of associations and usages within it. When we appropriate language for our own use, we inherit the moral history of the words we employ, even if we are attempting to do nothing more than use those words to get what we want. Words do not simply influence our thinking; they undergird it, they shape it, and they direct it.

In a curious way, contemporary theories of literature and language seem to support a view of human nature similar to the one expounded by St. Augustine more than 1500 years ago. By emphasizing the situated nature of discourse and the sobering limits of the self, current thinking about language agrees in important ways with the picture of humanity offered in Augustine's exposition of human finitude and fallenness. Nevertheless, Augustinian views of the self go against the grain of the Pelagianism that is dominant in contemporary American culture. Indeed, it might be said that the argument of this entire book is that many contemporary theories of language and literature are caught between Augustinian insights and Pelagian desires. Those theories seek to acknowledge the dark and mysterious side of human nature and affairs. But at the same time they also preach a gospel of liberation, whether that liberation is to come through the experience of art, the supplanting of dominant oppressive vocabularies, or the pragmatic exercise of the will in search of satisfaction.

Perhaps no one has presented the Pelagian implications of American culture as clearly as the literary historian Perry Miller did in a number of vital articles and books. The identity of any individual is the product of a series of decisions, Miller asserts, "and the great uniqueness of this nation is simply that here the record of conscious decision is more precise, more open and explicit than in most countries." For the history of the European settlement of America there is no mythical past; all the major events —

2. Gadamer, *Truth and Method,* 2nd rev. ed., trans. Joel Weinsheimer and Donald G. Marshall (New York: Crossroad, 1989), pp. 276-77.

the culture-shaping decisions — of that settlement were documented. As a result, the American conception of the self has stressed the roles of choice and volition to an unprecedented degree. In Miller's memorable phrase, "being an American is not something inherited but something to be achieved."[3]

Because it affirms that men and women have an unprecedented freedom to choose their identities and values, the ideology of American culture seems to run counter to Gadamer's argument that "the prejudices of the individual, far more than his judgments, constitute the historical reality of his being." And yet to confirm Miller's claim about American life, we need do little more than consider a representative list of our culture's "self-made" men and women, both historical and fictional: Benjamin Franklin, Ralph Waldo Emerson, Hester Prynne, Walt Whitman, Emily Dickinson, Thomas Alva Edison, Huckleberry Finn, Henry Ford, Jay Gatsby, and Martin Luther King, Jr. Each figure in this very diverse group is an individual who refused to accept the definition assigned by tradition and the social order into which he or she had been born.

All of these individuals are "protestants" who place the claims of conscience and innovation ahead of established practices or beliefs. Their cultural prototype is Martin Luther, who stood before the Holy Roman Emperor at the Diet of Worms and proclaimed:

> Unless I am convicted by Scripture and plain reason — I do not accept the authority of popes and councils, for they have contradicted each other — my conscience is captive to the Word of God. I cannot and will not recant anything, for to go against conscience is neither right nor safe. God help me. Here I stand, I cannot do otherwise.[4]

To be a "protestant" in this sense is to believe in the virtue of a defiant stand against corrupt authority. Such resistance takes a strenuous effort of the will and must be freely chosen to be considered virtuous.

In an essay on the novelist Henry James, W. H. Auden identified an emphasis upon volition as one of the distinguishing characteristics uniting Protestantism and American culture. The presupposition for which America "has come, symbolically, to stand," explains Auden, "is that liberty is prior to virtue, i.e., liberty cannot be distinguished from license, for

3. Miller, *Nature's Nation* (Cambridge: Harvard University Press, 1967), p. 13.
4. Luther, quoted in Roland Bainton, *Here I Stand: A Life of Martin Luther* (Nashville: Abingdon Press, 1978), p. 144.

freedom of choice is neither good nor bad but the human prerequisite without which virtue and vice have no meaning. Virtue is, of course, preferable to vice, but to choose vice is preferable to having virtue chosen for one."[5] Auden wrote this almost half a century ago, when it apparently was evident that Americans preferred virtue to vice. It is not at all clear that that is still the case; at least it is not clear that contemporary therapeutic culture shares Auden's understanding of virtue and vice. In cataloguing our list of virtues, some postmodern Americans are more likely than not to write "freedom of choice and preference" and close the book.

Especially in America, the romantic movement appropriated the volitional emphases of Protestantism. In responding to the ruptures caused by early modern science and Enlightenment skepticism, romanticism stressed the need for a *reaffirmation* of commitment *after* an experience of doubt and denial. In the words of Robert Langbaum, "it is not this or that political, philosophical, religious, or even aesthetic commitment that marks the romanticist. It is the subjective ground of his commitment, the fact that he never forgets his commitment has been chosen. . . . The commitment, no matter how absolutist and dogmatic, remains subordinate to the chooser."[6]

For Protestant Christians living in postromantic America, then, respect for tradition must always be coupled with an acknowledgment of cultural and psychological reality. Those who profess Christ must also confess that they have *chosen* to do so; adherence to any tradition of faith remains a matter of the will as much as one of habit. As we have seen, the early Puritans placed a great emphasis upon the need for individuals to confirm their standing before God through a wrenching process of conversion. This Puritan way of the spirit later became what Robert Bellah and his colleagues call the American pattern of "leaving home."[7] One of

---

5. Auden, *The Dyer's Hand and Other Essays* (New York: Random House, 1962), p. 318.

6. Langbaum, *The Poetry of Experience: The Dramatic Monologue in Modern Literary Tradition* (Chicago: University of Chicago Press, 1985), p. 21. Paul Ricoeur writes: "In every way, something has been lost, irremediably lost: immediacy of belief. But if we can no longer live the great symbolisms of the sacred in accordance with the original belief in them, we can, we modern men, aim at a second naïveté in and through criticism. In short, it is by *interpreting* that we can *hear* again" (Ricoeur, *The Symbolism of Evil*, trans. Emerson Buchanan [Boston: Beacon Press, 1967], p. 351).

7. Bellah et al., *Habits of the Heart: Individualism and Commitment in American Life* (Berkeley: University of California Press, 1985), pp. 56-62.

the paradoxes at the heart of the American experience is that this culture has developed a tradition of disdaining tradition; and any good citizen is obliged to learn the cultural pattern of spurning the cultural patterns of family and community. "Like other core elements of our culture, the ideal of a self-reliant individual leaving home is nurtured within our families, passed from parent to child through ties that bind us together in solitude as well as love."[8]

The expatriate poet T. S. Eliot understood very well that an American Protestant must will his or her connection to the church, to ethical values, and to God. His own life illustrated the paradox of a tradition of spurning tradition. In the late 1920s Eliot announced that he had become a royalist in politics, an Anglo-Catholic in religion, and a classicist in literature. Born in St. Louis and educated at Harvard, Eliot had been, in stages, a believer in republican democracy, a Unitarian Protestant, and a champion of the literary avant-garde. So his mid-life decision involved a major shift, a return to tradition. Yet Eliot knew that in the modern world all such returns are matters of the will. In a well-known essay dating from 1919 entitled "Tradition and the Individual Talent," he wrote that "tradition . . . cannot be inherited, and if you want it you must obtain it by great labour."[9]

The Identity of Goodman Brown

"Tradition cannot be inherited," for uncritical adherence to received belief is morally suspect in postromantic, Protestant America. Yet at the same time, the impoverishing limitations of American individualism make a return to tradition imperative for many Americans. How does one reconcile the cultural demand for rupture with the yearning for continuity? How strong is a commitment that is grounded in the act of conscious choice alone?

Questions such as these troubled the great nineteenth-century American fiction writer Nathaniel Hawthorne. In his stories and novels, this descendent of the Puritans continually explored the tensions engendered

8. Bellah et al., *Habits of the Heart*, p. 62. On this subject, see also Charles Taylor, *Sources of the Self: The Making of the Modern Identity* (Cambridge: Harvard University Press, 1989), pp. 32-40.

9. Eliot, "Tradition and the Individual Talent," in *Selected Prose of T. S. Eliot*, ed. Frank Kermode (London: Faber & Faber, 1975), p. 38.

by American culture's understanding of the past. The claim that "tradition cannot be inherited" is something that one of Hawthorne's best-known characters, Goodman Brown, would have understood very well. In "Young Goodman Brown," the central figure is a common man living in Puritan Massachusetts in the late seventeenth century. Like so many in that time and place, he is bedeviled by questions of authority and authenticity. On one night in particular, he has a harrowing experience outside Salem village, and he is forever devastated as a result of it.

As Hawthorne's story opens, Young Goodman Brown is leaving his bride of three months to go off on an unspecified journey at sunset. In spite of the pleas of his wife, Faith — "Pray, tarry with me this night, dear husband, of all nights in the year!" — Goodman Brown sets off on his journey, vowing to himself "after this one night" to "cling to her skirts and follow her to Heaven." Shortly after he has left Faith, he meets a man on his journey in the darkened forest. This person "had an indescribable air of one who knew the world," and he was distinguished by the strange staff he carried, which "bore the likeness of a great black snake, so curiously wrought, that it might almost be seen to twist and wriggle itself, like a living serpent."[10]

As they continue on the path ever deeper into the forest, through conversation and observation Goodman Brown learns shocking things about the Devil and his fellowship with the pious citizens of Salem village. The Evil One tells Goodman Brown how in the past he had assisted Goodman Brown's father and grandfather in such deeds as the flogging of a Quaker woman or the torching of an Indian village. Furthermore, he informs Goodman Brown that he continues to work closely with the notables of the village and the colony:

> "The deacons of many a church have drunk the communion wine with me; the selectmen, of divers towns, make me their chairman; and a majority of the Great and General Court are firm supporters of my interest. The governor and I, too — but these are state-secrets."[11]

Having heard firsthand of the Devil's past actions, Goodman Brown must now observe his present workings. He watches as revered residents of Salem consort with the Evil One. Their revel culminates in a Black

10. Hawthorne, "Young Goodman Brown," in *Hawthorne: Tales and Sketches*, ed. Roy Harvey Pearce (New York: Library of America, 1982), pp. 276-77.
11. Hawthorne, "Young Goodman Brown," p. 278.

Mass, at which even Goodman Brown's pure wife Faith is present. After the "congregation" sings a hymn, Goodman Brown and Faith are brought before the "altar." The Devil points to "the fiend-worshippers" and says to the young couple:

> "There . . . are all whom ye have reverenced from youth. Ye deemed them holier than yourselves, and shrank from your own sin, contrasting it with their lives of righteousness, and prayerful aspirations heavenward. Yet, here are they all, in my worshipping assembly!"[12]

As the Devil prepares to administer an unholy baptism, Goodman Brown cries out, "Faith! Faith! . . . Look up to Heaven, and resist the Wicked One!" And immediately he finds himself miraculously standing alone in the forest "amid calm night and solitude."

The next morning, Goodman Brown stumbles into town, only to recoil at the sight of the devil worshipers back at their normal pious activities — the minister meditating upon his sermon, Deacon Gookin at domestic worship, and Goody Cloyse catechizing a little girl. The contrast between the private, hellish world of the forest and the public purity of the village is too great for Goodman Brown to bear. Afflicted by his guilty awareness of the difference between what is and what seems to be, Goodman Brown becomes "a stern, a sad, a darkly meditative, a distrustful, if not a desperate man." And when he died, "they carved no hopeful verse upon his tomb-stone; for his dying hour was gloom."[13]

To understand this story, it is important to recall that the Puritans of Massachusetts adhered to "covenant theology" of a specific kind. They believed that God had elected them for eternal salvation and for the decidedly historical task of establishing his kingdom in the wilderness of the New World. In Puritan covenantal theology, though God had decreed the individual and collective future, members of the covenant had a solemn obligation to execute that covenant through the rigorous exercise of their wills. Every man and woman was called to confront a righteous God and to struggle to discern the signs of his favor.

As we have seen, because of the enormity of their task and because of their need to distinguish themselves clearly from heretics, the Puritan churches sought to preserve their purity and orthodoxy through a strict regulation of membership. Those who aspired to full status in the church

12. Hawthorne, "Young Goodman Brown," p. 286.
13. Hawthorne, "Young Goodman Brown," pp. 288-89.

were required to profess their conviction that they had been elected to the covenant of salvation. Sydney Ahlstrom, an American church historian, explains that the requirement of a narration of the experience of grace was "a radical demand." It marked the first time in the history of the church that "a state church with vigorous conceptions of enforced uniformity in belief and practice was requiring an internal, experiential test of church membership."[14]

At a distance of several centuries, it is difficult to take the full measure of the intensities and intricacies of the debate over the exclusion of individuals from the Lord's Supper. The arguments went to the heart of the question of how one could maintain a Christian identity in the New World. According to New England Calvinism, the only thing a person could be sure of inheriting was the legacy of Adam's sin. Through baptism one might also be welcomed into the fellowship of the covenantal community, but baptism provided no guarantee of forgiveness or salvation. One could receive this greatest of gifts only through a conscious decision, through a converting awareness of God's grace breaking the bonds of the hellish tradition of sin. A person could not claim this decision to be his or her own, of course, but had to wait for God to act. Individuals had to scrutinize their experiences for evidence that they had been called out of the communion of sinners and into the circle of saints.

In a study of Hawthorne's short stories, Michael Colacurcio has argued that when Goodman Brown journeys into the forest to meet the Devil, he does so as one who has only recently been admitted to *full communicant membership* in Salem church.[15] Safely within the inner sanctum of saints, young Goodman Brown feels secure enough to explore the demonic world. "Feeling himself justified," he assures himself that his wife Faith is "a blessed angel on earth" and that he will be able to follow her to heaven, *after* his adventures of a night. Born to the communion of sinners and elected to the fellowship of saints, Goodman Brown sets out to explore the moral opposite of his redeemed world. If he can see clearly what the members of the Devil's party are like, he may be better able to secure his own identity in his difference from them.

It is clear that Goodman Brown did not expect to find the commu-

---

14. Ahlstrom, *A Religious History of the American People*, 2 vols. (Garden City, NY: Image Books, 1975), vol. 1, p. 194.

15. Colacurcio, *The Province of Piety: Moral History in Hawthorne's Early Tales* (Cambridge: Harvard University Press, 1984), pp. 283-313.

nion saints within the Devil's grasp. After all, the premise of the church as a gathering of visible saints was the possibility of separating the sheep from the goats within history. But instead of finding the damnable opposite against which he could define himself, Goodman Brown is stunned to discover the blessed and damned carousing together:

> Aloft in the air . . . came a confused and doubtful sound of voices. Once, the listener fancied that he could distinguish the accents of town's-people of his own, men and women, both pious and ungodly, many of whom he had met at the communion-table, and had seen others rioting at the tavern. . . .
>   . . . But, irreverently consorting with these grave, reputable, and pious people, these elders of the church, these chaste dames and dewy virgins, there were men of dissolute lives and women of spotted fame, wretches given over to all mean and filthy vice, and suspected even of horrid crimes. It was strange to see, that the good shrank not from the wicked, nor were the sinners abashed by the saints.[16]

If the people Goodman Brown meets at the hallowed communion table are no different from those he comes upon reveling at the tavern, what can be the meaning of the demanding Puritan conversion experience?

Goodman Brown is caught in a genuine American cultural bind. He comes to doubt the power or efficacy of a *conversion* experience that claims to have released the self from bondage to the *tradition* of sin. And this is a dreadful realization for him, because the Puritan enterprise of which he was a part had promised a radical new beginning of life in Christ. From the earliest days, the Puritans had labored to free the redeemed members of the covenant community from the wicked past as well as from their wicked peers. The New England experiment was an extraordinary attempt to create a "city upon a hill." In the imagery of John Winthrop's sermon, in this city it just might be possible for members of the covenant community to expel the old Adam, when "Christ comes and takes possession of the soul and infuseth another principle, love to God and our brother."[17]

In the forest, Goodman Brown is shocked to find that those who labor by day to build the "city upon a hill" spend their nights frolicking with the Evil One. He is devastated to learn that human behavior provides

16. Hawthorne, "Young Goodman Brown," pp. 282-83, 285.
17. Winthrop, "A Model of Christian Charity," in *The Norton Anthology of American Literature*, 3rd ed., ed. Nina Baym et al. (New York: W. W. Norton, 1989), vol. 1, p. 37.

no convincing evidence for a distinction between the blessed and damned. Shocked as he is, Goodman Brown withdraws into a purifying isolation. When he had set out to meet the Devil, he had assumed that the sanctity of his neighbors was genuine. He had been confident that he would be able to persevere in the faith and return to the village unharmed. But when he saw the righteous members of the Salem church in the company of the Devil, he lost faith in all human virtue save his own. Goodman Brown "is left outside the bounds of all communion: his own unbartered soul is the only certain locus of goodness in a world otherwise altogether blasted."[18]

There is much that is characteristically American and curiously postmodern in Goodman Brown's righteous isolation. Like many cultural critics of today, Goodman Brown trusts his ethical perceptions when they expose the guilty secrets of others from the present or past, but he conveniently exempts himself from scrutiny. The hermeneutic of suspicion applies to everyone but the interpreter who uses it. Furthermore, like many in American culture, Goodman Brown somehow considers himself an island of purity in a sea of corruption. To be sure, he recognizes the hypocrisy of those who claim to be innocent but whose deeds are evil. Yet he repeats the very errors he condemns as he convinces himself that he can remain righteous by severing his ties to the corrupt world around him. For Goodman Brown, as for many of the heirs of Nietzsche, indignant disenchantment affirms and secures his virtue in a corrupt world. Todd Gitlin, a faculty member at Berkeley and a prominent student activist from the 1960s, implicitly recognized the "Goodman Brown" syndrome when he addressed a conference in the early 1990s on "The PC Frame-Up." According to the account of the conference, "Gitlin said academic leftists needed to be more politically savvy, recognizing that they are seen as pleading on behalf of special interests." In Gitlin's own words, "The amazing truth of American political culture of the last 20 years is that the right owns the White House while the left is fighting over the English department!"[19] While the hermeneutic of suspicion may convince theorists of their moral rectitude, it does nothing to rescue them from the banishment imposed by their own self-righteousness.

Unlike Hawthorne, other figures in the American experience —

18. Colacurcio, *The Province of Piety,* p. 302.
19. "'Frame-Up of Multicultural Movement Dissected by Scholars and Journalists,'" *The Chronicle of Higher Education,* 27 Nov. 1991, p. A-15.

including Emerson, Henry David Thoreau, and Walt Whitman — have resolved the problems of purity and virtue not by isolating themselves from those whom they take to be guilty but by proclaiming all men and women to be innocent. To the romantic poets and essayists, the problem of sin and guilt was one of perception, a problem we could be free of by discarding the distorting lenses inherited from the past. As Thoreau proclaims in *Walden:* "We loiter in winter while it is already spring. In a pleasant spring morning all men's sins are forgiven. Such a day is a truce to vice. . . . Through our own recovered innocence we discern the innocence of our neighbors."[20] And in *Song of Myself* Whitman uses the image of the communion meal to depict the transformation of America that he anticipates; when we see things as they are, we discover that all of us are saved, because none of us is guilty:

> This is the meal equally set, this the meat for natural hunger,
> It is for the wicked just the same as the righteous, I make
>   appointments with all,
> I will not have a single person slighted or left away,
> The kept-woman, sponger, thief, are hereby invited,
> The heavy-lipp'd slave is invited, the venerealee is invited;
> There shall be no difference between them and the rest.[21]

These images of the "meal equally set" effectively announce the final broadening of access to the communion table that the romantic movement signifies in the American experience. In his battle against those who sought to limit participation in the Lord's Supper, the Connecticut Valley pastor Solomon Stoddard had pointed to the success of the revival "harvests" in which he had invited all Christians to participate in communion. By inviting to the communion table even those who were uncertain of their election, Stoddard sought to provide an occasion for the working of God's grace. God could use the nourishment of the communion ritual to make men and women blighted by doubt ready for the harvest. In Whitman's poem, the poet announces himself as the great harvester, but the nature of the harvest is different. Whitman is also announcing that his miraculous winnowing has yielded no tares to be discarded but only pure grain to be

20. Thoreau, *Walden,* in *Thoreau,* ed. Robert F. Sayre (New York: Library of America, 1985), p. 573.

21. Whitman, *Song of Myself,* in *Whitman: Poetry and Prose,* ed. Justin Kaplan (New York: Library of America, 1982), p. 205.

gathered in. Proclaiming equality and forgiveness, Whitman sees himself as doing nothing less than ushering in the kingdom of God upon earth. "Let the physician and the priest go home," Whitman declares, for the poet has arrived.[22]

Whitman's promise — that the priests could depart, because the poet was ready to do their duties more effectively — became the premise of a powerful cultural minority in America during and after the romantic period. Taking its cues from Whitman, Thoreau, Emerson, and Margaret Fuller, this small but influential group of critics and artists set out to construct a social order based on Christian moral principles but independent of Christian theology and commitment. From the midpoint of the nineteenth century on, there was a pitched battle between orthodoxy and agnosticism. "It was a civil war," argues James Turner, and in that conflict "agnostics did not repudiate the churches' morality; they inherited it."[23] These agnostics appropriated the moral legacy of the Christian faith, fully confident that the sources of morality were hidden deep within nature and the human spirit. They believed that the romantic liberation of that spirit would do more to improve human history than any efforts conducted under the constraints of orthodoxy and authority. For some in the generation of Emerson and Hawthorne, it appeared likely that American culture would be able to preserve the seed of moral and spiritual vitality from the Christian tradition while winnowing the chaff of authority and history.

Yet for the Christian, history is something more than chaff to be winnowed or shackles to be broken. The past is a scene of liberation as well as bondage, the site of forgiveness and grace as well as injustice. There is admittedly much for which we need to repent in our individual and collective pasts. How can we comprehend *our* moral complicity in slavery, in Auschwitz, and in the Gulag? But there is also in the past much for which we need to be profoundly grateful. After all, it is in that past that we discover the history of redemption. God chose a *particular* people as his own, and Jesus was born, died, and raised again in a *particular* place at a *particular* time. Without that past, we would have no future. In converting to that tradition — a broad tradition of orthodoxy spanning denominational lines — we have been brought into the truth. We may only see the truth through a glass darkly; but for those who have seen that

---

22. Whitman, *Song of Myself*, p. 232.

23. Turner, *Without God, Without Creed: The Origins of Unbelief in America* (Baltimore: Johns Hopkins University Press, 1985), p. 244.

truth, gratitude and hope have the power to keep them from the gloom of Goodman Brown's dying hour.

The Scarlet Letter and the Failure of Interpretation

As a direct descendent of the Puritans, Hawthorne was ambivalent about his heritage. He was so ashamed of the role that one of his ancestors had played in the Salem witch trials that he changed his family name from Hathorne to Hawthorne. And while he feared that the stain of ancestral corruption might have seeped into his own character, he was also aware of what his forebears might have said about his chosen career as a writer of stories. In the introductory sketch to *The Scarlet Letter*, Hawthorne imagines his ancestors talking: "'What is he?' murmurs one gray shadow of my forefathers to the other. 'A writer of story-books! What kind of a business in life . . . may that be? Why, the degenerate fellow might as well have been a fiddler!' "[24]

As harsh as Hawthorne's judgments were about his Puritan ancestors, he also sensed that with the disintegration of Puritanism something profound had passed from the American scene. Nineteenth-century American culture lacked the ethical clarity of the first New England settlements. As oppressive as seventeenth-century Boston must have been, it was still a place where moral choices mattered, where questions of belief and behavior had eternal consequences. In every way, Hawthorne said, "morally, as well as materially, there was a coarser fibre" in the citizens of Puritan Boston.[25] The writing of *The Scarlet Letter* became, in the words of Quentin Anderson, an "adventure of imagining what his contemporaries could not give imaginative shape to: a town. In such an imagined town . . . adultery would not lead to indifferent snickers; it would be an issue of life and death."[26]

According to Hawthorne, the cohesiveness of seventeenth-century Boston should not be attributed to "the impulses of youth, but to the stern and tempered energies of manhood, and the sombre sagacity of age;

---

24. Hawthorne, *The Scarlet Letter*, in *Hawthorne: Novels*, ed. Millicent Bell (New York: Library of America, 1983), p. 127.

25. Hawthorne, *The Scarlet Letter*, p. 161.

26. Anderson, *The Imperial Self: An Essay in American Literary and Cultural History* (New York: Vintage Books, 1972), p. 80.

accomplishing so much, precisely because it imagined and hoped so little."[27] The early New England settlement knew what doctrines it believed, what actions it could countenance, and what practices it had to exclude at all costs. In seventeenth-century Boston, an individual's identity was distinct. At a time in history "when the forms of authority were felt to possess the sacredness of divine institutions," individuals were secure as long as they conformed to the demands of those who wielded authority.

But Hawthorne believed that absolute conformity was impossible in matters of faith and practice, for the human heart was bound to go astray. This was true for those who ruled as well as for those who were ruled. Who would judge the rulers of church and community if their virtues or beliefs were called into question? Who was to determine whether those who wielded kingdom authority had the right to abide in the virtuous realm they so assiduously guarded? And if the authorities had no experience of the actions they condemned, how could they understand anyone who went astray? Hawthorne says of the Puritan men who sat in judgment on Hester Prynne in *The Scarlet Letter:* "They were, doubtless, good men, just, and sage." But "out of the whole human family," it would have been impossible to choose a group of men "less capable of sitting in judgment on an erring woman's heart, and disentangling its mesh of good and evil."[28]

The plot of *The Scarlet Letter* is familiar even to many who have never read the novel: in seventeenth-century Boston, Hester Prynne has committed adultery and is forced to stand before the people of the town with a red letter *A* upon her dress and with her illegitimate infant, Pearl, in her arms. The town does not know the identity of her adulterous accomplice, and she refuses to reveal his name. To a great extent, the action of the novel consists of the inner struggles of Hester and of Arthur Dimmesdale, who is a highly revered minister and the father of Pearl.

In Puritan Boston, adultery was a serious breach of the marriage covenant and a clear violation of the commandment of God.[29] Hester's judges have no doubts about the righteousness of their punishment of Hester

27. Hawthorne, *The Scarlet Letter,* p. 172.

28. Hawthorne, *The Scarlet Letter,* p. 173.

29. In light of the severity of Puritan codes of punishment and practices, it might be argued that the punishment of Hester was lenient by their standards. "The Puritans followed the teachings of the Old Testament in believing that adultery was a sin of the deepest dye. . . . Their criminal codes made adultery a capital crime, and at least three people were actually hanged for it in the Puritan colonies" (David Hackett Fischer, *Albion's Seed: Four British Folkways in America* [New York: Oxford University Press, 1989], p. 88).

and the appropriateness of their interpretation of her sin. "A blessing on the righteous Colony of the Massachusetts, where iniquity is dragged out into the sunshine!" cries the magistrate who leads Hester, with her infant daughter, to the scaffold on which she must stand before the townspeople. When Hester refuses to divulge the name of her lover, a minister delivers

> to the multitude a discourse on sin, in all its branches, but with continual reference to the ignominious letter. So forcibly did he dwell upon this symbol . . . that it assumed new terrors in their imagination, and seemed to derive its scarlet hue from the flames of the infernal pit.[30]

By any meaningful standard, the Puritan leaders fail in their efforts to shame Hester into sharing their convictions about the meaning of the letter she wears. For Boston, the *A* stands for adultery, a lurid deed with wicked consequences committed by persons worthy of damnation; by punishing Hester with the wearing of the letter, the community excludes her from its ongoing moral life, while keeping her before the community as a lesson in moral failure. For Hester and Dimmesdale, however, the *A* has far different meanings. She discovers that the scarlet letter has given her new categories of understanding. Cut off from the community, she "felt or fancied . . . that the scarlet letter had endowed her with a new sense. . . . It gave her a sympathetic knowledge of the hidden sin in other hearts." As she guessed the secrets of others' hearts, Hester was tempted to believe "that the outward guise of purity was but a lie, and that, if truth were everywhere to be shown, a scarlet letter would blaze forth on many a bosom besides Hester Prynne's."[31]

Thus, "the effect of the symbol . . . on the mind of Hester Prynne herself, was powerful and peculiar." Though she conforms outwardly, Hester rebels inwardly as she contemplates the emblem she wears. Her meditations unsettle every one of her settled convictions, and she even considers whether it might be best for her to "send Pearl at once to heaven, and go herself to such futurity as Eternal Justice should provide." Faced with clear evidence that Hester has had anything but the change of heart the Puritans had hoped for, Hawthorne concludes that "the scarlet letter had not done its office."[32]

Like Hester, Arthur Dimmesdale experiences spiritual torment. He

30. Hawthorne, *The Scarlet Letter,* pp. 164, 176.
31. Hawthorne, *The Scarlet Letter,* p. 192.
32. Hawthorne, *The Scarlet Letter,* pp. 258, 261.

is burdened by the guilt of adultery and terrified by the prospect of public confession. Though he might find release by fleeing the confines of Boston, he relies for support upon the very structures that oppress him. "Mr. Dimmesdale was a true priest, a true religionist . . . ; it would always be essential to his peace to feel the pressure of a faith about him, supporting, while it confined him within its iron framework."[33] He conceals his specific deed, while repeatedly bewailing his general sinfulness to his rapt congregation. His own deception seems to mirror the deceitfulness at the heart of Puritan culture, and Dimmesdale finds the pressure of this massive hypocrisy to be all but unbearable. He is tormented by the discrepancy between appearance and reality in his own life and in his community, and he is all but crushed by the shame of deception.

Seeking release, Dimmesdale stumbles out one night to "confess" his crime. While standing in the public square, he witnesses the fall of a meteor in the sky. "Nothing was more common, in those days," Hawthorne writes, "than to interpret all meteoric appearances, and other natural phenomena, that occurred with less regularity than the rise and set of sun and moon, as so many revelations from a supernatural source."

> We impute it, therefore, solely to the disease in his own eye and heart, that the minister, looking upward to the zenith, beheld there the appearance of an immense letter, — the letter A, — marked out in lines of dull red light. Not but the meteor may have shown itself at that point, burning duskily through a veil of cloud; but with no such shape as his guilty imagination gave it; or, at least, with so little definiteness, that another's guilt might have seen another symbol in it.

While Dimmesdale reads the *A* in the sky as a confirmation of the judgment of God upon him, the people of Boston see something else entirely in the meaning of the meteor. The morning after Dimmesdale has stood on the scaffold, the sexton of his church tells him of the "great red letter in the sky, — the letter A, — which we interpret to stand for Angel. For, as our good Governor Winthrop was made an angel this past night, it was doubtless held fit that there should be some notice thereof!"[34]

Like Melville in *Moby Dick,* Hawthorne in *The Scarlet Letter* appears to have arrived at a very disheartening conclusion about his romantic heritage. Emerson had held out the promise that the study of nature and

---

33. Hawthorne, *The Scarlet Letter,* p. 223.
34. Hawthorne, *The Scarlet Letter,* pp. 251-52, 254.

the study of the self would yield the same discovery of a benevolent power at work in the self and in all of nature. Emerson and many other romantics had made the turn inward to find a refuge and foundation for the spiritual life, once orthodox belief seemed irrelevant. But in their fiction, Hawthorne and Melville discovered the poverty of the Emersonian ideal. The only certainties their main characters discover are the conflicts of the human heart; all truths that claim to speak of transcendent comfort or power turn out to be nothing more than fantastic projections cast upon the blankness of nature by illuminating minds. In their greatest fictions, these two nineteenth-century Americans anticipate postmodern arguments about the arbitrariness of language and the centrality of desire.

The incident on the scaffold at night leads to but one of the many conflicts of interpretation throughout *The Scarlet Letter*. In a climactic scene that takes place in the forest on the edge of town, Hester urges Dimmesdale to flee with her from Boston, to throw off the burden of those beliefs that afflict them and weigh them down. When he tells her of the agony of his sin — because of the "contrast between what I seem and what I am!" — she replies, "Your sin is left behind you, in the days long past." Sounding like Emerson inveighing against the "corpse of memory," Hester urges Pearl's father to "leave it all behind. . . . Meddle no more with it! Begin all anew!" She begs him to toss down this sin-stained and weary identity of his and to "exchange this false life of thine for a true one. . . . Preach! Write! Act! Do any thing, save to lie down and die!"[35]

Hester's faith is the romantic faith that a change of place will lead to a change of heart. This faith has been particularly potent in America, a culture predicated upon a belief in the transforming power of the frontier and the future.[36] Hester is a forerunner of postmodernist Richard Rorty, for like him she believes that moral quandaries are not resolved by repentance but by relocation or redescription. Not much distance separates the romantic woman who believes that "seven years' weight of misery" can readily be exchanged for a future "full of trial and success" from the pragmatic man who writes that "all any ironist can measure success against is the past — not by living up to it, but by redescribing it in his terms,

35. Hawthorne, *The Scarlet Letter*, pp. 283, 288-89.
36. On the history of "faith in the future" in American culture, see Ernest Tuveson, *Redeemer Nation: The Idea of America's Millennial Role* (Chicago: University of Chicago Press, 1968). On "faith in the frontier," see Henry Nash Smith, *Virgin Land: The American West as Symbol and Myth* (Cambridge: Harvard University Press, 1950).

thereby becoming able to say, 'Thus I willed it.' "[37] Both of them in turn have as their ancestor the great prototype of romantic rebellion — the figure of Satan in John Milton's *Paradise Lost*. At the beginning of that work, Satan boasts to his fellow fallen angels that "the mind is its own place, and in itself / Can make a Heaven of Hell, a Hell of Heaven."[38] By the fourth book of the epic, however, as he looks upon the innocence of Eden, Satan realizes that "which way I fly is Hell; myself am Hell."

Arthur Dimmesdale is beguiled by Hester's pleas, yet he finds comfort and strength in the same weighty theological system that Hester would have him abandon. Puritan covenantal theology crushes him with the guilt it induces, but it also supports him with the consolation and meaning it imparts to his life. Furthermore, Dimmesdale discovers that without the constricting framework of his beliefs, his moral life turns into a confusing array of destructive impulses. After he has agreed to flee with Hester, the change within Dimmesdale is so great that, as he returns to the town from the forest, it seems that "the intervening space of a single day had operated on his consciousness like the lapse of years." He realizes that he has experienced "nothing short of a total change of dynasty and moral code." Yet this revolution is not what he anticipated, nor would Emerson be likely to consider it the proper moral transformation he had envisioned for the romantic self. When Dimmesdale encounters a deacon of his church, he is tempted to blaspheme the Lord's Supper; when he meets a pious widow, he finds himself suddenly inclined to blast her faith in the immortality of the soul; he next meets a young maiden and struggles against the desire to seduce her; and when he comes upon a group of children, he has to resist the devilish urge to teach them "some very wicked words."[39]

These experiences shock Dimmesdale and the author who created his character. As an heir of the Enlightenment and romanticism, Hawthorne had wanted to believe that it would be possible to sustain Christian morality without the encumbrances of Christian doctrine. At every turn in his fiction, however, he found his experiences confounding his expectations. Through the struggles of his characters, Hawthorne repeatedly discovered that, while the will might readily be made free, it could not easily be made pure.

37. Rorty, *Contingency, Irony, and Solidarity* (Cambridge: Cambridge University Press, 1989), p. 97.

38. Milton, *Paradise Lost*, in *The Norton Anthology of English Literature*, 4th ed., ed. M. H. Abrams et al. (New York: W. W. Norton, 1979), vol. 1, pp. 1418, 1478.

39. Hawthorne, *The Scarlet Letter*, pp. 305-6, 308.

Seeking virtue, Hawthorne realized that he either had to commit himself to an established theological or ethical system or redefine the moral life so that the practices of the untrammeled individual would be considered inherently virtuous because they were the product of free choice. Because he was not able to do either of these things, his description of his friend Herman Melville also proved to be true of himself: "He can neither believe, nor be comfortable in his unbelief; and he is too honest and courageous not to try to do one or the other."[40]

At the close of *The Scarlet Letter,* Dimmesdale mounts the scaffolding a final time. He has rejected the idea of fleeing with Hester and is determined to confess his sin. He cries out as he rips open his shirt, "Stand any here that question God's judgment on a sinner? Behold! Behold a dreadful witness of it!" Yet even when he appears to confess, Dimmesdale shrouds himself in ambiguities. Among the many witnesses who claim to have seen the *A* on Dimmesdale's chest, there is great disagreement; some saw it as an emblem of his sacrificial attempt to identify with poor Hester, while others read it as a sign inflicted upon him by the wicked wizard, Roger Chillingworth; still others viewed it as a manifestation of an inward guilt that had finally gnawed its way out. There were some "highly respectable witnesses," however, who said they saw nothing at all on Dimmesdale's chest. According to them,

> After exhausting life in his efforts for mankind's spiritual good, he had made the manner of his death a parable, in order to impress on his admirers the mighty and mournful lesson, that, in the view of Infinite Purity, we are sinners all alike.[41]

To understand the impasse Hawthorne reaches at the end of *The Scarlet Letter,* we would do well to consider claims made by Emerson a decade or so before Hawthorne published his novel. Emerson had urged his American audience to trust its instincts in all phases of life: "If the single man plant himself indomitably on his instincts, and there abide, the huge world will come round to him," he promised.[42] "To believe your own thought," in effect to believe your own interpretation of a text or event, "to believe that what is true for you in your private heart is true for

40. Hawthorne, *The American Notebooks,* in *The Norton Anthology of American Literature,* vol. 1, p. 1314.

41. Hawthorne, *The Scarlet Letter,* p. 341.

42. Emerson, "The American Scholar," in *Emerson: Essays and Lectures,* p. 70.

all men, — that is genius. Speak your latent conviction, and it shall be the universal sense," he claimed in "Self-Reliance."[43] Emerson's assurance was nothing less than a promise that a person or community with integrity could bring others into line with its interpretation of the moral and spiritual life without exercising coercive authority.

In *The Scarlet Letter* Hawthorne set out to realize this Emersonian romantic ideal and failed at his task. "Hawthorne fails to resolve the central conflict of the novel," writes William Spengemann, "because he expected the symbol to do too much — to change the community as radically as the experience it embodies has changed Hester."[44] The Puritans stand upon their theological convictions and ethical beliefs, but Hester does not come round to them; Hester stands firm upon the moral instincts her shame has helped to develop for her, but she despairs of the prospect of moving the established morals of the community any closer to justice; and the symbol comes to have a special private meaning for Arthur Dimmesdale, who reads into the *A* all the tortured concerns of his troubled soul.

The events of *The Scarlet Letter* show for Hawthorne the folly of a romantic interpretation of the promise of America — that in a land of freedom, decent men and women can discard their prejudices and share an innocent, unifying vision of life. The romantic poets and essayists like Emerson had promised that shared symbols could free us from our painfully limited perceptions. The conflicts between different schools of thought and different theological positions would vanish when, as Thoreau puts it, with Christ-like power "through our own recovered innocence we discern the innocence of our neighbors."[45] Very reluctantly, Hawthorne came to the conclusion that innocent reading of this kind was forever behind us, in the Garden of Eden, or forever in front of us, in the mind of God. In history, such innocent interpretation is simply impossible, and no lasting community can be founded upon the premise of it.

One might expect the church to be the place where a unifying interpretation might be offered, but such is not the case in Hawthorne's fiction. The church fails because it cannot take to heart its own message about repentance, forgiveness, and restoration. No matter how much the pastors of Salem and Boston preach on those themes, in reality their

43. Emerson, "Self-Reliance," p. 259.
44. Spengemann, *The Adventurous Muse: The Poetics of American Fiction, 1789-1900* (New Haven: Yale University Press, 1977), p. 169.
45. Thoreau, *Walden*, p. 573.

communities live by innocence and forgetfulness rather than sin and forgiveness. In both "Young Goodman Brown" and *The Scarlet Letter*, the righteous presume their own innocence as they condemn the sin of others. As they strive to remain faithful to God and his commandments, the Puritans in Hawthorne's fiction cannot avoid overestimating their own virtue and underestimating that of others. They may proclaim a gospel of grace, but they cannot avoid building legalistic communities. The result is that in the world of Hawthorne's fiction, a sinner has only two options — pretension or banishment. Without the possibility of forgiveness, self-conscious sinners must either conceal their guilt or endure their ruin.

American Banishment

At the end of the first chapter of *The Scarlet Letter*, Hawthorne describes a wild rosebush "rooted almost at the threshold" of Hester's prison door. He imagines himself plucking one of the roses and handing it to his reader. "It may serve, let us hope, to symbolize some sweet moral blossom, that may be found along the track, or relieve the darkening close of a tale of human frailty and sorrow." Though the origin of this rosebush is uncertain, Hawthorne reports that there is "fair authority for believing" that it had "sprung up under the footsteps of the sainted Ann Hutchinson, as she entered the prison-door."[46]

The Anne Hutchinson to whom Hawthorne refers was at the center of the greatest controversy to rock the Massachusetts Bay Colony in its early years.[47] This Puritan woman was a follower of John Cotton, a popular preacher in Boston in the 1630s. She derived from Cotton's teaching a conviction that the Holy Ghost dwelt immediately within the justified person and that sanctification had no relationship to justification. By her logic, a truly justified person could discern the spiritual states of others, and she claimed to know which members of her community were under a saving covenant of grace and which labored under a damnable covenant of works. Hutchinson promoted her views through a series of weekly

46. Hawthorne, *The Scarlet Letter*, pp. 158-59.
47. See Edmund S. Morgan, *The Puritan Dilemma: The Story of John Winthrop* (Boston: Little, Brown, 1958), pp. 134-54; and Emery Battis, *Saints and Sectaries: Anne Hutchinson and the Antinomian Controversy in the Massachusetts Bay Colony* (Chapel Hill: University of North Carolina Press, 1962).

lectures in her home. These gatherings were intended for the purpose of discussing Cotton's sermons, but they effectively turned into meetings fomenting resistance against the civil and ecclesiastical authorities.

Governor Winthrop and his associates quickly recognized the rebellious potential of Anne Hutchinson and her movement. She was brought to trial before the General Court in November 1637, and although she proved to be more theologically astute and quick-witted than her interrogators, she was convicted, expelled from the church, and banished to Rhode Island. Like the fictional Hester Prynne, Hutchinson was sent away in hopes that her exile would bring her back to faith and under the authority of the gathered church.[48] In excommunicating her, the Reverend John Wilson told her, "*I doe cast you out* and in the name of Christ *I doe deliver you up to Sathan* that you may learne no more to blaspheme to seduce and to lye." The excommunication is meant to deprive her of the benefits of the very "Holy Ordinances of God" that she has "dispised and contemned." *"I command you* in the name of Christ Jesus and of this Church *as a Leper to withdraw your selfe out of the Congregation."*[49]

The fictional shaming of Hester Prynne and the actual banishment of Anne Hutchinson were acts of exclusion intended to purify the community as it toiled to bring in the kingdom of God. To a significant extent, the Puritan acts of exclusion were grounded in the biblical example of judgment and banishment. The parables of Jesus are replete with images of the eschatological separation of the sheep from the goats, the wheat from the tares. For the Massachusetts Puritans, the banishments of heretics and transgressors were acts that anticipated God's eschatological winnowing. In defending the witchcraft proceedings of 1692, for instance, Cotton Mather, the foremost Puritan historian, described "the New Englanders" as a "people of God settled in those, which were once the devil's territories." They are claiming the land of the New World for "our blessed Jesus," and

---

48. Like the scarlet letter, exile apparently did not do its office. A year after Anne Hutchinson had been excommunicated, the Boston church sent a delegation to see her in the wilderness. Upon their return, the group of three reported that when they told her that they had a message to her "from the church of christ in Boston," she declared that "she knew no church but one. . . . For our church she would not acknowledg it any church of Christs" ("Robert Keayne's Report of Boston Church Action," in *The Antinomian Controversy, 1636-1638: A Documentary History,* ed. David D. Hall [Middletown, CT: Wesleyan University Press, 1968], p. 392).

49. "A Report of the Trial of Mrs. Ann Hutchinson before the Church in Boston, March, 1638," in *The Antinomian Controversy, 1636-1638,* p. 388.

the outbreak of witchcraft is merely proof of the ire of the devil at those who are seizing his territory on behalf of his great enemy: "The devil is now making one attempt more upon us; . . . an attempt so critical, that if we get well through, we shall soon enjoy halcyon days with all the vultures of hell trodden under our feet."[50]

Over the course of the eighteenth century, that Puritan eschatological vision was transformed almost beyond recognition. Through a series of accommodations, the characteristics of the ideal redeemed church were transferred to nature in the New World and to the nascent republic itself. The seventeenth-century Puritans sought "the actual reign of the spirit of Christ, the amalgamation of the City of the World into the City of God." The enlightened citizens of the infant nation would obliterate the distinction between the two cities by declaring American civilization itself to be the kingdom of God.[51] At the conclusion of his sermon on Christian charity, John Winthrop reminded his fellow Puritans that they had "entered into covenant with [God] for this work" in the New World. If we are faithful to the terms of that covenant, Winthrop told them, "He shall make us a praise and glory"; if we "fall to embrace this present world and prosecute our carnal intentions, . . . the Lord will surely break out in wrath against us."[52] A century and a half later, the Frenchman St. Jean de Crèvecoeur also wrote of the covenant of the New World, but the covenant of which he wrote was no longer an agreement between a holy God and his church but a bargain between a benevolent nation and an aspiring individual. In "What Is an American?" Crèvecoeur gave a voice to nature in the New World. In his words, "our great parent" promises freedom and abundance to anyone who desires to come to this new land: "Welcome to my shores, distressed European; . . . If thou wilt work, I have bread for thee; if thou wilt be honest, sober, and industrious, I have greater rewards to confer on thee — ease and independence."[53]

50. Mather, "The Wonders of the Invisible World," in *The Norton Anthology of American Literature,* vol. 1, pp. 217-18. The racist and imperialist overtones of such a passage are sobering. All who inhabit the devil's territory — that is, the Native American Indians — must be the devil's minions. And, by implication, they deserve no better treatment than does the devil himself.

51. Tuveson, *Redeemer Nation,* p. 97.

52. Winthrop, "A Model of Christian Charity," in *The Norton Anthology of American Literature,* vol. 1, pp. 40-41.

53. Crèvecoeur, "What Is an American?" in *The Norton Anthology of American Literature,* vol. 1, pp. 567-68.

The significance of this shift might be illustrated best by considering the difference between Anne Hutchinson and Jonathan Edwards. In 1638, this Puritan woman and her family were exiled to the wilderness because she had crossed the boundaries of theological orthodoxy. In the late 1740s, Jonathan Edwards, the greatest theological mind this country has produced, found himself in an irreconcilable conflict over communion with his congregation in Northampton, Massachusetts. Edwards wished to enforce the standards of the "Half-Way Covenant" and require a testimony of conversion for participants in the Lord's Supper. He was in a minority, however, and was eventually forced from his church over the issue. He spent virtually the rest of his life in exile, ministering to Native American Indians at the frontier settlement of Stockbridge, Massachusetts.

Hutchinson was excommunicated for a theological heresy that the Puritan authorities realized might have ominous social significance. Edwards was dismissed for heretical social views — that is, for violating the amiable standard of inclusiveness that was coming to rule the church in his day. The theological heresy of the mid-seventeenth century had become the cultural orthodoxy of the next century. In almost every way, we in the pluralistic world of late twentieth-century America have more in common with the denizens of the American Enlightenment than they had in common with their ancestors of a century before. By the time of the American Revolution, the transformation of the original Puritan vision was all but complete. At the center of the "city upon a hill" was no longer a church but a marketplace, where preference was on its way to becoming the only principle.

CHAPTER 7   *The Bondage of Liberation: Marxism and the Romantic Legacy*

T HE DEBATE begun by the Puritans about American identity continues
    to this day. The terms may have changed, and the explicitly Christian
frame of reference for the debate may have vanished from sight, but the
arguments still involve fundamental disagreements over questions of inclusion and exclusion. In John Winthrop's theocratic Boston, only those
who adhered to orthodox doctrines and behavior had any chance to be
admitted to the communion table. To be included among those who had
fellowship with the risen Lord, an individual had to demonstrate the
indubitable work of Christ in his or her life. Failure on doctrinal, be-
havioral, or experiential grounds would lead to exclusion from the redeemed circle at the heart of the larger community.

But as we have seen, from the very early days of the Puritan
settlement there was pressure to loosen the standards for participation.
By 1700 Solomon Stoddard was offering the sacrament to all professing
Christians; in the early 1800s, Unitarian churches had come to make
few if any demands of belief upon those who wished to participate in
communion; and by the middle decades of that century, writers such as
Emerson and Whitman were seeking to effect the complete break of
American culture from the doctrines and particularities of Christian
belief. Emerson and Whitman sought to resolve the tension between
inclusion and exclusion by obliterating the distinctions between the saved
and the lost. According to Emerson, we are all Christs whose individual
limitations are only the products of our failures to have acquired proper

perception. For Whitman, the American nation itself represents the great banquet feast of heaven; all people are invited to join in "the meal equally set," which is "for the wicked just the same as the righteous, [for] I make appointments with all, / I will not have a single person slighted or left away."[1] The only ones who deserve to be cast into the outer darkness are those who believe in darkness at all.

The arguments over the Lord's Supper provide a cultural context for the current debates about the theories and practices of the modern university. In an age without allegiance to clear principles, the ideal of inclusiveness has assumed the status of an unshakeable principle. In the academic world, this fact has to a significant extent created a consensus on certain matters of rights for minorities, women, and homosexuals. Whether it is race, gender, or sexual behavior that is under consideration, the pragmatic individualism that rules in the contemporary university has no grounds for judging or excluding.

The indiscriminate mixing of things as diverse as race and sexuality presents genuine challenges for the Christian at work within the worlds of modern culture and academic life. Does a wholehearted commitment to civil rights for minorities obligate the Christian to support those same rights for homosexuals? And if the Christian supports equal civil rights for homosexuals, does that imply that the church should condone or sanction homosexual behavior? All Christians can and should declare themselves in favor of the extension of full civil rights to minorities; in many instances, the record of Christian communities in the past has been shameful, but overtly racist attitudes are now forbidden within the Christian community. On this matter, there should be little or no distance between the Christian community and the larger culture.

On issues of gender and sexuality there is a greater degree of ambiguity for one who professes the Christian faith. On the issue of the role of women, for example, the divergent opinions point to deep differences within evangelical and Reformed churches. Nevertheless, as divisive as this issue has proved to be, especially on the issue of the ordination of women, there appears to be a consensus that principled Christians can disagree strongly on this matter without having to call into question the faith of their opponents. The issue of homosexuality, however, would seem to put most Christians at odds with the reigning ideology of the cultural and

1. Whitman, *Song of Myself,* in *Whitman: Poetry and Prose,* ed. Justin Kaplan (New York: Library of America, 1982), p. 205.

intellectual elite. While many evangelical and Reformed Christians would support full civil and legal rights for practicing homosexuals, few would deny that the Bible condemns homosexual behavior and only a minority would support the ordination of practicing gays and lesbians.

In short, the question for the Christian is how to reconcile the love of goodness with the hatred of evil, how to embrace the truth while shunning falsehood, how to build a community founded upon love and trust while forbidding or punishing sinful behavior. The difficulty of these tasks should not obscure for the Christian critic the true nature of the bargains that many contemporary cultural theorists strike. They reconcile good and evil by denying the distinction; they resolve the conflict between truth and error by labeling both as derivatives of the primary reality of power; and they exclude from their communities only those who believe in the necessity of some form of moral or spiritual exclusion.

In the contemporary academic world, theories of language and knowledge have been drawn into the battle over rights and power. In this chapter and the chapter following, we will look at two of the dominant influences on contemporary theories of literature and interpretation: Marxism and poststructuralism. In both cases, these schools of thought originated in a European intellectual and cultural context, but they have long since made themselves felt in American humanities departments. And the trip across the Atlantic has brought changes to both movements. In being imported into American cultural life, both Marxism and poststructuralism have been reinterpreted to make them consistent with the pragmatic individualism that is deeply ingrained in the American character.

The Academic Marx

If, as Samuel Johnson once declared, patriotism is the last refuge of the scoundrel, then in the contemporary world university departments in the humanities seem likely to become some of the last sanctuaries of Marxist belief. At a time when Marxism has been decimated as an economic theory and abandoned as a political force throughout Europe, it nonetheless continues to enjoy a position of special privilege in many departments of literature across America. Even after the Soviet Union has abandoned Marxism and then been dissolved itself, a number of cultural critics in the West continue to read history and texts in Marxist terms, conscripting Marxism for service in a crusade for an undefined ideal of radical freedom.

"Marxism," Frederick Crews points out, "retains its hold on the imagination only where it has not yet been put into effect."[2]

The Marxism of contemporary literary theory has deftly managed to present itself as a radical alternative to the romantic tradition that we have been examining throughout this book. It has done so even as it has drawn upon the energies and appropriated key images of the romantic traditions in literature and philosophy. At a time when a number of observers are questioning the dominant liberal individualism of modern societies, Marxist theory claims to offer a sharp, convincing, and comprehensive alternative to the fragmentation and alienation of the individualist experience. Yet in fact the Marxism promoted in contemporary American theory represents a subtle form of the latest developments in romantic theory, rather than a dramatic alternative to that tradition.

To be fair, at this point a caveat ought to be entered. Some of the critics whom I am calling "Marxist" would be uneasy about claiming that label for themselves and their work. Instead of calling themselves Marxists per se, they often choose to work under the rubric of the New Historicism (a critical movement that includes many Marxists but is by no means limited to Marxists), cultural criticism, or materialist criticism. The reasons for these theorists' discomfort with the Marxist name are easy to understand, for the history of Marxist practice has been a saga of extraordinary oppression and cruelty. Since many cultural critics embrace Marxist theory as a tool in the fight for liberation from oppression, Marxist history is an embarrassment to them.

In their aversion to the Marxist label, the radical theorists of recent vintage seem strikingly different from the literary and cultural critics of the Depression years. Those figures, who included some of the foremost American men and women of letters in their day, were content to be known as Communists or Marxists, and they made no effort to mask their convictions that the Soviet enterprise under Joseph Stalin was the harbinger of a utopian future. The sweep of their vision is made clear in a memoir by Malcolm Cowley, a prominent poet, critic, and activist of the time. Forty years after the fact, Cowley was not ashamed to admit that he and his radical colleagues had anticipated nothing less than the transformation of the world by Marxist principles and practices.

Cowley writes that "the dream" he shared with others began with the notion that "capitalism and its culture were in violent decay" and

2. Crews, *Skeptical Engagements* (New York: Oxford University Press, 1986), p. 137.

on the point of self-destruction. "The workers" were the only class that would survive, and middle-class intellectuals had no option but to renounce their identities and declare their solidarity with the workers. As Cowley recounts it, a "religious feeling" pervaded the radical movement, with many of its members even sentimentally yearning for martyrdom. Countless individuals would be sacrificed in the struggle, but that did not matter, since "history [was] on our side." Even as Stalin starved the Ukrainian people and viciously purged his army and bureaucracy, Western intellectuals hailed him as a savior. Cowley recalls the spirit of that day: "All of us joined in brotherhood, our right fists raised in the Red Front salute, let us march forward into the classless society. The Soviet Union has shown us the way."[3]

Cowley's frankness and clarity contrast sharply with the obfuscation of Gayatri Chakravorty Spivak, a translator of Jacques Derrida and a noted contemporary theorist in her own right. Spivak goes to great lengths to distance herself from the consequences of Marxist theory in Marxist practice. In an interview about her work, she blames those who have put Marx into practice — in the former Soviet Union, China, Cuba, and elsewhere, one would presume — with having misread Marx. "If one identifies Marxism with a master narrative," she explains, "one is conflating the history of Marxism with the texts of Marx." This is a mistake, because it reduces the ironic, insightful, and playful Marx and turns him into a troubling thinker whose theories have contributed to the impoverishment and suffering of millions of people. After declaring "I'm not a fundamentalist," Spivak says that "the texts of Marx are precisely the place where there is no sure foundation to be found."[4]

If the history of Marxism represents a cruel set of practices inspired by a gross misreading of Marx, and if Marx himself offers no "sure foundation" for the organization of knowledge and society, what is the point of studying him? What power does he have? What help might his works offer? Though Spivak does not answer these questions directly, her scholarly views and practices give us a hint of what her answer might be. Like many other contemporary critics of culture who have an allegiance to Marxist thought, Spivak appears to be particularly attracted to its

3. Cowley, *The Dream of the Golden Mountains: Remembering the 1930s* (New York: Viking Press, 1980), p. 315.
4. Spivak, "The New Historicism: Political Commitment and the Postmodern Critic," in *The New Historicism*, ed. H. Aram Veeser (New York: Routledge, 1989), p. 287.

disruptive and subverting power. As one of the "masters of suspicion," Marx proves to be a splendid ally for all who would claim that they understand their texts and students much better than those texts and students understand themselves. In this version, Marx does not provide blueprints for the transformation of society but techniques for power reading.[5]

Spivak says as much as this in her interview. Her questioner mentions that a woman "from a Marxist teaching collective at Syracuse University" had told him to ask Spivak about "the violence of [her] teaching and writing." As convoluted as it is, Spivak's response is nonetheless revealing:

> I think the violence comes out of the conviction that the forces against which one is speaking are at their worst when they are most benevolent, and that they are most benevolent when embodied by the most vulnerable, that is to say, the students in the class. . . . When one realizes that the real battleground is the classroom and the real focus is the benevolent young radical in the bosom of the neocolonial production of knowledge, and that one has to take away from them their conviction of where they are at their best without leaving them with nothing but a breast-beating, which is also something that is part of the neocolonial production of knowledge — "I'm only a white male," etc., and then business goes on as usual — that very uneasy predicament is I think what she is implying as the recognizable violence rather than the socratic method revamped, where anxiety is felt throughout the classroom, and you can congratulate yourself as doing correct politics. I think that's where the violence comes from.[6]

In the welter of cumbersome syntax and garbled diction, Spivak seems to be saying that her students are at their wicked worst when they appear

5. Catherine Belsey offers a particularly self-satisfied version of one theoretical commonplace: "[Knowledge pertinent to the twentieth century] is discursive and subjectless. That is to say, it is inscribed in discourses which are independent of the individual wills, preferences or 'genius' of individual readers or critics. . . . Thus author and reader . . . no longer present the symmetrical poles of an intersubjective process understood as communication. Instead critical practice is seen as a process of releasing the positions from which the text is intelligible. Liberated from the fixity of the communication model, the text is available for production in the process of reading" (Belsey, *Critical Practice* [London: Methuen, 1980], pp. 139-40).

6. Spivak, "Political Commitment and the Postmodern Critic," pp. 284-85.

most "vulnerable" and "benevolent" and that she is at her charitable best when her "violence" levels her foes on the "battleground" of the classroom. Stalin himself could not have done a better job of mastering Orwellian doublespeak.

Though Spivak and others may go to great lengths to disclaim the name of Marxism while touting the virtues of Marx, other contemporary theorists of literature are unabashed in their Marxist sympathies. Two of them, Frank Lentricchia and Terry Eagleton, have written highly influential surveys of contemporary theory. Both Lentricchia and Eagleton attribute the inconsistencies of modern views of literature to the contradictions inherent in late capitalism. Their claim is that a highly developed consumer society cannot help but turn all works of culture into objects of pleasure and consumption. Lentricchia and Eagleton allege that the common denominator of such varied schools of thought as the New Criticism, archetypal criticism, and poststructuralism is that they all trivialize literature. According to the analysis of these Marxist critics, the aestheticism of such theories promotes literature as an escape from the tumult and pain of history and thus turns reading into yet another consumer's delight in capitalist society. "It is indeed the *extremism* of literary theory," laments Terry Eagleton, "its obstinate, perverse, endlessly resourceful refusal to countenance social and historical realities, which most strikes a student" of those modern theories that refuse to adopt a Marxist diagnosis of the role of literature in history.[7]

Marxist literary theorists claim to have abandoned the passivity of aestheticism and to be employing a powerful rhetoric of social change. The English critic Christopher Norris, for example, dismisses an entire school of theory — in this case, hermeneutical theory as exemplified by the work of Martin Heidegger and Hans-Georg Gadamer — as "merely a species of conservative pleading for the 'commonsense' status quo."[8] Similarly, Lentricchia disparages the willingness of the "self-conscious university intellectual to do nothing and sink into occupational nihilism." He strives against those who view literature as a form of compensation for the harshness of reality. By accepting a limited understanding of the scope and power of literary study, they accede to the oppressive powers that rule

7. Eagleton, *Literary Theory: An Introduction* (Minneapolis: University of Minnesota Press, 1983), p. 196.
8. Norris, *The Contest of Faculties: Philosophy and Theory after Deconstruction* (London: Methuen, 1985), p. 1.

capitalist society. Lentricchia would have the scholar become an agent of liberation: "I come down on the side of those who believe that our society is mainly unreasonable and that education should be one of the places where we can get involved in the process of transforming it."[9]

The move that Lentricchia makes in this quotation is typical of the strategies frequently employed by those who adhere to what Crews calls the "Left Eclecticism" of contemporary theory, and it is indicative of the degree to which the radical theory of today is deeply indebted to the legacy of oppositional thinking in the history of romanticism.[10] In effect, Lentricchia blasts an unbridgeable chasm between what he takes to be radically different viewpoints. In this case, Lentricchia says that the scholar must choose between education as the transmission of culture and education as the transformation of culture. He or she is forbidden to conceive of existing culture as something that empowers as well as restrains or that nourishes as well as frustrates. Furthermore, the scholar cannot find *within* culture itself the resources needed for the reform *of* culture. He or she is left with the options of capitulation to the established order or rebellion against it, for there is no middle ground. And given the rich history of the principle of rebellion within the romantic literary tradition, there is no doubt as to how Lentricchia would have the scholar decide. If, as he claims, "criticism . . . is the production of knowledge to the ends of power and, maybe, of

9. Frank Lentricchia, *Criticism and Social Change* (Chicago: University of Chicago Press, 1985), p. 2.

10. Crews explains:

Influential departments in several fields of study have begun to practice what I will call Left Eclecticism, a welcoming of many styles of anti-establishment analysis — not just orthodox Marxist but also structuralist, deconstructionist, feminist, gay, Lacanian, Foucauldian, and assorted combinations of these. The heart of Left Eclecticism is an understanding, ultimately borrowed from the Marxist ethos, that analytic and theoretic discourse is to be judged primarily by the evident radicalism of its stance. The schools of thought thus favored make sharply divergent claims, yet all of them set themselves against allegedly repressive Western institutions and practices. In dealing with a given painting, novel, or piece of architecture, especially one dating from the capitalist era, they do not aim primarily to show the work's character or governing idea. The goal is rather to subdue the work through aggressive demystification — for example, by positing its socioeconomic determinants and ideological implications, scanning it for any encouraging signs of subversion, and then judging the result against an ideal of total freedom. That, in essence, is the Marxist path. Thus we could say that the adversary Marxist animus, which long predated the other schools that make up Left Eclecticism, has perpetuated itself within them. (*Skeptical Engagements,* pp. 138-39)

social change," then the literary theorist must become the liberator of the oppressed, the one who frees those who are enslaved to the insidious ideologies of capitalist societies.[11]

In a society in which the most obvious battles for rights and political freedoms — those of speech, suffrage, and religion, among others — have been won, Marxist theory now serves to reinvigorate the romantic vision of the artist as redeemer. But it does so by replacing the artist with the critic. In Lentricchia's view, the critic or theorist is a vital agent in the war against the repressive ideological forces that control all activity in the Western democracies. In the following list of agents of the capitalist state, Lentricchia seems to exempt no figure of authority, save one, from condemnation:

> The powerful figures of identity-formation — such figures as parents, doctors, nurses in the so-called prepolitical period of childhood, and such figures, in later life, as foreman or employer — are vehicles of the hegemonic constitution of consciousness that is carried out more overtly in the educative, legislative, and constabulary levels of the political superstructure through its symbolic authorities and representatives.[12]

Thus, on one side stand all the oppressive agents of culture — including parents, the police, literature, and traditional criticism — marshalled together to rationalize and enforce the irrational demands of capital; while on the other side stand the lonely, oppressed self and its sole defender, the demystifying literary theorist.

In making such claims about the state of contemporary Marxist theory, it is not necessary to argue that Marxist critiques of literature and history have nothing of worth to offer Christian scholars; nor in objecting to Marxism must one remain insensitive to the injustices and distortions of a consumer culture and capitalist economy. Need it even be said that a Christian has resources that enable him or her to judge sins of economic or racial injustice without having to ascribe to the reductive materialism of Marxism? Indeed, one of the most lamentable consequences of the dichotomizing habit of mind is that it can imagine no middle ground between extremes. One must be either an oppressor or one of the oppressed, a master or a slave, a tyrant or a victim. Such a simplified splitting of human characters denies the truth of our experience and the

11. Lentricchia, *Criticism and Social Change*, p. 11.
12. Lentricchia, *Criticism and Social Change*, p. 77.

claims of the Scriptures. We are all *simul justus et peccator* — at the same time justified and sinful. The dichotomy established in contemporary radical theory represents a variation upon a dominant theme of the Enlightenment tradition. It is what Reinhold Niebuhr describes as the "the effort to derive evil from specific historical sources."[13] And while the belief that evil is rooted in institutions or groups has had a salutary effect in some instances — especially in the fight against slavery and against the exploitation of women and minorities — it has also had dreadful consequences. On the right in Fascism and on the left in Marxist-Leninism, this belief has been the engine of modern genocide.

That is not to deny that there are definite points of correspondence between certain Marxist beliefs and a Christian understanding of human nature. For example, in their skepticism about romantic claims concerning genius and self-transcendence, Marxists speak to those Christians who are uncomfortable with all human attempts, including sophisticated cultural efforts, to sanction self-deification. In addition, because they recognize the historical rootedness of literature, Marxists have a certain affinity with Christians who adhere to a faith rooted and revealed within history. And in rejecting the claims of disinterestedness made on behalf of the literary experience, Marxists share with Christians important convictions about the nature of action and commitment.

But these similarities may obscure the dramatic differences between Marxist naturalism and historic Christian orthodoxy. As many observers have pointed out, Marx borrowed heavily from the Messianic traditions of Judaism and Christianity for his vision of human liberation and redemption; Marxism's views of justice and historical destiny are secularized forms of ancient Christian hope.[14] Yet it remains true that the Marxist analysis of culture and history is grounded in scientific atheism and in an Enlightenment and romantic conviction about the essential innocence of the individual. Just as evangelical scholars were for decades susceptible to the romantic adaptation and exploitation of Christian imagery, so may

13. Niebuhr, *The Nature and Destiny of Man,* vol. 1: *Human Nature* (New York: Charles Scribner's Sons, 1943), pp. 96-104.

14. For a standard form of this argument, see Karl Löwith, *Meaning in History* (Chicago: University of Chicago Press, 1949), pp. 33-51. See also Alasdair MacIntyre, *Marxism and Christianity* (New York: Schocken Books, 1968). For a strong attempt to refute the thesis that the modern idea of progress — whether romantic or Marxist — depends for its legitimacy upon historic Christianity, see Hans Blumenberg, *The Legitimacy of the Modern Age,* trans. Robert W. Wallace (Cambridge: MIT Press, 1983).

contemporary Christian critics find themselves beguiled by the moral force and explanatory power of Marxist theory.

Marxism in the Contemporary Academy

We saw in an earlier chapter that various forms of liberal humanism shaped the university study of English up through the middle decades of this century. How, then, are we to account for the resurgence of Marxist thought in American literary study in the past two decades? In part, the answer lies in the political and cultural upheaval of the 1960s and its interaction with long-established romantic images of literature and its power. During that decade, an unprecedentedly large number of graduate students undertook the study of literature at the same time that American society was being shattered by the battle for civil rights, by political assassinations, and by the most unpopular war in the history of the republic. Frederick Crews attributes the "rapidly growing sway" of radicalism in the humanities to "the academy's mood of social pluralism, iconoclasm, and antinationalism — a mood deriving ultimately from revulsion against America's role in the Vietnam era."[15]

The young scholars of the sixties were being trained by teachers whose own ideas about the religious and cultural significance of literature were heavily romantic, and as Harold Bloom has argued in a number of books, at the heart of that romantic enterprise is the demand placed upon each new generation of poets and critics to supplant the previous generation.[16] Thus the revolutionary impulses of romanticism have made it inevitable that each new generation would receive the burden of the standard of radical originality. In true romantic fashion, Walt Whitman could write in *Song of Myself* that "he most honors my style who learns under it to destroy the teacher";[17] judging by the tenor of contemporary theory, the students of the humanities in the sixties and early seventies learned that lesson well for their role as theorists. Drilled in the tactics of romantic conflict, they would even-

15. Crews, "Whose American Renaissance?" *New York Review of Books,* 27 Oct. 1988, pp. 68-70.

16. See especially Bloom, *The Anxiety of Influence: A Theory of Poetry* (New York: Oxford University Press, 1973).

17. Whitman, *Song of Myself,* p. 242.

tually employ their skills and weapons against the very scholars who had trained them.

To understand the dynamics of contemporary Marxist literary theory and to see how it relates to the brief history sketched in the first half of this chapter, we might consider an essay written in 1965 by Lionel Trilling, a highly influential literary critic of his day. Like many students of American culture at mid-century, Trilling had been drawn to Marxism in the years between the two world wars, only to be driven away from Marx by Stalin and into the arms of Victorian humanist Matthew Arnold. Though less optimistic than Arnold about the power of literature to transform the world, however gradually, Trilling shared the Victorian essayist's conviction that literature and criticism ought to try to fill the void created by the demise of religious belief.

Trilling's essay, "The Two Environments," which is a chapter in his book *Beyond Culture,* begins with a discussion of the earliest stages of the academic study of literature in the vernacular in the schools of Victorian England. While citing the obvious differences between that world and modern America, Trilling asserts that for the last century there has been a consistent element in the various defenses of literature offered in the Western world. That common denominator has been a claim about literature's "unique effectiveness . . . in purging the mind of prejudices and received ideas, in making the mind free and active." The argument, Trilling says, has been that "the effect which the study of literature has upon the private sentiments of a student" will lead to "an improvement in the intelligence, and especially the intelligence as it touches the moral life."[18]

In trying to account for what has drawn so many students to the study of English in the years after the Second World War, Trilling says that "we may well conclude that it is in large part a moral impulse." This impulse is not the same one that drove the Victorian moralists, who were concerned, in the words of one of them, to "examine methodically the relation of Interest and Duty." Trilling argues that modern morality, as it dreams of "the sources of life" and desires to obtain control over them, "denies the contradiction between Interest and Duty. Typically in our culture, when a person of good will thinks of the control of the sources of life, he conceives of it as assuring the happiness both of the individual and of the generality of mankind. . . . What he wants

18. Trilling, "The Two Environments," in *Beyond Culture* (Oxford: Oxford University Press, 1980), pp. 183-84.

for others he thinks of as the guarantee of the fullness, freedom, and potency he wants for himself."[19]

Trilling believes that such confidence might lead one to believe that "perhaps at last we are on the way to being released from the old bondage to Necessity and have actually got one foot into the realm of Freedom." But to Trilling, Matthew Arnold's belief that "right" is ready to take over the rule from "force" represents a naive reading of modern moral life and liberal education. When Arnold spoke of the power of literature, Trilling writes, he saw criticism as a means of liberating an individual from a cramped, provincial world and leaving him "outside the cultural environment in which he was reared."[20] What we now have instead is a massive cultural and educational industry in which almost all the ills of the larger society have been replicated.

As Trilling explains, the critic envisioned by Arnold was to be a strong individual, one who would be willing to live outside the boundaries of conventionality and to sacrifice comfort and security for the pure privilege of a righteous moral position. Such a person would courageously exchange the pleasures of force for the deeper satisfactions of right. All of this sounds properly heroic, Trilling acknowledges, but the reality is that the student of literature in the 1960s "is not being sent into the wilderness alone, a banished man; . . . there stands ready to receive him another 'environment' in which he is pretty sure to be tolerably comfortable, an environment that is organized and that has its own roots in the general economy." And Trilling observes that "as we watch the development of the second cultural environment, we become less and less certain that it is entirely free of the traits that we reprobate in the first." To justify itself, the second environment has to maintain "*some* ethical or spiritual advantage over the first." It does so by delighting in the fact that its members shall never have "the actual rule of the world; if its personnel sometimes dreams of rule, it yet knows that it would become bored by the dreary routine that rulers must submit to: the blame for the ugly actualities of rule will therefore always rest on Philistine shoulders." It is ironic to Trilling that as students "find it ever easier to take their places in the second cultural environment, as they are ever surer of finding comfort and companions in it, we have to see that it shows the essential traits of any cultural environment: firm

19. Trilling, "The Two Environments," pp. 190-92.
20. Trilling, "The Two Environments," pp. 193, 196.

presuppositions, received ideas, approved attitudes, and a system of rewards and punishments."[21]

Contemporary Marxist theory has served as the most powerful weapon available in the battle for authority within this "second environment," and to a significant extent that theory seems designed to assure that those who do not have *force* — who are finally content to let the "ugly actualities of rule . . . rest on Philistine shoulders" — will at least have the moral satisfaction that falls to those who are convinced that *right* is their exclusive possession. At the end of the 1960s, the first isolated voices of Marxist dissent could be heard within the academy, as students appalled by war in Vietnam and violent divisions at home found themselves galled by the impotence of literature and the political reticence of literary critics. Richard Bridgman recalls how in 1969 Henry Nash Smith, president of the Modern Language Association, was forced to respond at the MLA's annual convention to charges leveled by dissident members that "because 'objective' scholarship, criticism, and teaching failed to question the existing social and economic orders, they therefore represented nothing more than an immoral neutrality."[22]

Indeed, this charge of *immoral neutrality,* brought by students and a small number of faculty members more than twenty years ago, has become a rallying cry for the theorists of the past decade. Soon after colleges and universities had been rocked by the conflicts of the larger society in the late 1960s, declining enrollments began to reduce dramatically the number of tenured places for those who sought, in Trilling's words, "comfort and companions" in the "second environment." In order to make its *original* mark and to position itself to achieve its political and social goals, the generation schooled in the sixties and early seventies had to displace those who controlled power in the "second environment."

To do so, many members of that generation have skillfully employed such things as the Marxist critique of ideology. An example of how such analysis serves the interests of the new generation of scholars can be found in the preface to a recent collection of essays entitled *Reconstructing American Literary History.* Written by Sacvan Bercovitch, the editor of the volume, the preface opens with a confident declaration: "The need for a new American literary history seems clear and unexceptionable." Four

21. Trilling, "The Two Environments," pp. 196-97.
22. Bridgman, "The American Studies of Henry Nash Smith," *The American Scholar* 56, 2 (Spring 1987): 268.

decades have passed since the publication of the "monumental" *Literary History of the United States,* and Bercovitch says that "a lot has happened, critically and creatively" in the years since that volume appeared. He cites two developments as crucial: "the political-academic upheavals of the late sixties and . . . the recent impact of European critical theories." The radicalism of these two "events" has helped to make sensitive readers of literature "increasingly uncomfortable," Bercovitch claims, about "the consensus that shaped our concept of American literary history." They specifically object to the "consensus on the meaning of the term *literary* that involved the legitimation of a certain canon, and the consensus on the term *history* that was legitimated by a certain vision of America." That canon, with its predominance of male Anglo-Saxon writers, was exclusionary and oppressive. To break the power of that consensus, "it will be the task of the present generation to reconstruct American literary history by making a virtue of dissensus."[23]

Bercovitch explains that the contributors to his volume were chosen for the "quality of their work and for their diversity of views and interests," and that their only common bond is that all of them "are Americanists trained in the sixties and early seventies." Because of their training and because of the supposedly unique political events of their day, "all of them express a distinctive generational experience of discontinuity and disruption."[24] As products of "the past two decades," a time when "consensus of all sorts has broken down — left and right, political and aesthetic," the essayists in *Reconstructing American Literary History* have had to travel beyond dogma and ideology.[25] Bercovitch implies that, unlike their "liberal" predecessors, the scholars of this new generation possess no oppressive convictions that they need to bury beneath the layers of their rhetoric and no secret schemes of power that motivate their work.

Bercovitch's disclaimers, however, seem more than a bit disingenuous when one considers that as soon as he has spoken of the virtues of *dissensus,* of the liberating power of the absence of ideology in the work of his authors, he goes on to list the "similar convictions" they share "about the *problematics* of literary history." (In many ways, Bercovitch's "convictions about problematics" seem to be "ideology" and "metaphysics" in ironic

23. Bercovitch, preface to *Reconstructing American Literary History,* ed. Sacvan Bercovitch (Cambridge: Harvard University Press, 1986), pp. vii-viii.

24. Bercovitch, *Reconstructing American Literary History,* p. viii.

25. Bercovitch, *Reconstructing American Literary History,* p. vii.

disguise.) The shared beliefs of Bercovitch's scholars include the conviction that "race, class, and gender" are "formal principles of art" and are essential to the analysis of any text; that "political norms are inscribed in aesthetic judgment" and thus are inevitably an element of all interpretation; and that "tropes and narrative devices" shape our understanding of the past and "may be said . . . to enforce certain views of the past."[26] The underlying assumption of a number of the contributors to Bercovitch's volume seems to be that language is primarily, if not exclusively, an instrument wielded with great and deceptive power by a skillful minority desperate to protect its vested interests.

Given these assumptions about the nature of language, it is not surprising that Bercovitch lists as the last shared interest of the contributors their *mission* as scholars, which is to liberate the self by demonstrating how it has been the unwitting victim of linguistic oppression. He says that, unlike the literary humanists of previous generations, the new literary historians do not seek to demonstrate that "art transcends culture." Instead, the wish is "to identify and explore the ideological limits of their time, and then to bring these to bear upon literary analysis in such a way as to make use of the categories of culture, rather than being used by them."[27] Once again we see language depicted as a web of entangling forces, all of which threaten the vital freedom of the desiring self. As the contemporary theorist Robert Scholes puts it: "Criticism is our last best chance to loosen the bonds of the textual powers in which we find ourselves enmeshed."[28]

The dichotomies implicit in these two statements by Bercovitch and Scholes are revisions of classic Enlightenment and romantic polarities — polarities between future and past, self and society, freedom and authority — and the visions they offer of the literary historian and theorist are clearly in the lineage of romantic heroism. Indeed, both Bercovitch and Scholes show how, in spite of its protestations to the contrary, contemporary literary theory does not represent so much a radical break with romantic theory as a variation upon the romantic theme of the artist as prophet and liberator. Only now it is the literary theorist rather than the poet who stands at the center of things; and it is liberation from ideology rather than freedom from kings and priests that contemporary theory can win for the imprisoned self.

26. Bercovitch, *Reconstructing American Literary History,* p. viii.
27. Bercovitch, *Reconstructing American Literary History,* p. viii.
28. Scholes, *Textual Power: Literary Theory and the Teaching of English* (New Haven: Yale University Press, 1985), p. 73.

"The New Americanists claim to belong to the first scholarly cohort that does *not* consist of ideologues," writes Frederick Crews. He quotes Bercovitch to the effect that ideology resides in "the 'absolute values' that a social system projects before its own gaze." By this definition, the purpose of ideology is always a conservative one of attempting "to keep power relations out of focus and thus safe from fundamental criticism. And if so, the investigators and critics of ideology, even if they subscribe to a definite radical politics of their own, are not to be thought of as ideologues but as unmaskers."[29] Relentlessly stripping away, these radical critics could never be accused of covering up.

Thus, through the appropriation of the Marxist critique of ideology and the interpretation of literary history according to the categories of scientific materialism, contemporary theorists have managed to attach themselves to the romantic tradition even as they have claimed to be breaking away from it. They have appropriated that tradition's view of the poet as a figure who is both representative and unique — a central figure in the culture and an isolated individual — and have shifted the focus from the poet or critic to the theorist. In effect, what they have argued is that they are saving the Enlightenment and romantic traditions from themselves and that they are saving others from the pernicious effects of the ideology of those traditions. According to contemporary Marxist theorists, most romantic theories, rather than serving as means of discovering truth and beauty, have been instruments in the service of the few for the oppression of the many. To the English romantic poet Percy Bysshe Shelley, poets may have seemed to be the unacknowledged legislators of the world, but in the world of contemporary theory, the critics have become the self-proclaimed liberators of the world.

Marxism and the Christian Critic

Contemporary Marxist literary theory attempts to position itself as a radical critique of the liberal individualism of Western culture — particularly the acquisitive and acquiescent consumer cultures of modern capitalism. For that reason alone, such radical theory may appeal to Christian critics who also question the premises of the post-Enlightenment societies of the West. In fact, in the first volume of his systematic theology, Helmut

---

29. Crews, "Whose American Renaissance?" p. 68.

Thielicke raises such a question about the premises of modern Western intellectual life. But, to be sure, his is hardly the question that a Marxist would raise: "It is odd to what extent the idea of suppression — along with other psychological categories — is used in interpretation of states of consciousness and modes of conduct, and yet it seldom seems to have occurred to anyone to investigate the element of suppression in the principle of self-resting finitude and the irrelevance of the transcendent."[30] Is it possible, Thielicke is asking, that modern cultures are engaged in the rigid suppression of a humbling awareness of the transcendent? What if, in spite of the power of their insights and the value of their contributions, philosophy since Descartes, theology since Schleiermacher, and literature since the romantics — or at least the dominant schools of thought in these different fields — are dramatically flawed in a foundational sense?

In his most recent books, Alasdair MacIntyre has repeatedly made note of the fact that the history of modern attempts to establish a morality free of the constraints of tradition has itself become the central tradition of the modern West; this observation is especially relevant to the academic Marxism of contemporary humanistic study. With its confidence in human nature and in unimpeded rationality, this modern tradition has suppressed or forgotten more ancient truths and standards. There is the possibility, MacIntyre argues, that "our consciousness of even fundamental precepts may be subverted by the distractions and corruptions of evil, so that the wrongness of a whole class of actions may cease to be evident to us. Thus, according to Aquinas there are absolute and unconditional prohibitions which a whole culture may infringe without recognizing that it is so doing."[31]

Thielicke and MacIntyre believe that it is appropriate to ask whether an entire tradition is fundamentally misdirected. If M. H. Abrams and others are accurate in their description of romanticism, they would ask, is it not possible that the entire romantic program is skewed at its foundations? According to Abrams, literature in the romantic tradition represented a deliberate attempt to salvage Christian values by reformulating them in distinctly post-Christian terms. Romantic authors undertook "to

---

30. Thielicke, *The Evangelical Faith*, vol. 1: *Prolegomena: The Relation of Theology to Modern Thought Forms*, trans. and ed. Geoffrey W. Bromiley (Grand Rapids: Eerdmans, 1974), p. 241.

31. MacIntyre, *Whose Justice? Which Rationality?* (Notre Dame: University of Notre Dame Press, 1988), p. 331.

save traditional concepts, schemes, and values which had been based on the relation of the Creator to his creation." They did so by recasting them within a "two-term system of subject and object, ego and non-ego, the human mind or consciousness and its transactions with nature," which has prevailed in Western thought since Descartes.[32]

The cultural history of the past two centuries is in some ways a tale of the fate of the paradigm of the godlike self in the romantic tradition. That self moves through various stages from the time of the French Revolution to the present — from Blake's and Wordsworth's revolutionary hopes for the poet as a co-creator with God, through Gustave Flaubert's retreat from action to art, through the humanism of Matthew Arnold, and finally to the many varieties of twentieth-century aestheticism. Just as the Christian faith became attenuated in the self-deifying schemes of the romantic movement, so too does the history of the past two centuries show the diminishment of the romantic image of the poet as God.

Faced with romantic elevation of the literary experience, both the Marxist and the Christian critic are likely to feel discomfort. For example, when the contemporary Marxist critic Jerome McGann scorns the pseudo-religious culture industry centered in the modern university, the Christian critic might nod approval: "Coleridge's views were to enjoy a truly remarkable triumph in England and America for one hundred and fifty years, particularly in those *petit bourgeois* enclaves which Coleridge called 'the clerisy,' that body of culture-guardians whose center today is in the academies."[33]

But though such Marxist attacks upon romantic aestheticism may at first seem to complement a Christian view, the Christian student of culture has good reason to retain a healthy skepticism about the contemporary Marxist critique of humanism. After all, the Marxist critic scorns the recent history of culture, not in order to *restore* a perspective that has been forgotten or suppressed by that culture, but in order to free the self from the supposed bondage of all pasts, all cultures.

For the Christian, such a reductive approach to social history is troublesome. An exclusively Marxist reading of human experience, texts, and history seems no more valid than a proclamation of the gospel that

32. Abrams, *Natural Supernaturalism: Tradition and Revolution in Romantic Literature* (New York: W. W. Norton, 1971), p. 13.

33. McGann, *The Romantic Ideology: A Critical Investigation* (Chicago: University of Chicago Press, 1983), p. 7.

concludes with the exposure of sin and fails to declare the word of forgiveness and grace. Of course, for the contemporary Marxist critic of culture there is a word and way of redemption — through the liberation of the oppressed self trapped within the ideological confines of capitalist culture. But by treating evil as the exclusive product of specific historical forces, the Marxist analysis of culture repeats the ancient gnostic error. In its pervasive use of such dichotomies as oppressor and oppressed, contemporary Marxist theory oversimplifies the complexity of evil and distorts the powerful understanding of sin given in the Scriptures and developed over the course of Christian history.

Furthermore, the Marxist analysis of the past is debilitatingly reductive if it is taken as the complete word about that past. Like so many post-Enlightenment movements in Western culture, Marxism sees the past as almost exclusively a history of limitation and injustice. History, however, is not only a record of oppression but also a record of liberation; it is not only a story of repression and sublimation and injustice but also a story of sublime sacrifice and redemptive suffering. The texts and cultural traditions embedded in that past have the power to heal and reveal as well as to wound and deceive. For the Christian in particular, the past is a source of freedom as well as bondage. After all, it was in the *past* that God chose a *particular* people as his own and delivered them from their bondage at the hands of a wicked ruler, and it was in the *past* that Jesus was born, died, and rose again. Without the past, the Christian has no future.

Yet suppose that, in spite of having foundational differences with Marxist thought, the Christian critic seeks to form an alliance of sorts with Marxist literary theory. What may happen? In all likelihood, this Marxist critic will dismiss the central tenets of Christian belief out of hand. For instance, in his study of romanticism, McGann explains that, although he finds some things of value in the work of Samuel Taylor Coleridge, he must dismiss the poet-critic's work — specifically because of the religious claims it makes: "Because his position is a conceptual-idealist defense of Church, State, and the class interests which those institutions support and defend, Coleridge's ideas are, in a Marxist view, clearly deplorable."[34] For most contemporary Marxist theorists, Christian belief is a particularly dangerous form of ideological control.

McGann further reveals his attitude toward Christian belief in an essay on the religious poetry of Christina Rossetti. In this study of the

34. McGann, *The Romantic Ideology*, p. 5.

nineteenth-century poet, McGann develops a historical argument to elevate the reputation of a neglected Christian author, while rejecting categorically the theological claims of her work. He writes that Rossetti, an ardent premillenarian and evangelical, was ignored for decades because her views did not coincide with the two reigning ideologies of criticism in the university — the Broad Church school (Arnold, Trilling, Abrams) and the High Church Anglo-Catholics (defined by T. S. Eliot and including such figures as the poets John Donne and Gerard Manley Hopkins). Though driven "out of the Great Tradition and its attendant anthologies," the poetry of Rossetti, "to us" at least, "seems peculiarly alive, *as poetry*, to her age's cultural contradictions."[35]

At this point, the Christian critic might feel gratitude toward McGann for his attempts to revive interest in a woman whose Christian poetry has been ignored. But as soon as McGann has bestowed his blessing upon Rossetti, he dismisses her religious beliefs as irrelevant. He writes that he is pleased to have discovered a "means for gathering the power of her work outside of its own religious self-representations. . . . The Christian and Adventist machinery in her work is a historically specific set of images which do not so much describe actual spiritual realities (like paradise and so forth) as they indicate . . . how difficult it seemed to imagine . . . a fully human life in the real world of her place and time."[36] Thus, the Christian reader has Rossetti's poetry given back to him or her, but at the cost of the explicit denial of the value of that poetry's deepest claims and concerns. To quote McGann at the conclusion of his essay:

> Her poetry contains a forcible and persistent reminder that the themes of Christian poetry — even the greatest of such themes, like those of guilt and redemption, of resurrection, of incarnation — are time and place specific, that they have had a beginning, and a middle, and that they will finally have an end as well. To imagine otherwise is a vanity and an illusion, a peculiar blindness from which only those who recognize their own historical backwardness will be exempt.[37]

It is one thing to say that Christian doctrines are "time and place specific," that they are rooted in historical events and movements. Any

35. McGann, "The Religious Poetry of Christina Rossetti," in *Canons*, ed. Robert von Hallberg (Chicago: University of Chicago Press, 1984), p. 275.

36. McGann, "The Religious Poetry of Christina Rossetti," pp. 271-72.

37. McGann, "The Religious Poetry of Christina Rossetti," p. 275.

credible Christian doctrine of special revelation should make a similar claim, for Christian faith is grounded in the saving acts of God in our individual and collective histories. But it is another thing entirely to claim that these doctrines "will finally have an end as well" and to say that "to imagine otherwise is a vanity and an illusion." Indeed, the Christian believes that they will have an end of sorts, though not in the cooling of a spent cosmos but in the consummation of Christ's kingdom. To say the least, there is a dramatic difference here.

McGann's treatment of Christian belief is fairly typical of contemporary Marxist criticism. As we have seen, both Lentricchia and Eagleton attack the tradition of "liberal humanism" that supplanted medieval hierarchicalism at the beginning of the modern era. "Modern European criticism was born of a struggle against the absolutist state," says Eagleton.[38] But because the secular bourgeois societies that supplanted the medieval theocracies have now themselves become oppressive ideological bastions of privilege, they too must be overthrown. In the dialectic of history, Christianity's hierarchicalism had its place and time, and so did bourgeois individualism. But now, Eagleton argues, it is time for the utopian promise and power of Marxist criticism to take hold. Having been born in the struggle against the state, the final section of *The Function of Criticism* proclaims, modern criticism must redefine itself. "Unless its future is now defined as a struggle against the bourgeois state, it might have no future at all."[39]

In an influential work of contemporary Marxist theory entitled *The Political Unconscious,* Frederic Jameson points to the limited and antecedent role that is the most that Marxist criticism is willing to concede to Christian belief. A comparison of Marxism and religion "may . . . function to rewrite certain religious concepts — most notably Christian historicism and the 'concept' of providence . . . — as anticipatory foreshadowings of historical materialism within precapitalist social formations in which scientific thinking is unavailable as such."[40] That is, the Christian narrative of history, with its images of spoiled innocence, of bondage and deliverance, of crisis and redemption, has served a *propaedeutic* function in preparing

---

38. Terry Eagleton, *The Function of Criticism: From the Spectator to Post-Structuralism* (London: Verso, 1984), p. 9.

39. Eagleton, *The Function of Criticism,* p. 124.

40. Jameson, *The Political Unconscious: Narrative as a Socially Symbolic Act* (Ithaca: Cornell University Press, 1981), p. 285.

the way for Marxist scientific truth. For Jameson, however, there is no question of the Christian and Marxist views of history living together in peaceful coexistence. Because both claim to offer *comprehensive* explanations for the workings of history, Marxist orthodoxy must displace Christian belief if it is to bring about the order of freedom and justice it envisions.

As Alasdair MacIntyre argues in one of his early works, "Marxism shares in good measure both the content and the functions of Christianity as an interpretation of human existence, and it does so because it is the historical successor of Christianity."[41] Because it grows out of the prophetic traditions of Judaism and Christianity and thus draws upon a profound tradition of concern for justice and truth, Marxism has a powerful appeal for the Christian critic of culture. And because it is comprehensive in its claims and in its explanatory power, Marxist theory approaches the interpretation of history and texts with a confident thoroughness that those trained in the Christian tradition can surely appreciate.

At the same time, however, the Christian student of culture needs to maintain a critical distance from the claims of Marxist cultural analysis, whose assessment of texts and events is inevitably implicated in a series of larger metaphysical claims.[42] Grounded as it is in a quasi-scientific materialism and in Enlightenment optimism about the self, Marxist theory finds itself in irreconcilable conflict with core beliefs of the Christian faith. Furthermore, the Christian critic of literature who looks to contemporary Marxist theory for deliverance from the confines of romanticism is bound to be disappointed, for the theory offered by the radical critics of today constitutes a subtle reworking of romantic motifs rather than a rejection or transformation of those motifs.

As Edward Mendelson describes it, W. H. Auden realized that the impasses of literary modernism meant that the *next step* in the development of culture, the step Auden eventually was to take as a Christian poet and

---

41. MacIntyre, *Marxism and Christianity*, p. 6.

42. In "George Lukács and his Devil's Pact," George Steiner offers a brilliant analysis of the price to be paid by the earnest Marxist critic: "At the outset of his brilliant career, Lukács made a Devil's pact with historical necessity. The daemon promised him the secret of objective truth. He gave him the power to confer blessing or pronounce anathema in the name of revolution and 'the laws of history'. But since Lukács's return from exile, the Devil has been lurking about, asking for his fee. In October 1956 [in the form of the Soviet invasion of Hungary], he knocked loudly at the door" (Steiner, *Language and Silence: Essays on Language, Literature and the Inhuman* [New York: Atheneum, 1986], p. 337).

social theorist, "cannot be one that moves *beyond* the last — as the idiom of progress would suggest — but one that moves in a different direction."[43] For the Christian critic of literature, this means a *return* to the resources of the Scriptures and the Christian tradition for the purpose of formulating creative responses to the impasses and needs of the contemporary world. We return to our past, that is, in order to discern how we, who live under the signs of grace and forgiveness, are to act in the present as agents of justice and mercy within that history of which God is the author and finisher.

43. Mendelson, *Early Auden* (New York: Viking Press, 1981), p. 22.

CHAPTER 8   *Deconstructive Therapy*

Soon after I had become a confessing Christian in the late 1960s, I became intrigued by a process that repeats itself in almost all areas of the Christian experience of culture. I might call this phenomenon *evangelical culture lag*. With this term, I am referring to the evangelical habit of adopting the practices of general American culture several years after they have become established in, and thus made safe by, the society as a whole. Rock music swept the youth culture in the 1960s but remained anathema in evangelical churches until the mid-seventies. We now have Christian heavy-metal bands and music videos and may see a Christian Madonna in the coming years. In the same way, many evangelicals, though certainly not all, tended to gaze with suspicion from afar at the development of television in the 1950s and 1960s. But once Johnny Carson had been on the air for a decade, the 700 Club and the PTL Club appeared on Christian channels; the PTL Club especially seemed to lift virtually every element from the Carson format: the band, the monologue, the guests promoting their own books and shows, and the portly straight man. In the course of evangelical life, "Jazzercise" seems inevitably to become "Praise in Motion," while Ralph Waldo Emerson returns as Dale Carnegie, who in turn metamorphoses into Norman Vincent Peale and now appears on television weekly as Robert Schuller.

Such examples are legion, and the reasons for their appearance are complex. From the standpoint of the social sciences, the predominantly middle-class nature of modern evangelicalism no doubt partially explains the derivative quality of evangelical cultural life.[1] But to understand this phenomenon fully, one must consider the theological dimension of the cultural dilemmas of American evangelicals. In the decades since their fundamentalist forebears split with modernism, evangelicals have largely seemed content to let other institutions in American life — especially schools and the media — set the cultural agenda. Lacking a sensible theory of culture, they have often responded to innovations with fear and then have waited for the bizarre to become, through time, domesticated. Familiarity may breed contempt for some; for evangelicals it often gives birth to the coziest feelings.

It is easy, of course, for educated Christians to make selective fun of the cultural ignorance of their benighted fellow Christians. Yet however proud they may be of their urbanity, educated Christians are not immune to this curious reactionary virus. We mock Christian cultural provincialism but greet new intellectual developments with our own subtly retrograde attitudes. We were trained several decades ago by scholars who had, for the most part, dispensed with the Christian faith. We have embraced their theories and methods and have made them Christian by reading them into the Bible and the tradition of the faith. In the field of literary studies, this process has occurred in a most extraordinary way. Christians in the arts have often followed the lead of Dorothy Sayers and others in making the romantic doctrine of the creative imagination — which was explicitly formulated by Blake, Emerson, and others as a means of going beyond the historic Christian faith — into a cornerstone of evangelical aesthetics. The heresy of the day before yesterday becomes the orthodoxy of today.

The reasons for this delayed response to theoretical developments are fairly clear. Since there are no avowedly Protestant graduate programs, evangelical scholars learn their theories and receive their professional training alongside everyone else in the secular academies. Most of today's

---

1. From a very different perspective, Gerald Graff examines the process of the assimilation of radical ideals by middle-class culture. See his essay "Co-optation," in *The New Historicism*, ed. H. Aram Veeser (New York: Routledge, 1989), pp. 168-81. Graff states:

> My own awareness of this phenomenon had been shaped less by Marcuse and the new Left than by earlier postwar American culture critics, like the critics of 'Masscult' and 'Midcult' in the 1950s, who had noticed that a good deal of mass-culture *Kitsch* derived from the heretofore 'adversarial' vocabularies of modern art. As early as the late 1950s, the domestication of the 'adversary culture' was being widely discussed by the so-called 'New York intellectual critics." ("Co-optation," p. 170)

evangelical and Reformed scholars attended American graduate schools between 1950 and 1980; in philosophy this most often meant training in the Anglo-American analytic tradition, and in literature it meant instruction in various systems of formalism, particularly the New Criticism. To those who adhere to the analytic philosophical tradition, the works of Friedrich Nietzsche, Martin Heidegger, and Michel Foucault may represent the most befuddling obscurantism imaginable; to literary formalists, they presage a world stripped of wonder and belief. While there is nothing inherently anti-Christian in analytic philosophy and the New Criticism, there is also nothing uniquely Christian about them. Yet they are now frequently conscripted by Christians to serve as allies in the battle against this latest heretical confusion.

It is disconcerting to see such reactions. No matter what they think about new theoretical developments at first glance, the troubling fact is that Christian thinkers often eventually appropriate such theories with little or no theological discrimination. In the case of one of the most powerful theoretical movements of the past two decades, known as deconstruction or poststructuralism, we have already begun to hear the sanctified deconstructive word from Christian critics.

Deconstruction and the Postmodern Era

What we know as deconstruction or poststructuralism has its roots in the work of the Swiss linguist Ferdinand de Saussure. In lectures and essays dating from the early years of this century, Saussure propounded a series of exceptionally influential arguments about the relationship of language to reality.[2] According to Saussure, the relationship of the signifier (a word) to the signified (the object to which we attempt to point with words) is always an arbitrary matter of the will and linguistic convention. There is no essential connection between a given word and what it connotes. Saussure's point is essentially a Nietzschean one. The arbitrary connection of a vocal sound to an object comes "after long use [to] seem firm, canonical, and obligatory." After a significant amount of time, what is a purely linguistic convention becomes in the mind of a people an indubitable, everlasting truth: "truths are illusions about which one has forgotten

2. For an introduction to the thought and influence of Saussure, see Jonathan Culler, *Saussure* (New York: Penguin Books, 1976).

that this is what they are. . . . To be truthful means using the customary metaphors — in moral terms: the obligation to lie according to a fixed convention."[3]

While Nietzsche used his insights to launch and justify a program of eccentric, demystifying interpretation, in Saussure's hands this view of language served more systematic ends. Saussure argued that the arbitrary nature of the relationship of signifier to signified meant that the meanings of words could only be understood through their formal relationships to one another, rather than by means of their relationships to objects in nature or events in history. The sounds of a language, that is, do not constitute facts with clearly defined properties but receive their identity as a result of their difference from other elements of the total system of language. "In language there are only differences," Saussure says. "Even more important: a difference generally implies positive terms between which the difference is set up; but in language there are only differences *without positive terms.*"[4]

Saussure's vision of language significantly diminishes the role assigned to the creative self in the romantic tradition. According to Saussure, any individual speaker is not the master of the language he or she uses but rather is caught in the web of relationships spun by that language and by the social order that nourishes and sustains it. In *Song of Myself,* Walt Whitman bragged of the power possessed by his creative, language-using self: "My voice goes after what my eyes cannot reach, / With the twirl of my tongue I encompass worlds and volumes of worlds."[5] Saussure would counter Whitman with the claim that in the most real sense it is language that contains the poet rather than the poet who contains language; it is language that speaks through the poet and not the poet who masters language in using it.

Saussure's work exerted a significant influence on European intellectual life, particularly in France, in the decades after the Second World War. It proved to be an especially useful tool for those who wished to develop a scientific study of the linguistic and visual signs that constitute any given

3. Nietzsche, "On Truth and Lie in an Extra-Moral Sense," in *The Portable Nietzsche,* trans. and ed. Walter Kaufmann (New York: Penguin Books, 1976), p. 47.

4. Saussure, *Course in General Linguistics,* ed. Charles Bally and Albert Sechehaye in collaboration with Albert Riedlinger, trans. Wade Baskin (New York: McGraw-Hill, 1966), p. 120.

5. Whitman, *Song of Myself,* in *Whitman: Poetry and Prose,* ed. Justin Kaplan (New York: Library of America, 1982), p. 213.

culture. At the same time, it also proved valuable in the study of different literary genres, since it enabled critics to perform structural analyses of poems, short stories, and novels. Figures such as Claude Lévi-Strauss, the French anthropologist, helped to make the structuralism of Saussure a dominant force, first in the social sciences and later in the humanities.

In America, structuralism became a subject of serious study at about the time that it was being supplanted by poststructuralism in Europe. In fact, it is possible to date the transition in European thought with some precision. In October of 1966, Johns Hopkins University served as host for a symposium called "The Languages of Criticism and the Sciences of Man." More than one hundred scholars in the humanities and social sciences attended this conference, and among them was a thirty-seven-year-old French philosopher named Jacques Derrida, whose paper "Structure, Sign, and Play in the Discourse of the Human Sciences" proved to be a deadly opening salvo in the Continental invasion of American universities.[6] The essay is a subtle but devastating critique of the structuralist thought of Lévi-Strauss; but it is also much more than that. Because Derrida takes structuralism to be only the latest form of a long-standing Western obsession with metaphysics, his dismantling of Lévi-Strauss also aspires to undermine the ingrained Western habits of reflection in philosophy and theology.[7]

Derrida goes about his critique of Lévi-Strauss by sharply questioning the anthropologist's distinction between nature and culture. Derrida says that the opposition between nature and culture is "congenital to philosophy. . . . [I]t has been relayed to us by means of a whole historical chain which opposes 'nature' to law, to education, to art, to technics — but also to liberty, to the arbitrary, to history, to society, to the mind, and so on."[8] Whatever is "*universal* and spontaneous" belongs to nature, while all that is dependent upon the "system of *norms* regulating society" belongs to

---

6. For an account of this conference and its place in American intellectual history, see Frank Lentricchia, *After the New Criticism* (Chicago: University of Chicago Press, 1980), pp. 157-77.

7. "The course of Western thought, in the terms of Derrida's argument, is governed by the positing of a metaphysical presence which abides through various fictive appellations, from subject to substance to *eidos* to *archē* to *telos*, transcendentality, conscience, structure, man, or the ultimate fiction of God" (Lentricchia, *After the New Criticism*, p. 164).

8. Derrida, "Structure, Sign, and Play in the Discourse of the Human Sciences," in *Writing and Difference*, trans. Alan Bass (Chicago: University of Chicago Press, 1978), pp. 282-83.

culture. Derrida argues that the work of Lévi-Strauss itself shows this distinction to be untenable. In discussing the prohibition against incest, Lévi-Strauss writes that "it constitutes a rule, but a rule which, alone among all the social rules, possesses at the same time a universal character."[9] Derrida writes that Lévi-Strauss calls this state of affairs a "*scandal,* that is to say, something which no longer tolerates the nature/culture opposition he has accepted, something which *simultaneously* seems to require the predicates of nature and of culture. . . . Obviously," Derrida concludes, "there is no scandal except within a system of concepts which accredits the difference between nature and culture." The incest prohibition is a clear sign that the difference between nature and culture, "which has always been assumed to be self-evident, finds itself erased or questioned."[10]

Why would the elimination of the distinction between nature and culture be a dramatic development? Derrida answers that without such a distinction in place, those who believe that there is a stable center to language and the world will find that there is no foundation for this belief. In Derrida's terms, the "myth of nature" calms the anxieties of those who fear that there is nothing but the "structure of culture." The "center" that men and women have forever posited for their structures serves not only to "orient, balance, and organize the structure" but also to "make sure that the organizing principle of the structure would limit . . . the *play* of the structure." The belief in a "centered structure" is rooted in the human wish to see the play of human language and culture "constituted on the basis of a fundamental immobility and a reassuring certitude, which itself is beyond the reach of play."[11]

Derrida's arguments are hardly new to the literature of the Western world. Many of Shakespeare's greatest tragedies — *Macbeth, Hamlet,* and *King Lear* in particular — grapple with the terrifying prospect of an ungrounded or "decentered" world. Furthermore, many of the finest romantic poets and essayists had to pass through a period of terrifying negation before affirming the redemptive power of the imagination. For example, Emerson had to undergo the crisis of his wife's death and his own departure from the Christian church before he could declare his blissful confidence in human destiny: "The nonchalance of boys who are sure of a dinner, and would disdain as much as a lord to do or say aught

9. Lévi-Strauss, quoted in Derrida, "Structure, Sign, and Play," p. 283.

10. Derrida, "Structure, Sign, and Play," p. 283.

11. Derrida, "Structure, Sign, and Play," pp. 278-79.

to conciliate one, is the healthy attitude of human nature."[12] Yet Emerson was able to celebrate this nonchalance because his doubt had led eventually to his confident discovery that the laws at work within the human spirit were identical to those at work within nature, thus assuring him that nature and history were grounded upon a rock of impermeable spiritual reality.

It is the devastating loss of that confidence that much of modern literature registers and to which poststructuralism claims to be responding. In "The Ballad of the Children of the Czar," for example, the American poet Delmore Schwartz focuses upon imagery of play in order to ponder the human condition in the disenchanted world of modernity. In the first section of the poem, Schwartz imagines the children at play:

> The children of the Czar
> Played with a bouncing ball
>
> In the May morning, in the Czar's garden,
> Tossing it back and forth.
>
> It fell among the flowerbeds
> Or fled to the north gate.
>
> A daylight moon hung up
> In the Western sky, bald white.
>
> Like Papa's face, said Sister,
> Hurling the white ball forth.

The poet meditates on the nature of history and guilt, and his tone becomes somber near the close of the poem:

> The ground on which the ball bounces
> Is another bouncing ball.
>
> The wheeling, whirling world
> Makes no will glad.
>
> Spinning in its spotlight darkness,
> It is too big for their hands.

12. Emerson, "Self-Reliance," in *Emerson: Essays and Lectures,* ed. Joel Porte (New York: Library of America, 1983), p. 261.

A pitiless, purposeless Thing,
Arbitrary and unspent,

Made for no play, for no children,
But chasing only itself.

The innocent are overtaken,
They are not innocent.

They are their father's fathers,
The past is inevitable.[13]

This image of the "wheeling, whirling world" that "makes no will glad" — this "pitiless, purposeless Thing" — resonates with many images from poems of this century. Robert Lowell's "Waking Early Sunday Morning" also concludes with the depiction of the earth as an abandoned planet:

Pity the planet, all joy gone
from this sweet volcanic cone;
peace to our children when they fall
in small war on the heels of small
war — until the end of time
to police the earth, a ghost
orbiting forever lost
in our monotonous sublime.[14]

The vision of the world as an untethered or ungrounded reality, then, hardly originates with Derrida. What is unique in his thinking is the claim that this sense of emptiness is not a product of the specific cultural and intellectual history of the modern West; instead, Derrida argues that the emptiness is at the very heart of language, which is always on the verge of self-betrayal because it carries within itself the acknowledgment that there is nothing behind or beneath it save the free play of desire. For Derrida, language begins to *deconstruct* itself even before a critic trains his or her gaze upon it. ("Language bears within itself the necessity of its own critique.")[15]

13. Schwartz, *Selected Poems (1938-1958): Summer Knowledge* (New York: New Directions, 1967), pp. 21, 23.
14. Lowell, "Waking Early Sunday Morning," in *Robert Lowell's Poems: A Selection*, ed. Jonathan Raban (London: Faber & Faber, 1974), p. 104.
15. Derrida, "Structure, Sign, and Play," p. 284.

In the Derridean view, structuralism served its purpose by demonstrating that all human activity takes place within a network of verbal signs whose connections to reality are always arbitrary and conventional. To this Saussurean understanding of language poststructuralism adds the insight that there is no possible center, no point of certainty or stability outside the world of the interpretive play of signs. In his address at the Johns Hopkins symposium, Derrida acknowledges that a formidable number of humanists and social scientists still dream of discovering "full presence, the reassuring foundation, the origin and the end of play." But he leaves little doubt as to his conviction that the poststructural viewpoint will win the day.[16]

Derrida believes that the demise of structuralism signals the end of

---

16. Derrida, "Structure, Sign, and Play," p. 292. It is instructive to compare the conclusion of Derrida's essay to the ending of a very well-known poem by William Butler Yeats called "The Second Coming" (in *Selected Poems and Three Plays of William Butler Yeats*, 3rd ed., ed. M. L. Rosenthal [New York: Collier Books, 1986]). Derrida concludes his essay thus:

> Here there is a kind of question, let us still call it historical, whose *conception, formation, gestation,* and *labor* we are only catching a glimpse of today. I employ these words, I admit, with a glance toward the operations of childbearing — but also with a glance toward those who, in a society from which I do not exclude myself, turn their eyes away when faced by the as yet unnamable which is proclaiming itself and which can do so, as is necessary whenever a birth is in the offing, only under the species of the nonspecies, in the formless, mute, infant, and terrifying form of monstrosity." ("Structure, Sign, and Play," p. 293)

The conclusion of Yeats's poem reads:

> Somewhere in sands of the desert
> A shape with lion body and the head of a man,
> A gaze blank and pitiless as the sun,
> Is moving its slow thighs, while all about it
> Reel shadows of the indignant desert birds.
> The darkness drops again; but now I know
> That twenty centuries of stony sleep
> Were vexed to nightmare by a rocking cradle,
> And what rough beast, its hour come round at last,
> Slouches towards Bethlehem to be born?
> ("The Second Coming," p. 90)

Yeats wrote his poem at the end of World War I, and it proved to be prophetic in anticipating the totalitarian terrors of the coming decades; hence it has a ring of authenticity to it. Derrida's ominous conclusion, however, rings hollow because the rhetoric of enormity and monstrosity hardly seems to fit with his social setting or to coincide with the ironic playfulness of his writings.

193

Enlightenment humanism, and he believes that this collapse may be interpreted in two very different ways. First, it can be read in the manner of Lowell and Schwartz, as a loss of meaning and order; this reading of the collapse of Enlightenment hope is the one given in much of existential philosophy and modern literature. It is the "saddened, *negative,* nostalgic, guilty, Rousseauistic side of the thinking of play." But there is another interpretation one might offer for the demise of metaphysics and the loss of the center. The "other side would be the Nietzschean *affirmation,* that is the joyous affirmation of the play of the world and of the innocence of becoming, the affirmation of a world of signs without fault, without truth, and without origin which is offered to an active interpretation."[17] This "world of signs without faults" is clearly Derrida's utopian ideal, a world in which intellectual history becomes a great video arcade, and every character or idea in that history is but one more game meant to heighten the pleasure of the postmodern player at the controls.

In ways that Derrida probably did not imagine when he delivered his Johns Hopkins address, political events soon hastened the development and influence of poststructuralism. In Europe and America, 1968 proved to be a pivotal year. In the United States that year saw the withdrawal in disgrace of an incumbent president from the election race; the assassination of Martin Luther King, Jr., and Robert Kennedy; rioting in many cities; the Tet offensive in Vietnam; and conflict in the streets of Chicago during the Democratic convention. Throughout the democracies of Europe, especially in France, there were waves of student protests and labor strikes. Terry Eagleton argues that poststructuralism was "a product of that blend of euphoria and disillusionment, liberation and dissipation, carnival and catastrophe, which was 1968." He sees deconstruction as a transformation of the forces that were defeated in the streets in that year: "Unable to break the structures of state power, post-structuralism found it possible instead to subvert the structures of language."[18] In this reading, poststructuralism is the perfect form of thought for people who seek the thrill of subversion without the risk of dangerous confrontation.

One does not have to share Eagleton's Marxist beliefs to discern the measure of truth in his judgments about the social role of poststructuralist thought. As we saw in our study of Marxism in the contemporary univer-

17. Derrida, "Structure, Sign, and Play," p. 292.
18. Eagleton, *Literary Theory: An Introduction* (Minneapolis: University of Minnesota Press, 1983), p. 142.

sity, the social upheaval of the 1960s worked its way into the patterns of thought of many in a whole generation of young scholars. As a doctrine that celebrates the subversive free play of language, deconstruction may serve nicely the purposes of those who wish to overturn dominant systems of value or truth without getting wounded in the process. In the hands of many of its practitioners, it has become a means of waging the intellectual equivalent of risk-free guerilla warfare.

Poststructural Pragmatism

No doubt there are many who doubt that today's Christian analytic thinker will become tomorrow's deconstructive philosopher, or that contemporary Christian heirs of Cleanth Brooks will become the next apostles of Derridean interpretive free play. But in response to such skeptics one might argue that a conceivable course for evangelical thinking has already been charted by Richard Rorty and begun to make itself evident in Christian approaches to contemporary culture. Over the past two decades, Rorty has gone from being an accomplished analytic philosopher to being a champion of literary culture and the therapeutic model of philosophy. In the introduction to *Philosophy and the Mirror of Nature,* Rorty writes: "The aim of the book is to undermine the reader's confidence in 'the mind' as something about which one should have a 'philosophical' view, in 'knowledge' as something about which there ought to be a 'theory' and which has 'foundations,' and in 'philosophy' as it has been conceived since Kant." Then, making use of two very intriguing metaphors, Rorty admits that his own work "is therapeutic rather than constructive. The therapy offered is, nevertheless, parasitic upon the constructive efforts of the very analytic philosophers whose frame of reference I am trying to put in question."[19]

Of special interest to the Christian student of intellectual history is Rorty's essay "Nineteenth-Century Idealism and Twentieth-Century Textualism." In this work, he links philosophy and literature and argues that literature has supplanted philosophy as the central discipline of the contemporary world, just as philosophy displaced theology several centuries ago. The essay begins with two disarmingly straightforward sentences: "In the last century there were philosophers [the idealists] who argued that

19. Rorty, *Philosophy and the Mirror of Nature* (Princeton: Princeton University Press, 1979), p. 7.

nothing exists but ideas. In our century there are people [the textualists] who write as if there were nothing but texts." Rorty claims that "both movements adopt an antagonistic position to natural science," and "both insist that we can never compare human thought or language with bare, unmediated reality." According to Rorty, idealism and textualism both see science as simply a vocabulary that has proved to be "handy in predicting and controlling nature." Superior to science is art — for the idealists because it puts us in touch with the spiritual dimensions of our being and for the textualists because "the ironic modernist's awareness that he is responding to texts rather than to things, puts him one up on the scientist."[20]

Many contemporary Christian philosophers and literary scholars appear to be idealists with reservations and modifications. They maintain a belief in transcendence because their theological commitments rule out a purely naturalistic view of the world. At the same time, however, most of them have been trained in the Kantian tradition, and they seem to have made their peace with what C. P. Snow has called the tension of the "two cultures" — the scientific and the literary. For example, standard evangelical statements about literature for the past several decades have accepted the sharp demarcation between these two cultures. Christian aestheticians have often argued that, yes, science and philosophy do accurately describe the rational and empirical side of human experience, but those disciplines fail to do justice to the sphere of the intuitive and imaginative. Literature opens that realm for us; it allows us the emotional and spiritual satisfactions that our "factual" life cannot provide. Almost everything vital that the Christian student of literature believes — about the existence of God, the trustworthiness of the Bible, or the death and resurrection of Jesus — belongs to the realm of facts, while what he or she feels about those great truths is part of the indispensable imaginative side of human nature.

This neat division of human experience has its roots in what Rorty and others have seen to be a dichotomous view most fully developed by Immanuel Kant. Rorty points to the distinction that Kant made between the determinate and the reflective judgment. The determinate judgment "ticks off instances of concepts by invoking common, public criteria," while the reflective judgment operates "without rules, . . . searching for

---

20. Rorty, "Nineteenth-Century Idealism and Twentieth-Century Textualism," in *Consequences of Pragmatism* (Minneapolis: University of Minnesota Press, 1982), pp. 139-40.

concepts under which to group particulars."[21] The determinate judgment provides us with our hard knowledge, while the reflective judgment gives us the pleasing pictures of life that our imaginations and spirits crave. It is clear that Kant thinks more highly of the work of the determinate judgment; this is, after all, the world of real knowledge. Thus, while the creative activity of the reflective judgment gives us the illusion of spiritual freedom, we are never to forget that it is just that — an illusion.

Crude as they may be, these distinctions may help us to understand the attitudes of some Christian academicians. They place in context the condescension Christian philosophers and scientists sometimes express about the activities of those in the arts. Because of the nature of their commitments, scientifically inclined Christians obviously acknowledge a realm beyond the rational and empirical, but some are not sure about its academic status.

The distinctions may also explain the defensiveness of those who teach and practice the arts. Science and philosophy may tell one kind of truth about life, they say, but we had better listen to the artists if we hope to nourish our impoverished spirits. In holding to this modified Kantianism, Christian thinkers are subscribing to a view that has undergone dramatic changes in recent years. And it is important to acknowledge that this view was itself a recent development in the history of thought in the West.

Rorty provides a provocative and troubling answer to the question of what will come next in the development of Western thought. Briefly put, to its own great benefit, philosophy will become more like literature. "Twentieth-century textualism wants to place literature in the center," he writes, "and to treat both science and philosophy as, at best, literary genres."[22] But before the Christian writer, painter, or musician cheers this triumph of the imaginative over the rational and empirical, he or she should consider whether this is not indeed the most Pyrrhic of all victories. Customarily, when Christian aestheticians have claimed the primacy of the imagination, they have done so with the assurance that at least philosophy, science, and history have the facts right, so we know where the truth is when we need it. The arts were like children sent out to play while their parents tilled the soil and tended to the affairs of home. What Rorty proposes would be, for these children, a form of parricide and matricide.

21. Rorty, "Nineteenth-Century Idealism," p. 143.
22. Rorty, "Nineteenth-Century Idealism," p. 141.

They would be asked to assume adult responsibility in a world in which their games and dreams were suddenly at the center of importance.

Rorty would seem to be happy to have this arbitrary, game-like quality regarded as the essence of all intellectual activity; for him, writing a great book or formulating a compelling theory is like inventing an intriguing game. He particularly likes the fact that literary genres can be created and transformed at will: "It is a feature of what I shall call 'literature' that one can achieve success by introducing a quite new genre of poem or novel or critical essay *without* argument."[23] This feature of literature that Rorty finds particularly attractive is one that Walter Ong traces back to the romantic movement: "With romanticism, the old agonistic poetic had been replaced by a new doctrine of creativity. The poet is irenic, or at least neutral, uncommitted, free of dialogic struggle with an audience, since for the 'creative' romantic imagination, the poem is no longer a riposte but a simple product, an 'object' rather than an exchange."[24] According to the New Criticism, the object produced by the imagination is the tightly constructed work of art. In Rorty's scheme of pragmatic poststructuralism, the product of particularly creative activity is a new paradigm that gives order to cultural life and intellectual endeavors.[25]

Rorty asks that we allow him to "call 'romanticism' the thesis that what is most important for human life is not what propositions we believe but what vocabulary we use." He then claims that this word *romanticism* points to the tie that binds nineteenth-century philosophical idealism and twentieth-century literary textualism. Having sprung from the minds of Kant and Hegel at the beginning of the nineteenth century, philosophical idealism suffered irreversible damage at the hands of Marx, Kierkegaard, and others, so that "by the end of the century the word 'philosophy' had

23. Rorty, "Nineteenth-Century Idealism," p. 142.

24. Ong, "From Rhetorical Culture to New Criticism: The Poem as a Closed Field," in *The Possibilities of Order: Cleanth Brooks and His Work,* ed. Lewis P. Simpson (Baton Rouge: Louisiana State University Press, 1976), pp. 160-61.

25. As Alan Jacobs observes in an essay on Stanley Fish, the pragmatic poststructuralists are not able to give a convincing account of the means by which cultures change paradigms or individuals change their convictions: "Fish's only criterion for intellectual health in a practice is that it 'is not standing still and that its shape and the shape of its projects are continually changing.' Clearly, for Fish, a practice can have no telos in the usual sense, for the only end of a practice, in his view, is to perpetuate itself" (Jacobs, "The Unnatural Practices of Stanley Fish: A Review Essay," *South Atlantic Review* 55, 4 [1990]: 91).

become what it remains today — merely the name . . . for an academic department where memories of youthful hope are cherished, and wistful yearnings for recapturing past glories survive."[26]

With the death of metaphysical idealism, what survived was romanticism: "the principal legacy of metaphysical idealism is the ability of the literary culture to stand apart from science, to assert its spiritual superiority to science." Kant had taken the first step to establish "literary culture" when he argued that the vocabulary of science was but one of several valid and available vocabularies; by showing "that everything can be changed by talking in new terms," Hegel had taken the second step. As Rorty tells the story, the final move was made by Nietzsche and William James, who "gave up the notion of truth as a correspondence to reality." They taught us that all intellectual activity was therapy: "Instead of saying that the discovery of vocabularies could bring hidden secrets to light, they said that new ways of speaking could help get us what we want." This "pragmatism" is metaphysical idealism or romanticism in a new guise. What distinguishes it is a "thorough-going abandonment of the notion of *discovering the truth* which is common to theology and science."[27]

Rorty divides the "textualists" into two groups, the "weak" and the "strong." Weak textualists (the New Critics, Northrop Frye, and the structuralists, for example) do their best to "imitate science," seeking a "*method* of criticism" and agreement once they have "cracked the code." The weak textualists want the "comforts of consensus," while the strong textualists (the heirs of Nietzsche) simply ask themselves the same question about a text that "the engineer or the physicist asks himself about a puzzling physical object: how shall I describe this in order to get it to do what I want?"[28] Having given up the hope of discovering the truth, of finding what Rorty calls a "*privileged vocabulary,*" the strong textualists view all reading, indeed all intellectual activity, as a form of therapy. One reads and thinks in order to get hold of what one needs in order to get by. The truth is that which helps us to cope. Any vocabulary — be it that of the literary New Critics, the analytical philosophers, or the devout Christian believer — points not toward the truth but only toward the needs of its user for a means of dealing with life's devastations and disappointments.

26. Rorty, "Nineteenth-Century Idealism," pp. 142, 147.
27. Rorty, "Nineteenth-Century Idealism," pp. 149-51.
28. Rorty, "Nineteenth-Century Idealism," pp. 152-53.

American Therapy

In a number of ways, the development of poststructuralism in the academic world simply parallels the progress of therapeutic ideals in the culture as a whole. In Philip Rieff's words, the cultural revolution of therapy gives the unimpeded self "a way of using all commitments, which amounts to loyalty toward none." Just as Derrida called for a "joyous affirmation of the play of the world and of the innocence of becoming," therapeutic culture holds that "thinking need not produce nausea or despair as its final answer . . . because men will have ceased to seek any salvation other than amplitude in living itself." In a deconstructive, therapeutic world, even religious experience can find its place. If all truth is a fiction and all moral effort a form of groundless play, "faith can then grow respectable again, as one entertainable and passing personal experience among others, to enhance the interest of living from communal purpose." It will be crucial to the well-being of faith, however, that it not make moral demands upon its adherents. If it does so, it risks losing its power to draw new members to its fellowship. "To paraphrase Marx and Engels, all morality, be it ascetic or hedonistic, loses its force with a therapeutic outlook."[29]

We recall Rorty's image of the philosopher as the parasitic therapist. That parasite finds its host in the dead body of Christian belief and practice, which still gives off enough heat to warm the enlightened intellectual contemplating the demise of metaphysics. If Rieff, Alasdair MacIntyre, and Robert Bellah are right, ordinary men and women in the West are now huddling around the corpse alongside the therapeutic masters. "Between them," write Bellah and his coauthors in *Habits of the Heart*, "the manager and the therapist largely define the outlines of twentieth-century American culture. . . . It is an understanding of life generally hostile to older ideas of moral order. Its center is the autonomous individual, presumed able to choose the roles he will play and the commitments he will make, not on the basis of higher truths but according to

---

29. Rieff, *The Triumph of the Therapeutic: Uses of Faith After Freud* (New York: Harper & Row, 1966), pp. 21-22. As Rieff puts it in another book, "In his negational genius, the therapeutic as therapist revalues his values whenever he grows displeased with them. These constant revaluations by psychological man may well be called 'therapy neuroses' or 'life-style' as a parody of true culture. Truth endures. Life-style always changes" (Rieff, *The Feeling Intellect: Selected Writings*, ed. Jonathan B. Imber [Chicago: University of Chicago Press, 1990], p. 363).

the criterion of life-effectiveness as the individual judges it."[30] MacIntyre concludes that there are three "central *characters*" in modern society: "the aesthete, the therapist, and the manager."[31] As we have seen, Rorty defines all intellectual activity as therapy, as a means of seeing how "new ways of speaking could help get us what we want" — in other words, thought judged according to "the criterion of life-effectiveness." And it is easy to detect the managerial metaphor buried in the question that Rorty says the modern intellectual must ask: "How shall I describe this in order to get it to do what I want?"

Bellah and his colleagues tell the story of "Margaret Oldham," a therapist in her early thirties. "I do think it's important for you to take responsibility for yourself," she tells the interviewer, "I mean, nobody else is going to really do it. . . . In the end you're really alone and you really have to answer to yourself." When asked whether she has a responsibility for her own children, Margaret can only say, "I would say I have a legal responsibility for them, but in a sense I think they in turn are responsible for their acts." Assessing "Margaret's" view of the world, which they take to be representative of contemporary middle-class values, the authors conclude that since "there is no wider framework within which to justify common values, all one can ask from others is that they do the work of communicating their needs clearly, and one must in turn try to be clear about one's own need and desires." And we are left with a crisis involving our "inability to make legitimate demands on others."[32]

What "Margaret" believes is what Alasdair MacIntyre critically defines as "emotivism": "The doctrine that all evaluative judgments and more specifically all moral judgments are *nothing but* expressions of preference, expressions of attitude or feeling, insofar as they are moral or evaluative in character."[33] The only foundation for morality in an emotivist culture is the one provided by the human will; all efforts at moral discourse become "the attempt of one will to align the attitudes, feelings, preferences, and choices of another with its own."[34] In pluralistic, therapeutic America one

---

30. Bellah et al., *Habits of the Heart: Individualism and Commitment in American Life* (Berkeley: University of California Press, 1985), p. 47.

31. MacIntyre, *After Virtue,* 2nd ed. (Notre Dame: University of Notre Dame Press, 1984), p. 30.

32. Bellah et al., *Habits of the Heart,* pp. 15-16.

33. MacIntyre, *After Virtue,* pp. 11-12.

34. MacIntyre, *After Virtue,* p. 24.

can simply let others believe whatever they need to believe in order to get by, as long as they do not disturb others as they pursue the object of their faith or fancy. Over two hundred years ago, St. Jean de Crèvecoeur made note of the relativizing power of the American ideal:

> The various Christian sects introduced wear out, and . . . religious indifference becomes prevalent. When any considerable number of a particular sect happen to dwell contiguous to each other, they immediately erect a temple, and there worship the Divinity agreeably to their own peculiar ideas. Nobody disturbs them.[35]

In the introduction to *The Triumph of the Therapeutic*, Rieff approvingly quotes Karl Barth (writing in 1939): "Is not the very fact that so wretchedly little binding address is heard in the church, accountable for a goodly share of her misery — is it not perhaps *the* misery."[36] If *Habits of the Heart* is right, this lack may be due to the fact that the contemporary church has too much invested in the self to challenge it with "binding address." As a number of recent studies point out, especially George Marsden's *Fundamentalism and American Culture*, American evangelicalism has ahistorical individualism at its roots.[37]

If René Descartes made belief in God dependent upon self-consciousness and doubt, then American evangelicals have often seemed to make God the captive of their well-being and health. Some of America's greatest novels — Hawthorne's *The Scarlet Letter*, Melville's *Benito Cereno*, Dreiser's *An American Tragedy*, Fitzgerald's *The Great Gatsby*, and Faulkner's *Absalom, Absalom!* — document our democratic culture's aversion to a tragic vision. Though a serious consideration of the effects of sin is written into the fundamentalist charter, superficial assumptions about human nature and sanctification have worked their way into evangelicalism. As a result, in many instances, the heirs to the fundamentalist heritage have been able to make their peace with the inherent American optimism about the self. While holding relatively low opinions of tradition, the church, and general revelation, the evangelical tradition has largely turned to the experiences of the self for its security and stability. A failure to ground

---

35. Crèvecoeur, "What Is an American?" in *The Norton Anthology of American Literature*, 3rd ed., ed. Nina Baym et al. (New York: W. W. Norton, 1989), vol. 1, p. 563.

36. Rieff, *The Triumph of the Therapeutic*, p. 19.

37. Marsden, *Fundamentalism and American Culture: The Shaping of Twentieth Century Evangelicalism: 1870-1925* (New York: Oxford University Press, 1980).

faith outside the desiring self may leave evangelical Christians with few options but to appropriate the deconstructive view of language and the self.

Christian Proclamation in a Deconstructive World

To respond with integrity to deconstruction, the Christian needs to remain clear about points of agreement and disagreement, for a failure to recognize differences will inevitably lead to error and confusion. The confusion may arise because at first glance the deconstructive agenda seems similar to the powerful contemporary Christian critiques of modernity and its impasses.[38] Deconstruction questions the claims to truth made by unaided reason and thus may appear to have much in common with Christian convictions about the noetic effects of sin; it judges the pretensions and abuses of moral systems and so may seem to echo the prophetic voice of judgment in Jewish and Christian faith; and in breaking with rigid forms of scientific discourse, deconstruction may appear to present itself as a potent ally for Christians who wish to reintroduce mystery into the human experience.

But to confuse Christian faith and deconstructive practice involves a dramatic misreading of the poststructuralist enterprise. Following the lead of Martin Heidegger, Derrida and others do not attack the Enlightenment tradition out of any desire to recover or restore those practices and beliefs that that tradition had supplanted. Indeed, the poststructuralists believe that the work of Cartesianism and the Enlightenment is only a recent variation upon a decadent theme that can be traced to the very origins of Western thought.[39] Rather than seeking to dismantle Enlight-

---

38. Of those critiques, three of the most impressive are offered by Helmut Thielicke, a German Lutheran theologian, Nicholas Wolterstorff, a Reformed philosopher, and Alasdair MacIntyre, a Catholic moral philosopher. See Thielicke, *The Evangelical Faith*, vol. 1: *Prolegomena: The Relation of Theology to Modern Thought Forms*, trans. and ed. Geoffrey W. Bromiley (Grand Rapids: Eerdmans, 1974); MacIntyre, *Whose Justice? Which Rationality?* (Notre Dame: University of Notre Dame Press, 1988); and Wolterstorff, *Reason Within the Bounds of Religion* (Grand Rapids: Eerdmans, 1976). Though each of these individuals is critical of Cartesian and Enlightenment foundationalism, none would endorse the poststructuralist's method of dismantling foundationalism.

39. For the classic statement of this position, see Heidegger, *Being and Time*, trans. John Macquarrie and Edward Robinson (New York: Harper & Row, 1962).

enment rationality alone, deconstruction seeks to subvert the various conceptions of truth and transcendence that have grounded Western experience since well before the time of Christ.

Christians may find themselves especially beguiled by the blandishments of deconstruction if they confuse poststructural indeterminacy with the idea of mystery. The concept of *mystery* is predicated upon a belief that all truth is eschatological; now we see through a glass darkly — the Revised English Bible has it that "at present we see only puzzling reflections in a mirror" — but one day we shall see "face to face" (1 Cor. 13:12, REB). There is a vast amount that we do not know, but all that is hidden from us has already been hinted at in what has been revealed to us. "What we shall be has not yet been disclosed," according to 1 John, "but we know that when Christ appears we shall be like him, because we shall see him as he is. As he is pure, everyone who has grasped this hope makes himself pure" (1 John 3:2-3, REB). In the New Testament, the *kerygma* of the gospel announces the *mysterion,* which is the eternal counsel of God, hidden for the ages but revealed in the cross of Christ. The full disclosure of the mystery awaits the *parousia* or return of Christ.[40]

The *indeterminacy* promoted in poststructuralism is a very different thing from a biblical sense of *mystery.* Whereas mystery speaks of a truth that encompasses men and women even as they fail to comprehend it fully,

---

40. See the *Theological Dictionary of the New Testament,* ed. Gerhard Kittel and Gerhard Friedrich, trans. Geoffrey W. Bromiley, abridged in one volume by Geoffrey W. Bromiley (Grand Rapids: Eerdmans, 1985), pp. 615-19.

G. S. Hendry describes mystery thus:

> In modern usage, a mystery may be defined as a secret or riddle to which the answer has not been found. . . . In the New Testament a mystery is a secret which has been, or is being, disclosed; but because it is a divine secret it remains a mystery and does not become transparent to men. (Hendry, "Mystery," in *A Theological Word Book of the Bible,* ed. Alan Richardson [New York: Macmillan, 1962], p. 156)

Throughout his career, Karl Barth proclaimed his belief in the eschatological nature of truth. In one of his final works, he offered a straightforward exposition of this faith. He prefaced his statement about truth and hope by acknowledging that all human effort stands accused — "the moral as well as the immoral, the pious as well as the impious, all human thought, will, and action. . . . There is no human work or word which can avoid becoming dust and ashes in the fire that proceeds from that source [of judgment]." Nevertheless, "when theology confesses its own solidarity with all flesh and with the whole world under God's judgment, it receives *hope* in the grace of God which is the mystery of this judgment" (Barth, *Evangelical Theology: An Introduction,* trans. Grover Foley [Grand Rapids: Eerdmans, 1979], pp. 148-49).

indeterminacy has to do with the vertiginous play of interpretation that has given up on truth and seeks its only comfort in the game-playing potential of language. In the scheme of mystery, the self is situated within a framework that it did not create and that it can never fully understand. The deconstructive critic also situates the self, but does so by placing it at the end of the history of error and oppression; the interpreting self in poststructuralism is seeking to free itself from the tangled web of language and history through acts of creative interpretation. Roland Barthes, for instance, hymns the praises of the *writerly text,* which he defines as "*ourselves writing* before the infinite play of the world."[41] To read a work in a "writerly" manner is to interpret it as an occasion for an indeterminate activity "unimpoverished by any constraint. . . . Nothing exists outside the text," except the freewheeling play of interpretation.[42] The liberated text and the liberated reader should be like "that uninhibited person who shows his behind to the *Political Father.*"[43]

The inability of Christian critics to keep clear the distinction between mystery and indeterminacy has led a number to misread poststructuralist intentions, and such misreadings are likely to proliferate in the coming years, as Christians belatedly come to grips with the movement. For example, in a recently published essay, the Christian philosopher Merold Westphal offers the following "confession": "For years I thought that if I

41. Barthes, *S/Z,* trans. Richard Howard (New York: Hill & Wang, 1974), p. 5.

42. Barthes, *S/Z,* p. 15. Uneasy about the implications of the interpretive freedom celebrated in poststructuralist theory and practice, Christian advocates of deconstruction often try to explain away that interpretive license. Gary John Percesepe argues in "The Unbearable Lightness of Being Postmodern" (*Christian Scholar's Review* 20, 2 [Dec. 1990]: 129) that

> it would be a mistake to think of deconstruction as merely some violence done to a text, or to a unity. Derrida makes it clear that a text deconstructs itself, as moments of undecidability point away from the stability of meaning. . . . Deconstruction operates under a lawlike necessity that is far from being the arbitrary freeplay-in-the-blue irresponsibility that critics (often getting their information from *Time* and *Newsweek*) have found it to be.

Given the actual practices of Derrida, Barthes, and most of the prominent American proponents of deconstruction, it is hard to imagine how anyone can say that deconstruction does not promote "arbitrary freeplay." Be that as it may, the claims that "a text deconstructs itself" and that "deconstruction operates under a lawlike necessity" appear to be instances of disingenuous evasion. They are attempts to avoid taking responsibility for the very actions that deconstruction has so long promoted with vigor.

43. Barthes, *The Pleasure of the Text,* trans. Richard Miller (New York: Hill & Wang, 1975), p. 53.

waited long enough Derrida and company would go away and I would be spared the work of reading them. I played the ostrich to this boogeyman." He then goes on to explain, however, how he eventually concluded that poststructuralism was too important a movement to be ignored, so he "began the long and often painful task of reading them [Lyotard, Foucault, and Derrida]."[44]

Westphal reports that his reading has led him to the discovery that "postmodernism can be seen as an extended meditation on several Pauline themes whose repudiation all but defines modernity." According to Westphal, "against modernity's claim to absolute knowledge," Paul presses the claim that our knowledge is not absolute but is part of the treasure that we carry in our "earthen vessels." Furthermore, Paul instructs us that our finitude and sin limit the power and range of our "cognitive equipment," and he thus confounds one of the central faiths of modernism. "Philosophically speaking, the main motifs of modernism are the attempt to have done, once and for all, with Paul and his gloomy followers, from Augustine through Luther and Calvin to Kierkegaard and Barth."[45]

To say that postmodernism is an extended meditation on Pauline themes is like saying that because Joseph Stalin shared Winston Churchill's fear and loathing of the Nazis, the Russian dictator's speeches to rally his countrymen were extended reflections on political democracy and economic freedom. It is accurate to say that, like Derrida, Augustine would assail the tenets of modernism, but it is misleading to imply that since the

---

44. Westphal, "The Ostrich and the Boogeyman," *Christian Scholar's Review* 20, 2 (Dec. 1990): 117. One of the lamentable consequences of poststructuralism has been the degree of obscurity it has brought to the prose of many of its advocates. Derrida and his followers have created some now popular neologisms, and they have given new meanings to common terms. As a result, Christian scholars trying to appropriate the habits of mind and patterns of speech of the poststructuralists often end up writing sentences such as the following:

> But Saussure demonstrates that the *sign* has presence for consciousness, nonetheless, that meaning is some sort of mysterious hypostatization of the history and intentions of its inscribing, and this too is not to be held to be uninteresting, for it remains at least as ominous and troubling to intellectual complacency as is the present-absence of the trace which Derrida imbues with wonder and enigma in exchange for its supreme usefulness to his cause. (Janet Blumberg Knedlik, "Saussure, Derrida, and a 'Christian' Literary Criticism?" *Christianity and Literature* 39, 3 [Spring 1990]: 299)

45. Westphal, "The Ostrich and the Boogeyman," pp. 115-16.

two of them would spurn Descartes, they would be eager to embrace each other. There is a vast, unbridgeable chasm yawning between the fifth-century church father and the twentieth-century philosopher. Consider, for example, the difference between Augustine and Derrida on the goal of human longing.

First, a passage from Augustine's *Confessions:*

With you our good is ever living, and when we turn our backs on it, then we are perverse. Let us return now to you, Lord, so that we may not be overturned, because our good is with you, living and without any defect, since you yourself are our good. And we need not be afraid of having no place to which we may return. We of our own accord fell from that place. And our home, which is your eternity, does not fall down when we are away from it.[46]

Then a passage from Derrida's *Speech and Phenomena:*

"There is no name for this": we read this as a truism. What is unnamable here is not some ineffable being that cannot be approached by a name; like God, for example. . . .

What we do know . . . is that there never has been and never will be a unique word, a master name. . . .

There will be no unique name, not even the name of Being. It must be conceived without *nostalgia;* that is, it must be conceived outside the myth of the purely maternal or paternal language belonging to the lost fatherland of thought. On the contrary, we must *affirm* it — in the sense that Nietzsche brings affirmation into play — with a certain laughter and with a certain dance.[47]

Following the lead of Nietzsche, Derrida disparages any human longing for a lost innocence or hidden truth; indeed, he considers the human spirit to be free only when men and women abandon altogether the idea of spiritual quests. In making these judgments, Derrida shows himself to be faithful to his structuralist origins. Since there is no natural connection between words and things in structuralist understanding, the only reality to which language can point is that of human desire; language

46. Augustine, *The Confessions of St. Augustine,* book 4, trans. Rex Warner (New York: New American Library, 1963), p. 89.
47. Jacques Derrida, *Speech and Phenomena and Other Essays on Husserl's Theory of Signs,* trans. David B. Allison (Evanston: Northwestern University Press, 1973), p. 159.

serves the purposes of the will and the will alone. For this reason, it would be absurd for the poststructuralist to claim that language about original innocence or the kingdom of God reveals anything more than the human compulsion to believe in fantastic notions.

The difference between Augustine and Derrida on this point is crucial. For Augustine, the problem of the self is not that it has loves and desires, but that its sin makes it love and desire the wrong objects; for Derrida, the problem of the self is its belief that there are any necessarily proper or improper objects of desire outside the web of language itself. In his explorations of love and desire in the *Confessions* and elsewhere, Augustine captures the paradox of a Christian understanding of history. To the person caught in sin and situated in the midst of history, desire is a matter of plausible regret and legitimate hope. Looking back to Eden and forward to the New Jerusalem, the person redeemed in Christ believes in the reality of what he or she has lost and hopes to receive it again.

Many modern and postmodern thinkers, however, reject the notion that our desires may point to a reality beyond ourselves as well as to realities within ourselves.[48] That rejection has as much to do with distinctly modern ideas of heroic and virtuous action as it does with anything else. As we saw in our chapter on modern gnosticism, a number of contemporary artists and theorists appear to welcome the alienation of the human spirit implicit in naturalism. If nature and history are blind forces that pay no regard to human purposes, then artists may represent themselves as heroic figures who do battle with all the lifeless forces arrayed about them. The creative temperament is able to congratulate itself for having imparted a measure of order, excitement, or delight to an otherwise wretched world.

For the Christian who does believe in spiritual states that are more than projections of desire, the difference between Eden and the New Jerusalem is as crucial as the distinction between Adam and Christ, the second Adam. The mystery of the gospel is that what we gain in Christ is greater than what we lost in Adam. The eternal home to which Augustine says we return is like the garden from which we were expelled but in no way identical to it. As T. S. Eliot explains in "Little Gidding," the last of the *Four Quartets:*

48. For an excellent discussion of this matter, see Paul Ricoeur, "Existence and Hermeneutics," trans. Kathleen McLaughlin, in *The Conflict of Interpretations,* ed. Don Ihde (Evanston: Northwestern University Press, 1974), pp. 3-24.

We shall not cease from exploration
And the end of all our exploring
Will be to arrive where we started
And know the place for the first time.
. . . .

And all shall be well and
All manner of thing shall be well
When the tongues of flame are in-folded
Into the crowned knot of fire
And the fire and the rose are one.[49]

Both Augustine and Eliot are speaking of the paradoxical tension between the simple innocence of Eden and the complex delights of the kingdom of God. And this tension — between a lost past and a desired future — is one form of the perennial struggle between past and future in the Christian faith. In the Christian church this dialectic is at the heart of the proclamation of the gospel, which comes to us from the past and yet liberates us for the future. In the life of any individual Christian, the past may indeed be viewed as a scene of sin and bondage, from which the grace of God in Christ has the power to deliver the sinner. But that grace can only be given through the proclamation of the gospel, first, and then through the fellowship and sacramental life that that proclamation establishes.

After all, it is essential to remind ourselves that it is a *treasure* that we carry in the "earthen vessels" of which Westphal takes note. As Paul explains, we carry that treasure to prove "that such transcendent power does not come from us; it is God's alone" (2 Cor. 4:7, REB). That is precisely the point: classic Christian faith holds that the mystery of the incarnation means that the Alpha and Omega has taken on human form and suffered unto death on our behalf. In Lutheran terms, ours is an *alien righteousness,* a righteousness given by God when he "sees the sinner as one with Christ. He forgives his sin and considers the sinner to be righteous for Christ's sake."[50] The righteousness and forgiveness imparted by God in Christ remind us of Adam's lost innocence and help us to anticipate the fullness of the kingdom of God.

49. Eliot, "Little Gidding," in *The Complete Poems and Plays* (New York: Harcourt, Brace & World, 1952), p. 145.

50. Paul Althaus, *The Theology of Martin Luther,* trans. Robert C. Schultz (Philadelphia: Fortress Press, 1966), p. 227.

This Christian view contrasts sharply with the picture of righteousness developed in the thought of Nietzsche and Derrida. If there is any source of holiness in their anthropologies, it is the playful will of the affirming self. The self is pure if it can offer "the Nietzschean *affirmation,* that is the joyous affirmation of the play of the world and of the innocence of becoming, the affirmation of a world of signs without fault, without truth, and without origin."[51] In a sophisticated gnostic fashion, deconstructive thinking offers the exhausted and embattled self release from guilty striving. By construing the history of human thought as a history of linguistic game playing without origin or reference, deconstruction seeks to free the guilty self. It does so by declaring that self both innocent of any charges the past might bring against it and free of all obligations to pursue any vision of the good which that past might offer.

In the end, George Steiner writes with refreshing clarity, "the issue is, quite simply, that of the meaning of meaning as it is re-insured by the postulate of the existence of God. 'In the beginning was the Word.' There was no such beginning, says deconstruction; only the play of sounds and markers amid the mutations of time."[52] At the very center of Christian faith is belief in the *logos:* "The Word was in God's presence, and what God was, the Word was. He was with God at the beginning, and through him all things came to be; without him no created thing came into being" (John 1:1b-3, REB). The Christian faith is inconceivable without belief in the divine Word that created the universe out of nothing and continues to sustain it in power and grace. Steiner wonders if all of our ideas about the intelligibility of texts and the possibility of truth are dependent upon this faith in the creative *logos.* When the springs of that faith are dammed up, then it is only a matter of time until truth and meaning evaporate. It is for this reason that Steiner can say that "*on its own terms and planes of argument,* terms by no means trivial if only in respect of their bracing acceptance of ephemerality and self-dissolution, the challenge of deconstruction does seem to me irrefutable."[53]

If Steiner is correct, then a Christian response to deconstruction might well begin with a credal affirmation of belief in the creative and

---

51. Derrida, "Structure, Sign, and Play," p. 292.

52. Steiner, *Real Presences* (Chicago: University of Chicago Press, 1989), p. 120.

53. Steiner, *Real Presences,* p. 132. See also Hans-Georg Gadamer, *Truth and Method,* 2nd rev. ed., trans. Joel Weinsheimer and Donald G. Marshall (New York: Crossroad, 1989), pp. 405-38.

sustaining power of the divine Word. While agreeing with the poststructuralist judgment upon the pretensions of the Cartesian and Enlightenment self, the Christian ought to be wary of the meaning that poststructuralism gives to the development of modernity. The poststructuralist move is to read the Enlightenment and romantic development of the self as a misguided attempt to internalize the divine, undertaken at a time when orthodox faith was effectively being eclipsed in science, philosophy, and culture. For the poststructuralist, the exposure of the errors of modernity assumes the acknowledgment of the prior folly of Christian claims to transcendence. For the Christian, on the other hand, there is a different way to read the Cartesian and Enlightenment projects — that is, they might be seen as efforts to suppress all awareness of genuine transcendence. The first chapter of Romans offers a succinct variation of this reading of modernity: "Knowing God, they have refused to honour him as God, or to render him thanks. Hence all their thinking has ended in futility, and their misguided minds are plunged in darkness" (Rom. 1:21, REB). Alasdair MacIntyre seems to have something like this in mind when he argues that "our consciousness of even fundamental precepts may be subverted by the distractions and corruptions of evil, so that the wrongness of a whole class of actions may cease to be evident to us. Thus, according to Aquinas there are absolute and unconditional prohibitions which a whole culture may infringe without recognizing that it is so doing."[54]

This judgment on the pretensions of the modern self does not deny the validity of much that is contained in the Enlightenment critique of Christian faith and practice. Nor is it to take issue with the power of postmodern analyses of the impasses of Enlightenment morality and epistemology. Instead, it is to claim that there are within the Christian tradition ample resources and precedents to support such criticism. Long before we had Nietzsche, we were given the Old Testament prophetic judgments on sin and folly; long before we had Freud, we possessed in Paul, Augustine, and Luther profound analyses of the deceptive powers of the tormented soul; and long before we had Marx, the prophetic books of the Old Testament and the teachings of Jesus himself indicted greed and the manipulation of power. The modern masters of suspicion and their deconstructive heirs have undoubtedly enhanced our understanding of the complexities of the will and the injustices of society. But for the Christian they cannot replace the scriptural beliefs and liturgical practices that sustain the life of the spirit.

54. MacIntyre, *Whose Justice? Which Rationality?* p. 331.

CHAPTER 9

Christ, Culture, and the Romantic Quandary

THERE ARE MANY, no doubt, who believe that changes in a field as obscure as contemporary literary theory are likely to have little effect upon the way in which Christians think or act, that the theories of the university are irrelevant to the everyday concerns of the citizen and are powerless to influence the life of faith. For those who think in this way, however, and for those who believe that Christian scholars are not likely to assimilate Marxism and deconstruction, the history of recent Christian reflection on the arts should give pause. Even some of the most astute Christian scholars demonstrate the pervasive influence of theories that those Christians have assimilated unreflectively. The derivative nature of modern Christian thinking about culture is evident, for example, in the works of such an astute critic as C. S. Lewis, as well as in many pronouncements on the arts by lesser-known evangelicals. In Lewis's specific theorizing about the nature of literary experience and in evangelical attempts to defend the arts, we can see the pitfalls of Christian reflection that uncritically appropriates the theories dominant in the discipline at the time.

As a Christian apologist, C. S. Lewis gave clear evidence of a profound involvement with the Christian tradition. As we read his writings we can detect the presence of Calvin, Aquinas, Augustine, and the apostle Paul, among many others. It is curious, however, that as a literary theorist Lewis uncritically adhered to a view of literature — a variation of romanticism — that is in many ways at odds with his most deeply held Christian beliefs. Although he maintained a healthy, constructive skepticism about received opinions in matters of belief and behavior, Lewis nonetheless readily adopted dominant theoretical notions about literature and the arts. He was a brilliant literary historian and an invaluable moralist, but as a literary theorist Lewis was in many ways inconsistent and unconvincing.

A Critical Experiment

An intriguing late work entitled *An Experiment in Criticism* represents Lewis's most extensive attempt at theoretical reflection. He sets out his purpose in the book's opening sentence: "In this essay I propose to try an experiment." Instead of judging an individual's tastes by the books he or she reads, Lewis suggests "reversing the process." He proposes the following: "Let us try to discover how far it might be plausible to define a good book as a book which is read in one way, and a bad book as a book which is read in another." Lewis then defines what he considers to be "right reading" and seeks to justify his focus on the reader's experience as the central criterion for the assessment of a book. He concentrates upon the reader because he believes that the collective response to a book provides the best empirical evidence of its worth and power. "The accepted valuation of literary works varies with every change of fashion," he argues near the end of the book, "but the distinction between attentive and inattentive, obedient and wilful, disinterested and egoistic, modes of reading is permanent; if ever valid, valid everywhere and always."[1]

Lewis's argument is suspect because convictions about what makes for good reading have changed dramatically over the course of centuries. Far from being "valid everywhere and always," Lewis's own criteria are clearly products of the Kantian revolution in epistemology and the arts. Such things as his conception of right reading as a process of dispossession, his radical distinction between the passive reception and active use of a book, and his creation of a wide chasm between life and art — these central aspects of Lewis's theoretical system reflect developments in aesthetics over the past two centuries rather than timeless principles of judgment. In fact, one can go so far as to argue that Lewis's criteria bear a closer relationship to the work of Kant and nineteenth-century English critics of culture than

1. Lewis, *An Experiment in Criticism* (Cambridge: Cambridge University Press, 1961), pp. 1, 106.

they do to the traditions of the church and the actual realities of our reading practices.

At the heart of Lewis's "experiment in criticism" is his sharp distinction between the "use" and the "reception" of a work of art. This distinction is rooted in a view of aesthetics that arose in the last decades of the eighteenth century and still exerts a powerful explanatory force in contemporary theory. "The distinction can hardly be better expressed," writes Lewis, "than by saying that the many *use* art and the few *receive* it."[2] Lewis elaborates upon this claim by distinguishing between works of art on the one hand and toys and religious icons on the other. These latter objects may possess intrinsic beauty, but such beauty is never unadulterated. Unlike true works of art, such objects exist only to be used as a means to a greater end. When we pick up a toy, we do so in order to fulfill a need for pleasure or diversion; when we handle an icon, we seek to use it as a means of mediating the experience of God to us. "Its purpose is, not to fix attention upon itself, but to stimulate and liberate certain activities in the child or the worshipper." In both cases, we come to the object with needs and expectations to which we expect it to conform.[3]

All is different or should be different with a work of art. "Real appreciation demands . . . [that] we must begin by laying aside as completely as we can all our own preconceptions, interests, and associations," Lewis says. "We sit down before the picture in order to have something done to us, not that we may do things with it. The first demand any work of any art makes upon us is surrender. Look. Listen. Receive. Get yourself out of the way."[4]

This is the standard of good reception, according to Lewis, but since many use and only few receive, it is obvious that most "reading" falls short of the ideal. In discussing "the reading of the unliterary," Lewis concentrates upon the love that such people have for stories and their inattentiveness to the subtle textures of language. The "unliterary" majority wish to read "strip stories," "the news," and "swift-moving narratives" in which something is always "happening." They seek excitement, the satisfaction of intense curiosity, and vicarious pleasure. For such readers, the work of art becomes merely a means to pleasurable ends. And even though these ends may not be bad in themselves, Lewis argues that they should not

2. Lewis, *An Experiment in Criticism*, p. 19.
3. Lewis, *An Experiment in Criticism*, p. 17.
4. Lewis, *An Experiment in Criticism*, pp. 18-19.

become a primary part of the experience of a work of art. "Let us be quite clear that the unliterary are unliterary not because they enjoy stories in these ways, but because they enjoy them in no other."[5]

Lewis acknowledges, however, that even the "few" who truly *receive* the work of art must pass through the world of unliterary experience. Like the sensitive spirit beset by sexual drives and natural hungers, the good reader must satisfy some basic desires before attending to his or her special calling. "We do not enjoy a story fully at the first reading. Not till the curiosity, the sheer narrative lust, has been given its sop and laid asleep, are we at leisure to savour the real beauties. Till then, it is like wasting great wine on a ravenous natural thirst which merely wants cold wetness."[6] In one sense, then, all of us are condemned to "use" works of art in some way. We cannot get around our desires, but if we are disciplined enough we may learn to transcend them. Only when we have achieved such transcendence will we have a chance to join the few good readers capable of receiving what great works offer.

Because we all have certain basic needs, even the best works of art can be experienced in bad ways. Lewis cites the example of the prurient man who uses Tintoretto's painting *Three Graces* as a pornographic stimulant. "A good work of art may be used in the wrong way," but it is less likely to be used in this manner; the lustful man will gladly turn from fine paintings to dirty pictures, if the latter are readily available, for "more ham and less frill."[7]

But Lewis argues that the reverse is not possible. "A bad picture cannot be enjoyed with that full and disciplined 'reception' which the few give to a good one." He cites the example of a billboard at which he gazed one day while waiting for a bus. This picture of a man and a woman drinking beer in a pub seemed appealing at first glance, but its merits "diminished with every second of attention. . . . There was nothing in the composition to satisfy the eye." Those who seem to enjoy such a bad picture do not actually take pleasure in the picture itself but rather in the ideas suggested to them by the bad object. And though it may be legitimate or necessary to view a picture or read a book in this manner, "the real objection to that way of enjoying pictures is that you never get beyond

5. Lewis, *An Experiment in Criticism*, p. 38.

6. Lewis, "On Stories," in *Of Other Worlds: Essays and Stories*, ed. Walter Hooper (New York: Harcourt Brace Jovanovich, 1975), p. 18.

7. Lewis, *An Experiment in Criticism*, p. 20.

yourself. . . . You do not cross the frontier into that new region which the pictorial art as such has added to the world."[8]

Lewis and Modern Theory

At the beginning of this chapter I stated that Lewis's moral and theological writings offer a more satisfying view of aesthetic experience than do his explicit statements about literary theory. The best way to demonstrate this point is by contrasting Lewis's observations in *An Experiment in Criticism* with a portion of the opening paragraph of one of Lewis's finest sermons, "The Weight of Glory":

> If you asked twenty good men today what they thought the highest of the virtues, nineteen of them would reply, Unselfishness. But if you had asked almost any of the great Christians of old, he would have replied, Love. . . . The New Testament has lots to say about self-denial, but not about self-denial as an end in itself. We are told to deny ourselves and to take up our crosses in order that we may follow Christ; and nearly every description of what we shall ultimately find if we do so contains an appeal to desire. If there lurks in most modern minds the notion that to desire our own good and earnestly to hope for the enjoyment of it is a bad thing, I submit that this notion has crept in from Kant and the Stoics and is no part of the Christian faith. Indeed, if we consider the unblushing promises of reward and the staggering nature of the rewards promised in the Gospels, it would seem that Our Lord finds our desires not too strong, but too weak. We are half-hearted creatures, fooling about with drink and sex and ambition when infinite joy is offered us. . . . We are far too easily pleased.[9]

The Lewis who criticizes the ideal of "unselfishness," claiming that "this notion has crept in from Kant and the Stoics and is no part of the Christian faith," is the same man who, when writing as a literary critic, sees a crucial distinction between what he called "Egoistic" and "Disinterested" castle-building. In *An Experiment in Criticism* Lewis describes "egoistic" castle-building as a process in which "the day-dreamer himself

---

8. Lewis, *An Experiment in Criticism*, pp. 20-22.
9. Lewis, *The Weight of Glory and Other Addresses,* ed. Walter Hooper (New York: Collier Books, 1980), pp. 3-4.

is always the hero and everything is seen through his eyes." The "egoistic castle-builder" sees himself as the hero of the story; in the tales he dreams of, he has a caustic wit, owns an expensive yacht, and wins the beautiful women. The disinterested castle-builder, on the other hand, "is not the hero of the day-dream . . . ; he will be present in the fiction, but not as hero; rather as spectator." He is the type who will have a fantasy about a holiday in Switzerland, but instead of skiing down a grand slope with a beautiful woman, he will be standing and looking at the mountains.[10]

According to Lewis in *An Experiment in Criticism*, all reading, whether disinterested or egoistic, involves escape from "immediate, concrete actuality." The important question has to do with what we escape *to* when we leave reality behind us. Readers in "the lowest class" easily lapse into egoistic castle-building, which may either consist of harmless fantasizing or turn into something "brutal, prurient and megalomaniac." More sensitive and sophisticated readers "escape into mere play, *divertissements* which may be exquisite works of art — the *Midsummer Night's Dream* or the *Nun's Priest's Tale*," or into "disinterested castle-building, 'conducted', by, say, the *Arcadia, The Shepheards Sirena*, or *The Ancient Mariner*."[11]

Though members of the higher "literary" class are not likely to engage in egoistic castle-building, Lewis does cite "a fault in reading which cuts right across our distinction between the literary and the unliterary. . . . Essentially, it involves a confusion between life and art, even a failure to allow for the existence of art at all." For "the lowest type of reader," this means an insatiable appetite for narrative that pretends to be "news," while "on a higher level it appears as the belief that all good books are good primarily because they give us knowledge, teach us 'truths' about 'life.' "[12]

According to Lewis, both the "low" and the "high" readers forget that life does not have the order that is found in art. In a tragic drama we have catharsis and closure, but in life the real story goes on: "There is no grandeur and no finality." Stories may provide idle diversion from the pain and boredom of life, or they may provide glimpses of a glory to come in another world, but they must not be mistaken as comments on the actual order of our present lives. To lose sight of the fact that poems and novels

10. Lewis, *An Experiment in Criticism*, p. 52.
11. Lewis, *An Experiment in Criticism*, p. 69.
12. Lewis, *An Experiment in Criticism*, p. 74.

are primarily "carefully made objects" and to look to them for reflections upon life or for moral guidance "is a flagrant instance of 'using' instead of 'receiving.'"[13]

Throughout *An Experiment in Criticism* we encounter aesthetic categories that come straight from Kant, the eighteenth-century moralists, and the romantic poets — categories that we may see as clearly present in contemporary theories of literature. Frank Lentricchia devotes an entire chapter of his book *After the New Criticism* to "Versions of Existentialism," and the views he describes uncannily resemble those put forth by Lewis.[14] According to Lentricchia, such figures as theorists Northrop Frye and Frank Kermode and poet Wallace Stevens share a perception of the world as a place in which "human desire, conscious of itself as 'lack,' . . . confronts a grim reality which at every point denies us our needs. . . . Our 'environment' is alien, but . . . its very alien quality beckons forth our creative impulses to make substitutive fictive worlds."[15]

For Northrop Frye, the glory of literature consists in its ability to transform the alien environment of natural life into the blissful home of human desire; literature for Frye serves ultimately as a secular surrogate for the kingdom of God. Without question, C. S. Lewis would reject Frye's conception of the "body of literature" as the kingdom of God; but he might well stand in sympathy, at least in his literary theory if not in his moral and theological writings, with Frye's depiction of the world as an alien natural environment. For Stevens, the power of literature resides in its ability to give us the illusion of order as well as the ironic awareness of this order as an illusion; such a conception of language coincides with Lewis's radical distinctions between greedy use and disinterested reception and his warnings about the folly of confusing art and life. Finally, when Kermode calls narrative the power to shape the random processes of human life, Lewis seems to nod in agreement when he writes near the end of "On Stories": "If the author's plot is only a net, and usually an imperfect one, a net of time and event for catching what is not really a process at all, is life much more?"[16]

As a moralist and apologist, Lewis remained profoundly wary of the

13. Lewis, *An Experiment in Criticism,* pp. 78, 83.
14. Lentricchia, *After the New Criticism* (Chicago: University of Chicago Press, 1980), pp. 29-60.
15. Lentricchia, *After the New Criticism,* pp. 33-34.
16. Lewis, "On Stories," p. 20.

claims of romanticism and modernism. Yet as a literary thinker he dealt freely in the grand dichotomies of romantic thought — science vs. art, reason vs. intuition, and reality vs. imagination. For example, Lewis's descriptions in *An Experiment in Criticism* of the goal of literary experience give clear evidence of his indebtedness to romantic images of selfhood. Replete with metaphors of solitude and confinement, *An Experiment in Criticism* depicts the reading process as humanity's most effective way, short of faith in Christ, of joining self to self and escaping the prisons of our desires. The goal of reading is to "get out of our own skins," Lewis writes. We never reach the goal, but we can "make at least some progress towards it" by eliminating "at least the grosser illusions of perspective." In a figure reminiscent of Plato's "Allegory of the Cave," Lewis declares that "if I can't get out of the dungeon I shall at least look out through the bars. It is better than sinking back on the straw in the darkest corner."[17]

As he tries to justify reading in this manner, Lewis labors with a Cartesian view of the self's place in the world and with a decidedly romantic view of the interpretive process. "In coming to understand anything," Lewis writes near the conclusion of *An Experiment in Criticism*, "we are rejecting the facts as they are for us in favour of the facts as they are." The primary impulse of the self is aggrandizement, but a vital "secondary impulse is to go out of the self, to correct its provincialism and heal its loneliness. In love, in virtue, in the pursuit of knowledge, and in the reception of the arts, we are doing this."[18]

Present in these passages from Lewis is what Hans-Georg Gadamer terms the "one prejudice of the Enlightenment that defines its essence: the fundamental prejudice of the Enlightenment is the prejudice against prejudice itself, which denies tradition its power."[19] As we discussed in earlier chapters, the legacy of the Cartesian tradition in the West has been a vision of the self as an entity of boundless capacity and desire hemmed in by tradition and prejudice. To understand anything properly, we commonly tell ourselves, the self must set aside its assumptions and see the world as it truly is. More than anyone else, Descartes established the radical antithesis between reason and tradition, and under his influence Enlightenment and romantic theorists elaborated the implications of this dichotomy for the reading of texts.

17. Lewis, *An Experiment in Criticism*, pp. 101-2.
18. Lewis, *An Experiment in Criticism*, p. 138.
19. Gadamer, *Truth and Method*, 2nd rev. ed., trans. Joel Weinsheimer and Donald G. Marshall (New York: Crossroad, 1989), p. 270.

Descartes's influence is readily apparent in the case of Friedrich Schleiermacher. Descartes argued that accepted beliefs ought to be held in skeptical abeyance and held up to the light of reason to test their worth. In a similar fashion, Schleiermacher claimed that "interpretation is the art of avoiding the misunderstanding that follows automatically from every unregulated attempt to understand, for understanding fails naturally and of its own."[20] Instead of being the product of an unusual breakdown of mediating tradition, misunderstanding is for Schleiermacher an unavoidable reality of the human condition. We are all isolated within the cells of our prejudices and must seek, through method and intuition, to break through the walls of our assumptions and gaze upon the world as others see it. Schleiermacher sees interpretation as a "divinatory process, a placing of oneself within the whole framework of the author, an apprehension of the 'inner origin' of the composition of a work, a re-creation of the creative act."[21]

The influence of Schleiermacher's definition of interpretation is evident in the final pages of *An Experiment in Criticism*. Lewis tries to explain why we should fill our mind with fictions that can prompt in us possibly damaging vicarious feelings. "The nearest I have yet got to an answer is that we seek an enlargement of our being," he claims. "We want to see with other eyes, to imagine with other imaginations, to feel with other hearts, as well as with our own." And what is the source of this desire? Nothing less than our wish to break free of the confinement of our own imprisoning consciousness:

> We are not content to be Leibnitzian monads. We demand windows. Literature as Logos is a series of windows, even of doors. One of the things we feel after reading a great work is 'I have got out'. Or from another point of view, 'I have got in'; pierced the shell of some other monad and discovered what it is like inside.

The alternatives to right reading are imprisonment within the self or imprisonment within an impersonal collective, for "the man who is contented to be only himself, and therefore less a self, is in prison. My own eyes are not enough for me, I will see through those of others." Or, as the concluding paragraph of *An Experiment in Criticism* argues:

20. Joel Weinsheimer, *Gadamer's Hermeneutics: A Reading of "Truth and Method"* (New Haven: Yale University Press, 1985), p. 140.
21. Gadamer, *Truth and Method,* p. 187.

Literary experience heals the wound, without undermining the privilege, of individuality. There are mass emotions which heal the wound; but they destroy the privilege. In them our separate selves are pooled and we sink back into sub-individuality. But in reading great literature I become a thousand men and yet remain myself. Like the night sky in the Greek poem, I see with a myriad eyes, but it is still I who see. Here, as in worship, in love, in moral action, and in knowing, I transcend myself; and am never more myself than when I do.[22]

Cross Purposes: Theory and the Moral Vision in Lewis

It is ironic that in his literary theoretical writings Lewis is willing to demand of the reading self a greater righteousness and stringency than he is willing to require, in almost all places, for the self's love of God. Throughout *An Experiment in Criticism,* he presses the case for seeing the highest form of reading as a process of dispossession, a means of getting out of our apprehensive and acquisitive selves. But in his explicitly moral and theological writings, Lewis says repeatedly that these are the very selves from which we cannot escape. "It would be a bold and silly creature," he writes in *The Four Loves,* "that came before its Creator with the boast 'I'm no beggar.'"[23] As a Christian thinker reflecting upon the nature of human beings, Lewis recognizes clearly the corrupt complexity of the human heart. The greedy "Need-loves" are in constant conflict with the selfless impulse of "Gift-love." But rather than chastising us for failing to achieve the disinterestedness of true "Gift-love," God, according to Lewis, calls upon us to accept with gladness our own utter need, selfish as it may be. Only a work of grace can lead us to a "childlike and delighted acceptance of our Need, a joy in total dependence. We become jolly beggars. The good man . . . is not sorry at all for the innocent Need that is inherent in his creaturely condition."[24]

This is quite similar to the point noted earlier that Lewis makes in "The Weight of Glory" when he questions the modern preoccupation with unselfishness: "If there lurks in most modern minds the notion that to desire our own good and earnestly to hope for the enjoyment of it is a

22. Lewis, *An Experiment in Criticism,* pp. 137-38, 140-41.
23. Lewis, *The Four Loves* (New York: Harcourt Brace Jovanovich, 1960), p. 14.
24. Lewis, *The Four Loves,* pp. 180-81.

bad thing, I submit that this notion has crept in from Kant and the Stoics and is no part of the Christian faith." Lewis vigilantly guarded against Kantian encroachments in the moral life, while at the same time he gladly allowed romanticism to prevail as the reigning theory in his thinking about the arts.

Behind the modern aesthetic ideal of disinterestedness, Gadamer detects that pervasive "prejudice against prejudice" that is rooted to a significant extent in the work of Descartes and becomes the "global demand of the enlightenment." When Lewis speaks in the final pages of *An Experiment in Criticism* of "separate selves," "Leibnitzian monads," and the "shell" of the isolated self — and of the desperate need of the isolated self to break out of its imprisonment — he is conceiving of the self in fundamentally Cartesian terms. According to Gadamer, however, *prejudices* are not imprisoning irrationalities that block understanding but rather are the necessary foundations for all interpretation. Though the word *prejudice* now has powerful negative connotations, in the history of the law the word means something far different from "groundless assumption." As Gadamer explains, "In German legal terminology a 'prejudice' is a provisional legal verdict before the final verdict is reached." Only through the Enlightenment critique of religion did the word come to mean "unfounded judgment."[25]

In claiming that proper understanding is possible only when prejudices have been swept aside, the Cartesian and Enlightenment traditions have set an impossible goal. As Heidegger and Gadamer argue, all understanding involves the projection of assumptions; there is no such thing as a perfectly disinterested reading of anything, whether it be another person, nature, or a text. In Gadamer's conception of the self, there is no such thing as the completely isolated "Leibnitzian monad" that Lewis describes in *An Experiment in Criticism.* That solitary perceiver does not exist because each of us belongs, through language and through the patterns of behavior to which language points, to larger communities and more extensive traditions. We are not solipsistic entities shut off from communion with the outer world and isolated within our prejudices. Rather, we are creatures who have received hosts of assumptions about ourselves and about the nature of things; we are connected to vast communities, past and present, whether or not we will these connections or are even aware of them.

Prejudices, then, serve as the necessary foundation for all understand-

25. Gadamer, *Truth and Method,* p. 270.

ing. The goal of all thinking, and all reading, should not be to cast these assumptions aside in order to take on those belonging to another person (in Lewis's words, "The man who is contented to be only himself, and therefore less a self, is in prison. My own eyes are not enough for me, I will see through those of others"). Rather, the goal of thinking and reading is to test, clarify, modify, and expand our assumptions in order to bring them more in line with the truth of things.

According to Gadamer, human understanding is most fruitfully conceived of as a form of dialogue in which the horizon of our prejudices is fused with that of the other's as we both gaze upon the object or truth in question: "The task of hermeneutics is to clarify this miracle of understanding, which is not a mysterious communion of souls, but sharing in a common meaning."[26] To understand another person, or a book, then, one does not put on another's glasses to see the object through entirely different eyes; instead, one looks with another upon the object and enters into dialogue in search of understanding.

Lewis says virtually the same thing as Gadamer, not in *An Experiment in Criticism*, but in *The Four Loves*. In distinguishing between "Friendship" and "Eros," Lewis offers separate images of the way in which partners in these two relationships perceive one another. Under the spell of Eros, lovers stand and gaze into each other's eyes, searching for an ineffable something, while friends stand together and look upon a shared truth or delight. "Hence we picture lovers face to face but Friends side by side; their eyes look ahead."[27] According to the hermeneutical theory of Gadamer and Paul Ricoeur, a "friendship" model of this kind is far more appropriate for interpretation than is the romantic image of isolated souls straining to reach each other across the voids of time and space.

Gadamer's description of human understanding calls into question the categorical distinction established by Lewis between "reception" and "use." We recall how Lewis described "right reading" as the passive reception of the thoughts of another, in contrast to the active "self-interest" inherent in our use of anything. For Lewis, the arts are to be prized because they lend themselves to such disinterested activity much more readily than do any other forms of human endeavor. There is a two-stage process at work in our encounters with literature, according to Lewis. First we *hear*, as we are filled with the thoughts of the author who has written what we

26. Gadamer, *Truth and Method*, p. 292.
27. Lewis, *The Four Loves*, p. 98.

read; we are able to hear, Lewis says, because we have become detached and unselfish. Then, when that experience of hearing has ended, we return to our everyday tasks and ordinary desires. We may be able to *make use of* what we have received by applying the truth to our lives. Yet all the while we are aware, Lewis appears to say, that our mundane use is derivative and inferior to the experience in which we had our initial disinterested encounter.

In contrast to this two-stage approach, Gadamer argues in *Truth and Method* that understanding and application are inextricably intertwined. There is no reception, in other words, without some kind of use; if a text is to have any power over us, we must sense how it applies to our lives. "This bears repeating: without application there is no understanding," explains Joel Weinsheimer. Judges apply the law to themselves in their very understanding of it because they recognize its superiority to their own understanding, "and this recognition of authority is all the more true of the theologian interpreting the word of God."[28]

Given Gadamer's Lutheran background and commitments, it is hardly surprising that there is a theological analogy in the background here. Just as texts offer themselves to multiple interpretations and uses, so did God in Jesus Christ sacrificially offer himself to humankind. The fact that interpretation always involves application — receiving is also using — no more endangers the identity of the text than God's revelation of himself in Christ threatens or diminishes his eternal and unchangeable nature. Paul Althaus writes in explaining Martin Luther's theology of the cross, "God shows that he is God precisely in the fact that he is mighty in weakness, glorious in lowliness, living and life-giving in death."[29]

As a theological thinker, Lewis would have found much with which to agree in this image of God. As a critic of literature, however, Lewis remained under the powerful influence of theories that often worked at cross purposes to his moral and theological beliefs. Had he trusted his own theological instincts more fully — that is, had he developed their implications for literary study — Lewis might well have avoided many of the confusing contradictions inherent in the theoretical position he adopted and espoused.

---

28. Weinsheimer, *Gadamer's Hermeneutics,* pp. 195-96.

29. Althaus, *The Theology of Martin Luther,* trans. Robert C. Schultz (Philadelphia: Fortress Press, 1966), p. 34.

Christians and the Arts

Like Lewis, American Christians have often found it difficult to articulate a consistent and convincing theory of the arts. Whether they are practitioners or critics, evangelical Christians especially seem to grope for appropriate arguments to justify their involvement in artistic activity and to reconcile it with their religious commitments. They frequently press their case for the arts with little awareness of the history of reflection on aesthetics and with scant understanding of the theological doctrines at stake in their own arguments.

A good way of illustrating this is to consider one of Nathaniel Hawthorne's lesser-known stories. This work of fiction has a special relevance for Christians who are attempting to assess their own responses to American culture. Hawthorne published "The New Adam and Eve" in 1843, the year that William Miller and his followers predicted would be the year of Christ's return. In the opening paragraph of the story, Hawthorne asks us as readers to use our imaginations to "loosen those iron fetters, which we call truth and reality." We are to conceive, he says, "good Father Miller's interpretation of the prophecies to have proved true. The Day of Doom has burst upon the globe, and swept away the whole race of men." Yet even though every man and woman has disappeared from the face of the earth, all the artifacts of their lives — their tools, homes, clothes, food, and books — are left behind. It is into such a world that Hawthorne introduces his new Adam and new Eve. These innocent two have "been created, in the full development of mind and heart, but with no knowledge of their predecessors, nor of the diseased circumstances that had become encrusted around them." Adam and Eve would easily be able to distinguish between art and nature; they would intuitively "recognize the wisdom and simplicity of the latter," while the former, "with its elaborate perversities, would offer them a continual succession of puzzles."[30]

As they make their way through the deserted streets of Boston, they stumble upon a dry-goods store, a church, a courthouse, a statehouse, a mansion with its table set for dinner, a jeweler's shop, and the Bunker Hill monument. Repeatedly, as they gaze at these objects whose use and purpose they cannot fathom, Adam and Eve feel frustrated by their inability to

---

30. Hawthorne, "The New Adam and Eve," in *Hawthorne: Tales and Sketches,* ed. Roy Harvey Pearce (New York: Library of America, 1982), p. 746.

understand the significance of the artifacts they discover. Adam appears to desire to know the meaning of these objects, while Eve is happy to remain ignorant of their purposes. "Eve, Eve! What can this thing be?" he cries out as they stand before a gallows. Eve's response — in this and other instances — is one that seeks to dismiss all such considerations. What are the gallows? "I know not," answers Eve, "but, Adam, my heart is sick!" Though Adam is curious, Eve is desperate to remain ignorant. Adam wants to struggle to decipher the mysterious "hieroglyphics," while Eve prefers to leave them as they stand, mute and uninterpreted.[31]

But in the Harvard University Library, Adam stumbles upon one mystery that seems too tantalizing to resist. Having picked up a large book, he "stands poring over the regular columns of mystic characters . . . ; for the unintelligible thought upon the page has a mysterious relation to his mind, and makes itself felt, as if it were a burthen flung upon him." Enchanted by this book, Adam tells Eve that "nothing is so desirable as to find out the mystery of this big and heavy object with its thousand thin divisions." Eve, however, has no interest in objects of this kind. She calls upon her husband to "fling down that stupid thing; for even if it should speak, it would not be worth attending to." Adam replies, "I cannot help thinking that the interpretation of the riddles amid which we have been wandering all day long might here be discovered." But Eve remains firm: "It may be better not to seek the interpretation. . . . If you love me, come away!"[32]

Hawthorne seems happy to report that Eve "prevails, and rescues [Adam] from the mysterious perils of the library. Happy influence of woman!" Had the new Adam stayed and learned how to read that book, we would have had to record "the downfall of a second Adam. The fatal apple of another Tree of Knowledge would have been eaten." The new Adam would have learned about all the things recorded in human books — the "perversions and sophistries," the "false wisdom" and "narrow truth, so partial that it becomes more deceptive than falsehood," all of "the wrong principles and worse practice, the pernicious examples and mistaken rules of life," the "specious theories," and "the sad experience, which it took mankind so many ages to accumulate, and from which they never drew a moral for their future guidance." Had he learned to read, "the whole heap of this disastrous lore would have tumbled at once upon

31. Hawthorne, "The New Adam and Eve," p. 752.
32. Hawthorne, "The New Adam and Eve," pp. 760-61.

Adam's head." And he would have had nothing to do but "take up the already abortive experiment of life" and labor wearily under its weight. The new Adam's only hope is that, having failed to learn how to read, he might remain "blessed in his ignorance" and thus "still enjoy a new world in our worn-out one."[33]

"If you love me, come away!" Eve demands of Adam. And so he does. He comes away from the pain, ambiguity, and sin of history, away from all that might contaminate him in his innocence. "If you love me, come away!" This phrase sounds familiar to a student of poetry, and, indeed, it is echoed in lines that appear in an early poem by William Butler Yeats:

> *Come away, O human child!*
> *To the waters and the wild*
> *With a faery, hand in hand,*
> *For the world's more full of weeping than you can understand.*[34]

While not using the specific language of Hawthorne's story, a passage from a very different source echoes Eve's questions about the worth of knowledge. In a work published early in this century, the fundamentalist Baptist preacher Isaac Massey Haldeman wrote:

> For six thousand years [a] break in the faith relationship has been written in human history. For six thousand years man has continued to eat of the tree of knowledge. For six thousand years he has battled with the problem of good and evil. For six thousand years, he has studied and thought, searched and investigated. He has attained to much knowledge.
> [But] by wisdom he knows not God.
> He knows good and evil.[35]

And finally, in an essay by American evangelical novelist Wesley Ingles, there is a passage that portrays the Christian artist as a person who, like Adam in Hawthorne's story, remains curiously aloof from the very world he inhabits:

> The way of the Christian artist is to clothe the timeless in the timely, to express in contemporary forms the Eternal Word. He will not be

---

33. Hawthorne, "The New Adam and Eve," p. 761.
34. Yeats, "The Stolen Child," in *Selected Poems and Three Plays of William Butler Yeats*, 3rd ed., ed. M. L. Rosenthal (New York: Collier Books, 1986), p. 3.
35. Haldeman, *The Signs of the Times*, 5th ed. (New York: Charles C. Cook, 1914), pp. 69, 72.

swept by the sensate culture of his time, fractured into a thousand atoms. He will be in it, aware of his age, speaking to it, but also above and beyond it.[36]

The similarity of these passages is not a matter of coincidence, for in the writings of romantic poets, fundamentalist preachers, gospel song-writers, and evangelical artists one can detect uncanny familial resem-blances. The similarities are there because to a significant extent modern Christian views of literature and the arts represent the union of distinctively American attitudes toward history and tradition with romantic ideas about the nature of art and with fundamentalist views of culture.

Hawthorne's Adam, who refuses to gain understanding by entering history, choosing instead ignorance and the innocent Eve, resembles innumerable Americans in their attitudes toward the past. Indeed, as many critics of American culture have observed, the figure of Adam early became the archetype for men and women in early New England. For example, in 1630 John Winthrop told his fellow Puritans that though all of them had been born as children of the old Adam, the sinful hold of that earlier parentage lasts only "'til Christ comes and takes possession of the soul, . . . [and] so by little and little expels the former."[37] While Winthrop's Adam is reliant upon God in Christ for saving grace, it is possible to trace in this early Puritan image the outlines of later doctrines of cultural perfectionism. Winthrop's God-fearing individual is the an-cestor of what one observer has called the "radically new personality" who became the hero of American mythology: the "individual emanci-pated from history, happily bereft of ancestry, untouched and undefiled by the usual inheritances of family and race; an individual standing alone, self-reliant and self-propelling."[38]

While the Puritans remained skeptical about the potential of the new Adam, in eighteenth-century American culture doubts about his powers gradually faded away. By the time of the last decades of that century, what the Puritans had called the crippling sins of men and women became the amendable *errata* of which Benjamin Franklin wrote in his *Autobiography*. The new Adam as Winthrop and others in the Massachusetts Bay Colony

36. Ingles, "Art as Incarnation," *Christianity Today,* 1 March 1963, p. 15.
37. Winthrop, "A Model of Christian Charity," in *The Norton Anthology of American Literature,* 3rd ed., ed. Nina Baym et al. (New York: W. W. Norton, 1989), vol. 1, p. 37.
38. R. W. B. Lewis, *The American Adam: Innocence, Tragedy, and Tradition in the Nineteenth Century* (Chicago: University of Chicago Press, 1955), p. 5.

saw him could only grow in grace through a covenantal relationship with God in Jesus Christ; by the end of the eighteenth century, this devout Adam had been transformed into the ideal American depicted by the Frenchman St. Jean de Crèvecoeur. This ideal American was actively "leaving behind him all his ancient prejudices and manners" in order to be "melted into a new race of men."[39] And by the middle of the following century, Henry David Thoreau would argue that not humankind's sins but "the very tedium and ennui which presume to have exhausted the variety and joys of life are as old as Adam."[40] For Thoreau, the past is a record of timidity and failure and not an authoritative repository of truths about human possibilities:

> But man's capacities have never been measured; nor are we to judge of what he can do by any precedents, so little have been tried. . . .
>
> You may say the wisest things you can old man, — you who lived seventy years, not without honor of a kind, — I hear an irresistible voice which invites me away from all that. One generation abandons the enterprises of another like stranded vessels.[41]

Such American attitudes toward the past have exerted a powerful influence on evangelical thinking about the arts. George Marsden has observed, for example, that traditional American convictions about the irrelevance of the past and the American habit of making a sharp separation between the past and the future were partially responsible for the fundamentalist embrace of dispensationalism and other nondevelopmental views of history.[42]

In turn, this fundamentalist heritage helped to make many Christians receptive to aesthetic theories that celebrate the radical originality of the creative act. American evangelicals have shown a special fondness for an analogy, elaborated in the works of Dorothy Sayers and others, that likens the human artist to God the Creator.[43] Despite their attempts to temper the analogy, Christian advocates of the arts often depict the artist as a

---

39. Crèvecoeur, "What Is an American?" in *The Norton Anthology of American Literature,* vol. 1, p. 561.

40. Thoreau, *Walden,* in *Thoreau,* ed. Robert F. Sayre (New York: Library of America, 1985), p. 330.

41. Thoreau, *Walden,* pp. 330-31.

42. Marsden, *Fundamentalism and American Culture* (New York: Oxford University Press, 1980), pp. 225-28.

43. Sayers, *The Mind of the Maker* (London: Methuen, 1941).

god-like spirit brooding over a formless void. For example, evangelical novelist Wesley Ingles claims that

> all significant art is an attempt to give form to the chaotic, disorganized elements of experience, and to give a measure of permanence to the evanescent, the fleeting elements of experience. It is the God-like, creative energy of man, shaping a lump of clay and blowing the breath of life into it; turning water to wine.[44]

Or, as Christian musician Harold Best has argued:

> Culture is his [man's] handiwork, his fingerprint on the creation, and it is in the realm of his imagination that he comes closest to the godly prerogative of *ex nihilo*. He yearns for mastery over materials, to create shapes and articulate relationships. . . .
> . . . If God senses faith at work, faith which makes us free of conditioned reflexes, he smiles, whatever the supposed level of achievement *at the time*. And the important words are *at the time*, because he ever expects us to be on the move. The question to us is not, "What have you achieved?" but, "What is your next move?" Only when we are in this restless attitude is the Spirit free to work a newness.[45]

The latter quotation is particularly informative, for it points to the way in which three separate influences — an American disdain for the past, romantic theories of poetic power, and fundamentalist ideas about culture — blend to form an evangelical approach to the arts. The definition of culture given here — "[man's] handiwork, his fingerprint on the creation" — assumes that imaginative activity makes men and women resemble God. Culture is not the record of a sustained response to God, nature, and the past, but is instead the recorded legacy of intermittent bursts of human creativity, the saga of creaturely deeds that rival the creative achievements of God.

Like Adam in Hawthorne's tale, the artist envisioned in this quotation has little to learn from the past; indeed, the artist-as-Adam staggers beneath the weight of past achievements as he struggles to keep his creative balance and preserve his god-like prerogatives. The literary critic Harold

---

44. Ingles, "Art as Incarnation," p. 11.
45. Best, "Christian Responsibility in Music," in *The Christian Imagination: Essays on Literature and the Arts,* ed. Leland Ryken (Grand Rapids: Baker Book House, 1981), pp. 404, 407.

Bloom has written extensively on the anxiety over influence that has afflicted poets since the time of the romantics; anxiety of this kind drove the new Adam to discard the uninterpreted book, and it prompts Christian theorists to celebrate cultural discontinuity as a liberating force that allows the artist to act like God.

In earlier chapters of this book, we explored several facets of the complex historical movement known as romanticism. The influence of that movement on American evangelicalism in general and on Christian aesthetics in particular is very strong. Three very different examples illustrate how once radical romantic ideas have worked their way into the Christian tradition. Each passage employs one of the favorite metaphors of the romantics — that of the human spirit as an Aeolian harp that is called into song by powerful forces. The first excerpt is from a well-known work by the English romantic poet Percy Bysshe Shelley:

> Make me thy lyre, even as the forest is:
> What if my leaves are falling like its own!
> The tumult of thy mighty harmonies
>
> Will take from both a deep, autumnal tone,
> Sweet though in sadness. Be thou, Spirit fierce,
> My spirit! Be thou me, impetuous one!
>
> Drive my dead thoughts over the universe
> Like withered leaves to quicken a new birth!
> And, by the incantation of this verse,
>
> Scatter, as from an unextinguished hearth
> Ashes and sparks, my words among mankind!
> Be through my lips to unawakened Earth
>
> The trumpet of a prophecy! O Wind,
> If Winter comes, can Spring be far behind?[46]

The next excerpt is from a gospel song by Georgiana Taylor:

> Oh, to be nothing, nothing,
> Only as led by His hand;

---

46. Shelley, "Ode to the West Wind," in *Shelley's Poems* (London: J. M. Dent, 1907), p. 331.

A messenger at His gateway,
   Only waiting for His command,
Only an instrument ready
   His praises to sound at His will,
Willing, should He not require me,
   In silence to wait on Him still.[47]

The final excerpt is from an early essay by Thomas Howard, who has written widely on the arts for more than three decades:

Alas for the man for whom the vision of beauty . . . becomes . . . a searing agony that ravages him daily, hourly, in images too sweet to bear. . . .

[The artist] finds himself wounded with stabbing visions of some aching and elusive joy, some burning fever of desire; and he knows that in order to be true to his own being, he must *invite* the shafts and ask where in God's name they come from, while the rest of us must offset and quell these lance-like imaginings with practical consideration in order to make our way in the world and keep our sanity.[48]

In each of these passages, we encounter a sensitive soul waiting passively to be filled with power, either by the spirit of God or by the spirit that animates all of life. Ravished and quickened by that spirit, that soul then becomes an agent of healing in the world. In Shelley's poem the artist who is played upon by the spirit becomes a source of moral, aesthetic, and political regeneration; in Taylor's hymn, once the empty vessel is filled, it becomes "for the Master's use made meet"; and in Howard's essay, the ravaged artist commits himself to "the plastic immortalization of human beauty and the effort to shape visibly the chaotic phenomena of life." Though the goals of these three writers differ significantly, the poet, the hymn writer, and the essayist share an allegiance to the powerful image of the isolated individual who appears powerless but has been called and then filled in order to do a great work.

We can account for this similarity in part by noting the distinctly Protestant tone of a great deal of romanticism. As we have seen, many of the great romantic artists sought to resuscitate the battered body of Chris-

47. Taylor, "Oh, to Be Nothing," quoted in Marsden, *Fundamentalism and American Culture*, p. 76.

48. Howard, "Arts and Religion: They Need Not Clash," *Christianity Today*, 21 Jan. 1966, p. 9.

tian belief. They sought to breathe life into that tradition by claiming for the imaginative human spirit the rights and responsibilities traditionally attributed by theism to a transcendent God. In doing so, however, they emphasized the poverty of the natural world in contrast to the abundance of the human imagination. As a result, with romanticism the stripping of sacramental significance from nature and ritual that was begun in the Reformation was now complete. Nature and the past lay "without form and void" before the potent human spirit, as perfect material to be molded by that shaping agent. The earth, Thoreau wrote, and "the institutions upon it, are plastic like clay in the hands of the potter."[49]

Fundamentalists and evangelicals have been careful to avoid making precisely these kinds of Promethean claims about the power of the artist. Yet evangelicals have come very close to saying such things and have been ever so sympathetic to the substance and rhetoric of the romantic tradition. That sympathy grew out of perceptions of culture held by romantics and fundamentalists alike, with both groups prone to view themselves as the rightful proprietors of a world from which they had been displaced. Ann Douglas has documented the way in which liberal ministers, women, and serious artists were disestablished in nineteenth-century America.[50] Stripped of power in a culture ruled by men and the marketplace, these groups took what solace they could from their ability to influence those who exercised power.

Douglas's conclusions pertain to the first half of the nineteenth century, when, as Marsden claims, evangelical Protestants "thought of America as a Christian nation" and "considered their faith to be the normative American creed." That "old order of American Protestantism," however, built as it was "on the interrelationship of faith, science, the Bible, morality, and civilization, . . . was about to crumble."[51] Late in the century, faced with threats from higher criticism of the Bible, from Darwinian theory, and from the secular mores of an increasingly urban and industrial America, evangelicals suddenly found themselves on the outside looking in. As Marsden documents, the evangelicals' feeling of alienation was to lead, among other things, to the fundamentalist embrace of dispensational premillennialism and to the definition of Christian life as an existence untainted by a short list of social vices.

49. Thoreau, *Walden*, p. 568.
50. Douglas, *The Feminization of American Culture* (New York: Avon Books, 1978), pp. 17-93.
51. Marsden, *Fundamentalism and American Culture*, pp. 11, 17.

In the categories employed by H. Richard Niebuhr, the evangelicals of the early nineteenth century embraced a "Christ of culture" position because they saw America as a Christian nation, an antitype fulfilling the promise of biblical types. Their fundamentalist heirs, however, could hardly hold to the "Christ of culture" view in the late nineteenth century. As they witnessed what one observer has called "the demise of biblical civilization" in the last years of that century,[52] evangelicals came to adopt what Niebuhr terms the "Christ against culture" position. In the spirit of the modern gnosticism we discussed earlier, by adopting this view the fundamentalists run the risk of denying the sovereignty of God over the course of nature and history. Niebuhr argues that the "rejection of culture" by the "Christ against culture" radicals "is easily combined with a suspicion of nature and nature's God." Their dependence on Christ is often changed "into a reliance on the Spirit immanent in him and the believer." This emphasis upon a spiritual inwardness as opposed to outward barrenness eventually leads the radicals "to divide the world into the material realm governed by a principle opposed to Christ and a spiritual realm guided by the spiritual God. . . . At the edges of the radical movement the Manichean heresy is always developing."[53]

Niebuhr's description allows us to see a striking similarity between aesthetics in the high romantic tradition and fundamentalism. The early fundamentalists, of course, would hardly have seen the parallel and would not have appreciated having it pointed out to them. They had neither the time nor the inclination to write essays on aesthetic theory. Indeed, when the arts are even mentioned in fundamentalist works from the first half of this century, it is usually for the purpose of calling into question either their use or their value. In the writings of the early twentieth century, some forms, such as theater, dance, and film, seem by their very natures to belong to this "material realm governed by a principle opposed to Christ," while other forms, including fiction and poetry, appear to waste precious time that might be better spent in pursuing the goals of the kingdom.[54]

52. Grant Wacker, "The Demise of Biblical Civilization," in *The Bible in America,* ed. Nathan Hatch and Mark A. Noll (New York: Oxford University Press, 1982), pp. 121-38.

53. Niebuhr, *Christ and Culture* (New York: Harper and Brothers, 1951), p. 81.

54. For example, it is difficult to find any treatment of the arts in issues of the *Christian Fundamentalist* from the early 1930s. But in a magazine such as *Christian Life* there is a marked increase of interest in the late 1940s. The July 1948 issue, for instance, contains several letters that express doubt as to whether non-Christian actors should or

At the mid-point of this century, a different tone began to appear in evangelical writing on the arts. About this time we begin to find articles extolling the virtues of the arts in the life of the Christian. In fact, some of these articles proclaim the centrality of the arts and claim, as we have seen, that in their agony artists somehow come closer to God than any of the rest of us do.[55] But what remains constant in the aesthetic theory of conservative Christians — what provides the continuity between fundamentalist opponents of the arts and evangelical advocates for them — is a tendency to divide the world into opposing camps. One side is controlled by God, while the other belongs either to Satan or to the unshaped void. Modern Christians have been far more subtle than their fundamentalist forebears in promoting this dualistic vision. Yet they have largely accepted the bifurcation that pervades not only the fundamentalist tradition but also a great deal of aesthetic theory from the romantics to the postmoderns.

In retrospect, it seems quite logical that when evangelical students of culture began to emerge from the dusky passageways of fundamentalism, their eyes would be dazzled by the enchanting romantic tradition. Because of its skepticism about the relevance of the past and because of its sense of being alienated both from unadorned nature and from mass culture, romantic theory has offered an appealing sight to those whose aesthetic lenses have been ground in the shop of American fundamentalism. Because they see literature through the lenses of romantic expressivism, modern Christian theorists have often failed to bring into focus the considerable resources of their own theological traditions. We have seen this to be true, whether these Christians have been philosophers and literary scholars encountering poststructuralism, or the distinguished literary historian C. S. Lewis appropriating modernist theories of art, or countless Christian artists and teachers attempting to justify their calling in the contemporary world.

---

could accurately portray Christians in the many evangelistic films beginning to appear at that time. This particular issue of *Christian Life* also contains two Christian short stories written according to predetermined formulas of the victorious life.

55. This is an explicit theme in many of the essays appearing in *Eternity* and *Christianity Today* in the 1960s and 1970s.

CHAPTER 10   *Theory, Therapy,*
and the Christian

THROUGHOUT THESE CHAPTERS, we have been exploring a number of related phenomena that I have identified by various names — "perspectivism," "postmodernism," and "therapeutic culture" among them. In one sense, each of these names points to a different reality. "Perspectivism," for instance, is a viewpoint in epistemology, while "postmodernism" is the name given to the broader movement of culture in the contemporary West, and "therapeutic" designates a specific understanding of the nature of the self and its relations to structures that place demands upon it. As descriptive terms, *perspectivism* is most pertinent to philosophy, *postmodernism* to literature and the arts, and *therapeutic* to psychological and sociological analyses. Yet in spite of the distinctions among these phenomena, more than anything else they are all facets of the singular "culture of interpretation."

What those different facets reveal is a distinctly American pragmatism that is preoccupied with the usefulness of language, yet is skeptical about the power of language to reveal truth or to serve legitimately as an instrument of ethical obligation. Claiming that words point only to their origins in the individual or collective will, this contemporary pragmatism focuses upon language as an instrument of power and as a tool for the marketing of goods and services. In an "interpretive" culture as we now know it in the United States, the truthfulness of any idea is bound to appear secondary to its relevance, its marketability.

Modern theories of interpretation that have their roots in the ro-

236

mantic movement almost inevitably undercut any interpretation that claims to do more than announce the discovery of a particular potential or achievement of the self. In the time of Kant, Schleiermacher, and Emerson, of course, this stress upon the self did not appear to threaten truth because the romantic poets and philosophers considered the inner realm to be a bastion of virtue and epistemic certainty. When Emerson told his Harvard audience in 1837 that "the ancient precept, 'Know thyself,' and the modern precept, 'Study nature,' [have] become at last one maxim,"[1] he was expressing his serene faith that within each human soul there were sufficient resources, as he would say, "for the world." For the likes of Schleiermacher and Emerson, the apologetic effort to recast the gospel could do no harm to the truth, for buried within the self were the same inexhaustible troves of truth and virtue that previous generations had mined.

The apologetic model espoused by the romantics had undeniable power in their own day, but with the dramatic changes in conceptions of truth and the self over the past century, that model has become a thing of questionable worth in the defense of the Christian faith. If, as many postmodern theories of knowledge allege, the self has no inherent truth within it to disclose, interpretation can do no more than document the power of desire in language, and apologetics is left with the sad task of pouring contemporary experience into the hollow shell of empty Christian language. In this scheme of things, interpretation is reduced to the art of helping the self achieve satisfaction by all available means. For those who believe that religious language refers to nothing more than various stages or aspects of the self, therapy supplants truth as the goal of understanding, and theology becomes a mere footnote to the primary text of anthropology.[2]

Pragmatic Theology

We can see the effects of romantic and pragmatic understandings even in the work of such a stellar figure as the American theologian Reinhold

---

1. Emerson, "The American Scholar," in *Emerson: Essays and Lectures,* ed. Joel Porte (New York: Library of America, 1983), p. 56.

2. Helmut Thielicke, *The Evangelical Faith,* vol. 1: *Prolegomena: The Relation of Theology to Modern Thought Forms,* trans. and ed. Geoffrey W. Bromiley (Grand Rapids: Eerdmans, 1974), p. 53.

Niebuhr. For example, throughout his writing Niebuhr gave a central place to the doctrine of the resurrection; indeed, the whole of *Human Destiny* (the second volume of *The Nature and Destiny of Man*) relies upon the symbolic power of the resurrection to assure us that God redeems and fulfills the course of human history. As Niebuhr wrote to the Scottish philosopher Norman Kemp Smith in 1940, the wisdom of the resurrection is "the idea that the fulfillment of life does not mean the negation and destruction of historical reality (which is a unity of body-soul, freedom-necessity, time-eternity) but the completion of this unity." But even as he argued for the relevance of the resurrection, Niebuhr sought to reassure Smith that he was not a supernaturalist: "I have not the slightest interest in the empty tomb or physical resurrection."[3]

Because of the prevailing scientific naturalism of the twentieth century, Niebuhr felt that he could not possibly believe in the resurrection as an "event" of any kind. As a *symbol* the resurrection might have great power, but ultimately it can refer to nothing more than our faith in the meaningfulness of life. The word does not correspond to any state of affairs or event in history but is instead the most powerful expression we have of our belief in the coherence of meaning: "The Christian hope of the consummation of life and history . . . is an integral part of the total Biblical conception of the meaning of life."[4] Niebuhr wanted to salvage the noetic significance of the resurrection while dismissing any claims about its ontic actuality.

The example of Niebuhr is evidence of the fact that in the tradition of Schleiermacher and the romantics the desire to accommodate Christian doctrine to the reigning paradigms of science and epistemology is so strong that questions about the descriptive power of Christian symbols can only be dismissed as fruitless or irrelevant. If naturalism makes

3. Niebuhr, quoted in Richard Wightman Fox, *Reinhold Niebuhr: A Biography* (New York: Pantheon Books, 1985), p. 215. In another context, Niebuhr wrote: "Incidentally, most modern Biblical scholars take it for granted that Christ's resurrection was not a public event in the same sense as the crucifixion, but rather a spiritual experience of his disciples" (quoted in Merrill Tenney, *The Reality of the Resurrection* [New York: Harper & Row, 1963], p. 193).

4. Niebuhr, *The Nature and Destiny of Man*, vol. 2: *Human Destiny* (New York: Charles Scribner's Sons, 1943), p. 298. In a characteristic paragraph discussing the resurrection, Niebuhr calls it a *symbol*, a *hope*, and an *idea*, but never a *fact*, an *event*, or a *reality*. See *Human Destiny*, pp. 311-12.

the idea of the bodily resurrection of Jesus distasteful, then one must reinterpret the symbol to season it for the tastes of the modern intellectual palate. If we must abandon belief in the empty tomb in order to maintain the magical power of all that the word *resurrection* conjures up, so be it.

That there are clear parallels between Niebuhr's theology and the broader cultural tradition of romanticism would seem to be confirmed by the following observation made by the contemporary British novelist Iris Murdoch:

> It is equally interesting that after a period of irreligion or relative atheism there have been signs of a kind of perceptible religious renewal in certain changes in theology. . . . In England one is experiencing a demythologization . . . of theology which recognizes that many things normally or originally taken as dogmas must now be considered as myths. In this there is something which might have a profound impact on the future which, for the ordinary person, might return religion to the realm of the believable.[5]

The bargain that Murdoch seems to offer here to the church is still that of Schleiermacher: if the church gives up its claims to authority and truthfulness by discarding its antiquated dogmas, then the people, the "ordinary persons," will recompense the church with their assent, their approval. This is a questionable assumption and a questionable bargain.

There is admittedly in the Christian life always a tension between the Scriptures in themselves and the need to *apply* them to the demands and patterns of present reality. But for Niebuhr, Murdoch, and innumerable others in the culture of interpretation, the temptation is to make all human understanding a matter of accommodation and application. In this line of thinking, the Bible and Christian doctrine may console our spirits and help to organize the categories of our thought, but they have lost the power to *reveal,* to speak to us with a *binding address.* When all knowledge becomes application, eventually there may be nothing left to apply.[6]

5. Murdoch, quoted in Peter S. Hawkins, *The Language of Grace* (Cambridge, MA: Cowley Publications, 1983), pp. 134-35.

6. "Inquiry into the act and possibility of faith hardly leaves time for the content of faith. Intensive preoccupation with the question of method blinds us to what methodologically purified perception should show us. 'They are continually sharpening knives and

In his most recent book, Richard Rorty demonstrates with exceptional clarity the fate of Christian language in the romantic and Nietzschean interpretive traditions. In "The Contingency of Language," the first chapter of *Contingency, Irony, and Solidarity,* Rorty writes that "the suggestion that truth . . . is out there is a legacy of an age in which the world was seen as the creation of a being who had a language of his own." For centuries faith in the Logos bound Western men and women to the illusion that providence and truth governed reality. But Rorty takes the distinguishing mark of postmodernity to be its discovery that no power outside language and the human will rules the world. According to him, the revolutionaries and poets of the late eighteenth century "glimpsed" a truth that only perspectival postmodernism has come to see clearly: "that anything could be made to look good or bad, important or unimportant, useful or useless, by being redescribed."[7]

The romantics had only a "dim sense" that those whose language changed "so that they no longer spoke of themselves as responsible to nonhuman powers would thereby become a new kind of human beings." Yet by the end of the twentieth century, the outlines of that new human being have become more clear to Rorty. The new human is the liberal ironist, the one who takes delight in the satisfactions of language without ever making the pretentious error of trying to assert that that language reflects some kind of "truth as a deep matter."

> An ideal liberal society is one which has no purpose except freedom. . . .
> It has no purpose except to make life easier for poets and revolutionaries

---

no longer have anything to cut' (Karl Rahner)" (Thielicke, *Evangelical Faith,* vol. 1, pp. 52-53).

As Dorothy Sayers complains, we do Christ

> singularly little honour by watering down His personality till it could not offend a fly. Surely it is not the business of the Church to adapt Christ to men, but to adapt men to Christ.
>
> It is the dogma that is the drama — not beautiful phrases, nor comforting sentiments, nor vague aspirations to lovingkindness and uplift, nor the promise of something nice after death — but the terrifying assertion that the same God who made the world lived in the world and passed through the grave and gate of death. Show that to the heathen, and they may not believe it; but at least they may realize that here is something that a man might be glad to believe. (*Christian Letters to a Post-Christian World,* ed. Roderick Jellema [Grand Rapids: Eerdmans, 1969], p. 26)

7. Rorty, *Contingency, Irony, and Solidarity* (Cambridge: Cambridge University Press, 1989), p. 7.

while seeing to it that they make life harder for others only by words, and not deeds. It is a society whose hero is the strong poet and the revolutionary because it recognizes that it is what it is, has the morality it has, speaks the language it does, not because it approximates the will of God or the nature of man but because certain poets and revolutionaries of the past spoke as they did.[8]

When he entitled his Gifford Lectures *The Nature and Destiny of Man,* Niebuhr was confident that he could affirm the centrality and truthfulness of Christian doctrine even as he interpreted the Bible as a symbolic expression of human desire that was at the same time a miraculous revelation of the will of God. At a point in Western history when fascism and Stalinism appeared to make Christian views of sin more relevant than they had appeared for several centuries, Niebuhr's apologetic revivified classic doctrines. Ironically, however, it was precisely Niebuhr's exclusive emphasis upon the usefulness of those doctrines as philosophical and psychological interpretations that made them appear to many to be expendable once they had lost their timely explanatory power. In a perspectival, therapeutic culture, language can only be seen as an extension of human need, and when one way of talking no longer seems useful — say, the way governed by words such as *sin, forgiveness, grace, God,* and *judgment* — then one must drop that vocabulary and start speaking another vocabulary that might prove more efficient in the pursuit of human happiness. " 'The nature of truth' is an unprofitable topic," Rorty concludes, "resembling in this respect 'the nature of man' and 'the nature of God.' . . . But this claim about relative profitability, in turn, is just the recommendation that we in fact *say* little about these topics, and see how we get on."[9]

Rorty is confident that all of the languages of truth, whether they be those of Christian orthodoxy, Cartesian rationalism, or Baconian empiricism, will inevitably grow so uninteresting as to become obsolete.

Once upon a time we felt a need to worship something which lay beyond the visible world. Beginning in the seventeenth century we tried to substitute a love of truth for a love of God, treating the world described by science as a quasi divinity. Beginning at the end of the eighteenth century we tried to substitute a love of ourselves for a love of scientific

8. Rorty, *Contingency, Irony, and Solidarity,* pp. 7, 60-61.
9. Rorty, *Contingency, Irony, and Solidarity,* p. 8.

truth, a worship of our own deep spiritual or poetic nature, treated as one more quasi divinity.

The line of thought common to Blumenberg, Nietzsche, Freud, and Davidson suggests that we try to get to the point where we no longer worship *anything*, where we treat *nothing* as a quasi divinity, where we treat *everything* — our language, our conscience, our community — as a product of time and chance.[10]

In Rorty's radically contingent world, interpretation can never represent anything more than my effort to understand how the claims of other persons and texts can threaten or be useful to me; the power of interpretation can be nothing more than the power to shape the world to my own private ends, whatever they might be.

In an earlier chapter, I referred to the conflict of interpretive paradigms surrounding the departure of Bill Curry from the University of Alabama coaching job. Curry's father found the biblical story to be a convincing and adequate description of the struggles of his son, while the university trustee relied upon a vocabulary of perspectivism to assess the coach's dilemma. Rorty would undoubtedly understand the conflict between these two paradigms. After all, he writes in *Contingency, Irony, and Solidarity*, "interesting philosophy . . . is, implicitly or explicitly, a contest between an entrenched vocabulary which has become a nuisance and a half-formed new vocabulary which vaguely promises great things."[11] In a culture enamored of efficiency and self-fulfillment, and committed to no ideal higher than indeterminate freedom, the biblical story is likely to seem little more than a nuisance, while perspectivism indeed seems vaguely to promise "great things."

No matter how useful they find these new vocabularies of usefulness to be, Christian interpreters have something essential at stake in the "entrenched vocabulary" that the therapeutic model is seeking to supplant. For instance, there is a vast difference between Dietrich Bonhoeffer's search for a secular way of talking about God and Christian doctrine and Rorty's longing for a "half-formed new vocabulary which vaguely promises great things." Bonhoeffer's desire was to find a valid, honest way of addressing secular people with the claims and promises of the gospel; he distrusted religious language because he feared that its familiar irrelevance would

10. Rorty, *Contingency, Irony, and Solidarity*, p. 22.
11. Rorty, *Contingency, Irony, and Solidarity*, p. 9.

obscure the very truths to which it was to point. Only months before he died, he wrote to Eberhard Bethge of how much he had been learning about the "profound this-worldliness of Christianity." He quickly qualified that statement in a way that could serve as a rejoinder to the cultured weariness of Rortyan postmodernism: "I don't mean the shallow and banal this-worldliness of the enlightened, the busy, the comfortable, or the lascivious, but the profound this-worldliness, characterized by discipline and the constant knowledge of death and resurrection."[12]

To a significant extent, the history of interpretation since Schleiermacher and the romantics has been an effort to carry on the epistemological revolution of Spinoza and Descartes by other means. The therapeutic selves glamorized in contemporary theory differ from the self envisioned by the Cartesian tradition mainly in the degree to which the moderns have exchanged the language of truth for the vocabularies of perspective and interpretation. As Christian interpreters grapple with the reigning paradigms of postmodernism, they need to be reminded, in the words of Helmut Thielicke, that "God's Word is not interpretative; it is creative. It brings forth being out of nothing. It thus transcends all analogies and all supposedly common planes. . . . Being an active rather than an interpretative . . . word, God's Word changes the self rather than disclosing it."[13]

In effect, romantic hermeneutics internalizes all of human history, making of the past a saga of development and liberation whose goal has been my present. The past has authority and relevance only insofar as it makes present freedom possible or serves to illuminate some otherwise darkened corner of contemporary reality. Emerson's view of history as a parable of self-development is a variation upon Hegel's theme that the history of philosophy reached its end in his own system.[14] Emerson and Hegel in turn anticipate postmodern perspectivism, for which the past may have aesthetic power but never ethical authority.

---

12. Bonhoeffer, *Letters and Papers from Prison*, ed. Eberhard Bethge (New York: Collier Books, 1971), p. 369.

13. Thielicke, *Evangelical Faith*, vol. 1, p. 156.

14. "An obvious conclusion is that Hegel's philosophy is not just a new system but that all previous philosophies from the Pre-Socratics to Kant are elements in it, are taken up into it, and are seen to be stages in the self-consciousness of the spirit. Unconsciously, they have all helped the self-consciousness of the spirit to reflection. They have been precursors like John the Baptist. Hegel himself is the Christ of knowledge. He has come as a kind of philosophical Savior" (Helmut Thielicke, *Modern Faith and Thought*, trans. Geoffrey W. Bromiley [Grand Rapids: Eerdmans, 1990], pp. 370-71).

To believe in Christ, however, means in a sense to *belong* to the past, to a community and tradition of faith established and sustained by the redemptive acts of God. This community existed long before any of us came into being and, by the grace of God, may continue long after all of us have passed from historical life. Again, it is Rorty who provides a sharply contrasting view to this one. He argues that instead of accepting the defining power of our history, we should follow Nietzsche's example and "seek consolation, at the moment of death, not in having transcended the animal condition but in being that peculiar sort of dying animal who, by describing himself in his own terms, had created himself."[15] To this ideal of redescription the Christian might respond with Alasdair MacIntyre's claim that "only in fantasy do we live what story we please. In life, as both Aristotle and Engels noted, we are always under certain constraints. We enter upon a stage which we did not design and we find ourselves part of an action that was not of our making."[16]

The self-description that Rorty sees as an act of liberation St. Augustine took to be a sign of sin. In the opening chapters of the *Confessions*, Augustine analyzed how he had acquired language in infancy: "Little by little I began to become conscious of where I was, and I wanted to express my desires to those who could satisfy them." Because those desires were "inside" him, he had no means of expressing them to "those who could satisfy them." As a result, he spent a good deal of time jerking his limbs and becoming "angry with my elders for not being subservient to me, and with responsible people for not acting as though they were my slaves." Eventually, though, Augustine learned to speak by observing how adults make use of the power of naming. When others spoke and turned toward objects, "I saw and grasped the fact that the sound they uttered was the name given by them to the object they wished to indicate." By imitating them, Augustine learned how to "share with those about me in this language for the communication of our desires."[17]

15. Rorty, *Contingency, Irony, and Solidarity,* p. 27.

16. MacIntyre, *After Virtue,* 2nd ed. (Notre Dame: University of Notre Dame Press, 1984), p. 213. "In my drama, perhaps, I am Hamlet or Iago or at least the swineherd who may yet become a prince, but to you I am only A Gentleman or at best Second Murderer, while you are my Polonius or my Gravedigger, but your own hero. Each of our dramas exerts constraints on each other's, making the whole different from the parts but still dramatic" (*After Virtue,* pp. 213-14).

17. *The Confessions of St. Augustine,* book 1, trans. Rex Warner (New York: New American Library, 1963), pp. 21, 25-26.

To Augustine, the worthiness of what was said was more important than the abstract right to say it. Unlike many postromantic thinkers, Augustine did not take the conflict between the dead world of matter and the vital world of the will to be humanity's central dilemma. Instead, for Augustine the most important questions had to do with the nature of the will and the objects of its worship. In large measure, he considered worthiness and worthlessness to be qualities inherent in objects and actions and not merely values imposed by the will. By their very nature, some things deserve our praise and adoration, while others are clearly unworthy.

To be sure, Augustine and many others in the Christian tradition have acknowledged the expression of desire as one of the valid and undeniable functions of language. C. S. Lewis wrote movingly about the power of human longing to anticipate the joys of heaven, while Dante brilliantly examined the power of desire in *The Divine Comedy*. But at the same time, Christians have also claimed emphatically that language does more than chart the course of our longings. For the Christian, language is not only expressive but also mimetic; language can tell us something about the nature of God and his actions as well as about our motives and needs. The stories of the Bible may help to illuminate our individual struggles, but fundamentally they speak of the creative, judging, and redeeming power of God in nature and human affairs. A Christian apologetic that does not reach beyond the romantic tradition will find in the Bible nothing more than a record of human aspiration and oppression, and in finding nothing more than that it will have neglected the central redemptive message of the Scriptures.

To point to the dilemmas posed by the romantic self and romantic theories of interpretation is not, of course, the same thing as arguing that it would somehow be possible to move back to a time before the self became a pressing concern for Western culture in general and for theology in particular. No, the goal of the Christian interpreter should not be to deny intellectual history but to have the courage to address that history with authority when it has suppressed the truth. As Thielicke has argued, "we need to consider whether the elimination of the question of transcendence from the reflective consciousness is not perhaps due to Neronic suppression, to what Paul calls 'holding down the truth in unrighteousness'" (Rom. 1:18).[18] In declaring that truth and transcendence are lodged only in the reigning paradigms of language, the perspectival or therapeutic

18. Thielicke, *Evangelical Faith*, vol. 1, p. 241.

view of knowledge involves nothing less than the massive suppression of an entire dimension of the truth.

After all, there is a vast difference between saying that we see the truth as through a glass darkly and claiming that all we can do with language is attempt to make nature mirror our own power. What the Christian looks for in creation is something greater than the stunning reflection of his or her own desiring countenance. What the Christian listens for in the proclamation of the Word of God is more than the echo of his or her own clamoring voice. If this were not so, then we would be of all people "most to be pitied" (1 Cor. 15:19, REB).

The Question of Truth

From one vantage point, the assertions of the previous paragraph would seem to beg the most important question of all, that of truth. What good does it do to say that Christians want to see more in nature than their own reflections or hear more in the Bible than echoes of their own voices if one cannot at the same time prove that nature is divinely ordered or that the Bible is the revealed Word of God? Without irrefutable arguments and convincing evidence, are not all claims about the character and power of God pitiful cases of wish fulfillment?

These questions need be answered in the affirmative only if one accepts the premise that truth must have indubitable foundations. Those who believe that relativism is the only alternative to skepticism accept the Cartesian criteria of truth as indubitable certainty. They believe that if an assertion can be shown to be under the influence of a prejudice, it can be rejected as an irrational claim. By a curious logic, these Cartesians assume that their own prejudice against prejudice is an indisputable fact and that their criterion of mathematical certainty constitutes an indubitable standard; when claims to truth do not measure up to their standards, the heirs of Descartes are liable to dismiss them with charges of skepticism or relativism.

It is ironic that in their zeal to establish irrefutable arguments and unshakeable evidence for the truth, Descartes, Spinoza, and others made possible the relativism and nihilism of our present century. The rationalist philosophers were seeking to strengthen belief rather than to undermine faith, but by claiming that reason builds a stronger foundation for faith than the one provided by church, tradition, and the Scriptures, the early modern philosophers helped to pave the way for postmodern disbelief. Following the lead of Descartes and Spinoza, many thinkers lashed the Christian faith to the vessel of reason piloted by the lonely self. When that vessel broke upon the rocks of the modern experience, many Christians could do nothing but gaze wistfully as their faith sank beneath the waves.

The Cartesian search for an indubitable proof of the existence of God and the truthfulness of the Scriptures continued, of course, through the Enlightenment and the romantic period. Except for the isolated cases of a few prominent French *philosophes,* the Enlightenment was generally open to Christian belief. To be sure, the Christianity promoted in the Enlightenment was a dramatically pared down version of medieval and Reformational supernaturalism. Yet no matter how strenuously they objected to elements of Christian belief and practice, the Enlightenment critics did not generally dispute the existence of God. In the words of historian James Turner, "disbelief in God remained scarcely more plausible than disbelief in gravity," and as a result "the known unbelievers of Europe and America before the French Revolution numbered fewer than a dozen or two."[19]

While open disbelief may have been rare, the questioning of traditional formulations of the faith was common in the Enlightenment. As we have seen, such questioning led to a search for rational proofs of God, a search that culminated in Kant's denial of the possibility of such proofs. After Kant, romanticism tried to secure a place for God and the truth by locating their source within the imaginative, intuitive reaches of the self. The English romantic poets, the American transcendentalist essayists, and the German theologian Schleiermacher all tried to provide a ground for belief in the inner reaches of human feeling or imagination. As the romantics searched for truth, their confidence was grounded in their faith in the correspondence between the unimpeded self and the spirit at work in creation.

With the demise of the romantic enterprise over the past two centuries, Western men and women have found themselves left with the residue of the expressive self. The postmodern self is more or less the romantic will shorn of its ethical abilities and epistemological powers. In contemporary theories of interpretation, the desires and intuitions of the romantic self are no longer seen to correspond to some deep order in the nature of things. Instead, those desires themselves have become the only

19. Turner, *Without God, Without Creed: The Origins of Unbelief in America* (Baltimore: Johns Hopkins University Press, 1985), p. 44.

ground of a number of contemporary theorists of language and the only source of certainty for many in the postmodern West. The creed of preference in the contemporary university and the triumph of perspectivism in interpretation indicate that for many individuals in the West whimsy and willfulness provide the only grounds for human actions.

Proclamation and Interpretation

"On all fronts foundationalism is in bad shape," Nicholas Wolterstorff asserts in *Reason Within the Bounds of Religion*.[20] By "foundationalism" he means that understanding of knowledge in the West which seeks to establish "a body of theories from which all prejudice, bias, and unjustified conjecture have been eliminated." For the foundationalist, that body of theories needs to rest upon "a firm foundation of certitude."[21] Because Western conceptions of truth have been wedded to foundationalism since the late Middle Ages, Wolterstorff says, we reflexively assume that the truth is endangered when foundationalism comes under attack. Yet such fears are mistaken, because from the difficulties of foundationalism "it does not follow that there is no structured reality independent of our conceivings and believings. . . . Nor does it follow that we can never know the truth."[22]

In a Christian understanding of knowledge, truth is something other than the indubitable certainty essential to technology and science. In the scientific understanding of knowledge, if you desire to master something or someone, you treat that person or thing as an object and learn the laws that govern it so that you might put it under your control; to do this work of manipulation most effectively, you must have indubitable knowledge that discloses the predictable ways in which the object of your attention acts. In a Christian understanding of things, however, knowledge is always partial and personal. The Christian faith holds that our ability to know is limited by our finitude and fallibility as knowing subjects. Instead of being a matter of indubitable proof, knowledge for the Christian involves a dynamic interplay of data and experience. To be a Christian is to bear witness to what you have discovered and what has been revealed to you,

20. Wolterstorff, *Reason Within the Bounds of Religion* (Grand Rapids: Eerdmans, 1976), p. 52.
21. Wolterstorff, *Reason Within the Bounds of Religion*, p. 24.
22. Wolterstorff, *Reason Within the Bounds of Religion*, p. 53.

and to bear witness is not to prove the truth indubitably but to proclaim it confidently.

To be sure, proclamation must take into serious consideration its audience and the state of knowledge in the world it addresses. In the words of Dietrich Bonhoeffer, what must bother the Christian "incessantly is the question what Christianity really is, or indeed who Christ really is, for us today."[23] For instance, it is senseless to create a stumbling block by confessing God in terms of a medieval, Ptolemaic cosmology, and it is futile to proclaim God's sovereignty without considering the difference between the agrarian world of the Bible and the urban world in which modern persons live and work.

But it is one thing to consider the concerns of an audience and quite another matter to allow those concerns to dictate the message one proclaims. The temptation to tailor convictions to fit the desires of an audience is especially strong in a society in which the market has determining power. Instead of demanding proof of the truth, consumers in a market economy are more likely to insist that the messages preached to them satisfy specific desires. In a consumer culture, the hermeneutical principle of application is in danger of becoming a mere marketing tool. With the history charted in this book having run its course, Descartes, who sat alone gazing at his fire and scouring his mind for indubitable truth, is doomed to recognize as his proper heir the solitary soul couched in front of a television set, seeking satisfaction for unspecified needs and ineffable desires.

The modern descendent of Descartes is much like the protagonist of Theodore Dreiser's novel *Sister Carrie*. Carrie Meeber is a young woman who travels from the country to Chicago in the late nineteenth century. Having been drawn away from the rural world of her childhood, she quickly succumbs to the appeals of a salesman who seduces her with a gift of $20: "The money she had accepted was two soft, green, handsome ten-dollar bills."[24]

Throughout *Sister Carrie*, the symbolic power traditionally associated with icons in religious experience is transferred to money and the objects it obtains. Cash has the power to draw Carrie away from the religious and ethical training of her youth, and it forever beckons her with its promises of delight. For all of its power to allure, however, that money does not

23. Bonhoeffer, *Letters and Papers from Prison*, p. 279.
24. Dreiser, *Sister Carrie*, ed. Neda Westlake et al. (New York: Penguin Books, 1986), p. 62.

have the power to satisfy Carrie. The last we hear of her in the novel is when she is fantasizing about a man she has recently met. In his typically overwrought prose, Dreiser describes Carrie's despondency:

> All her nature was stirred to unrest now. She was already the old, mournful Carrie — the desireful Carrie, — unsatisfied.
>
> Oh, blind strivings of the human heart. Onward, onward it saith, and where beauty leads, there it follows. . . .
>
> Carrie! Oh Carrie! ever whole in that thou art ever hopeful, know that the light is but now in these his eyes. Tomorrow it shall be melted and dissolved. Tomorrow it shall be on and further on, still leading, still alluring, until thought is not with you and heartaches are no more.[25]

This depiction of Carrie, written almost a century ago, demonstrates that Dreiser intuited one of the crucial traits of modernity and one of the central arguments that we have been making in this book. He saw that in the modern world the ideal of the self disinterestedly seeking truth has given way to a vision of the self as a unit of consumption seeking to slake its unquenchable thirsts.

While Dreiser and others like him intuited the bankruptcy of Cartesianism become consumerism, offering judgment in novelistic form, many recent works in philosophy, theology, and hermeneutics have provided theoretical critiques of the Cartesian approach. For instance, philosophical hermeneutics has pressed points about human understanding with which Christians of many different persuasions ought to be able to agree. Hans-Georg Gadamer and Paul Ricoeur might be especially helpful to the Christian defending a principled pluralism in matters of interpretation and the truth. Following the lead of Gadamer and Ricoeur, the Christian critic might challenge claims that truth is either indubitable or relative by affirming that the meaning of any text or action is neither single nor limitless. We can say a number of true things about any passage from the Bible, a historical document, or a novel, but not everything we say is necessarily true.

Ricoeur is particularly instructive on the question of conflict among interpretations. In *Freud and Philosophy*, he argues for the hermeneutical significance of the great modern "masters of suspicion" — Marx, Nietzsche, and Freud. The intention they shared was that of looking "upon

---

25. Dreiser, *Sister Carrie,* p. 487.

the whole of consciousness primarily as 'false' consciousness." Thus, ironically enough, they take up the Cartesian stance of doubt, but they do so by carrying "it to the very heart of the Cartesian stronghold." The philosopher who has been trained "in the school of Descartes" doubts everything but his or her own consciousness; for it is supposed that "in consciousness, meaning and consciousness of meaning coincide. Since Marx, Nietzsche, and Freud, this too has become doubtful. After the doubt about things, we have started to doubt consciousness."[26]

Ricoeur claims that after Marx, Freud, and Nietzsche we would be naive to believe that there is only a single legitimate meaning to any written work.[27] In making this point, he is not arguing that a Marxist or Freudian interpretation could offer an exhaustive reading of any text or action. Instead, Ricoeur is pressing the claim that contemporary interpretation must account for subconscious meanings in texts as well as for meanings consciously built into them. Texts and actions give evidence of such things as economic interest, the workings of the subconscious, and the presence of a will to power. In "Existence and Hermeneutics," Ricoeur explains that different hermeneutical schemes display the "dependence of the self — its dependence on desire glimpsed in an archaeology of the subject, its dependence on the spirit glimpsed in its teleology, its dependence on the sacred glimpsed in its eschatology."[28] Many stories can be told about a book or an action — about its subterranean origins in the subconscious regions, its purposive moral and aesthetic dimensions, and its spiritual significance and properties of mystery.

Ricoeur's complex hermeneutic has rich implications for Christian apologetics. It provides a means of incorporating the powerful insights of the hermeneutics of suspicion without denying the claims of the Christian gospel. The dimensions of which Marx, Freud, and others have written so

26. Ricoeur, *Freud and Philosophy: An Essay on Interpretation,* trans. Denis Savage (New Haven: Yale University Press, 1970), p. 33.

27. The acknowledgment that multiple meanings might exist for a single text is not, of course, an exclusive development of modern hermeneutical thinking. For example, medieval Catholicism developed an elaborate scheme of "fourfold interpretation." For a succinct discussion of medieval interpretive beliefs and practices, see Stephen Ozment, *The Age of Reform 1250-1550: An Intellectual and Religious History of Late Medieval and Reformation Europe* (New Haven: Yale University Press, 1980), pp. 63-72.

28. Ricoeur, "Existence and Hermeneutics," trans. Kathleen McLaughlin, in *The Conflict of Interpretations: Essays in Hermeneutics,* ed. Don Ihde (Evanston: Northwestern University Press, 1974), p. 24.

compellingly are elements of the complexity of life as it is led by finite, sinful men and women. It is neither necessary nor desirable to set a Christian understanding of human experience directly against a Freudian understanding of the power of sexuality or a Marxist reading of the power of economic motivation. Instead of denying the legitimacy of the hermeneutics of suspicion, Christian interpreters and apologists would do well to seek to incorporate those insights into their own master narrative of the sovereignty and grace of God. Attempts to affirm Christian truth by denying sexual, economic, or psychological reality are doomed to fail and discredit the very truth they set out to defend.

While contemporary hermeneutical theory may help the Christian to comprehend the power of modern schools of interpretation, it cannot be of much assistance in formulating an explicitly Christian response to questions about the validity of any particular interpretation. Martin Heidegger, Gadamer, and Ricoeur, for instance, each had extensive training in Protestant theology, but none has made explicit and consistent Christian claims in his work. Heidegger seems clearly to have left Christian faith behind and to have replaced it with something like a mystical faith in language. Both Ricoeur and Gadamer frequently say things that might lead one to believe them to be Christian theorists, but in each case their references to the Christian faith remain tantalizingly obscure.

In working to replenish the depleted stores of twentieth-century epistemology, Heidegger, Gadamer, and Ricoeur have self-consciously labored as philosophers rather than as theologians. They have sought the starting point for reflection not within the life of the church nor in a revealed word but rather within the resources and residue of language itself. As a result, any Christian critic employing their insights will need to engage critically the conceptions of truth and the assumptions about religious language with which they work. While Christians from disparate theological traditions have different emphases in their professions and confessions, all Christians concerned with orthodoxy agree that truth is revealed to us through the Scriptures and the history of God's dealings with his people. But in philosophical hermeneutics Scripture and tradition tend to be conflated and to become a *linguistic tradition* that *embodies* (instead of *pointing to*) the truth.

Helmut Thielicke is especially instructive about the theological limitations of modern hermeneutical models. "To the degree that theological interest focuses on appropriation," writes Thielicke, "faith becomes a matter of understanding." Thielicke argues that in spite of its efforts to break out of the confines of Cartesianism, the Heideggerian tradition has remained bound to the question of the human subject. For example, though Heidegger and Gadamer seek to ground the interpreting self in tradition, their break with Cartesianism consists more of an acknowledgment of the power of the collective human consciousness, subtly manifested in the history of language, than of a discovery of a revelatory truth imparted to humanity. Thielicke describes the difference between a strict "hermeneutical" understanding of the Scriptures and classic confessional claims about them:

> Being an active rather than an interpretative or "apophantic" word, God's Word changes the self rather than disclosing it. Hence it does not permit of prior principles of understanding. As the existence which is being understood is given up to death, so its principles of understanding are given up to death.[29]

Gerald Bruns, one of the most perceptive contemporary interpreters of Heidegger and Gadamer, argues that the truth disclosed within history does not reach beyond history. He writes, "these versions [of the truth of anything as it is disclosed in the process of interpretation] are not representations of anything hidden behind or beneath history, or at history's end. They are just whatever makes its appearance in time, which is all, I believe, that anything ever does."[30] Such a view of truth directly opposes the Christian conception of the creative and revealing Word of God, the Alpha and Omega of creation. Truth is not simply something that *emerges from* history and is *disclosed* in it; in historic Christian theology, it has always been something *revealed* to men and women *in* history by the one who claims to be the author of that history.

The Recovery of Authority

To call God the *author* of history is to use a word whose original meaning has been all but lost to modern usage. For centuries, the primary meaning of *author* — which has its roots in the Latin word *auctor* — was not "writer" but "originator" or "creator." For instance, in the late fourteenth

---

29. Thielicke, *The Evangelical Faith,* vol. 1, p. 156.

30. Bruns, *Inventions: Writing, Textuality, and Understanding in Literary History* (New Haven: Yale University Press, 1982), p. 14.

century Geoffrey Chaucer employed this meaning of *author* in "The Parson's Tale," where he wrote of the "author of matrimony, that is Christ," and in his long poem, *Troilus and Cressida,* where he praised "thou Love, O author of nature!"

From this latter sense of the word, our word *authority* received its meaning. Authority is rooted in the idea that legitimate power resides ultimately in God as the source of life and intermediately in the agents that represent God in nature and history. Throughout the history of the West, authority has been ascribed to certain figures or offices. In the ancient Greece of Homer, the heroic man — the warrior and ruler — was seen to be the final human authority; in the Catholic church, the hierarchy, beginning with the priest and extending to the pope, exercised ultimate, legitimate authority; in the Middle Ages, the philosophy of Aristotle was seen by many, Catholic and Muslim alike, to have unparalleled authority in matters of metaphysics and morals; in the sixteenth and seventeenth centuries, the kings of France and England increasingly had recourse to a doctrine of divine right to justify their authority; and throughout human history, diverse arguments have often been made that authority resides inherently or uniquely in the male gender.

Beginning with the Reformation, however, and then with the Enlightenment, Western conceptions of authority began to undergo vast changes. These involved the gradual transfer of authority from institutions and hierarchies to individuals. In the Reformation specifically, *sola scriptura* was intended to remove the church hierarchy from its position of authority in the spiritual life of Protestants.[31] "No believing Christian," explained

---

31. There are several reasons why I say that the principle of *sola scriptura* only *ostensibly* removed the church hierarchy from a position of authority in the spiritual life of Protestants. First, regardless of the ideal, the reality was that social and ecclesiastical forces continued to mediate the spiritual experience of Protestants. Furthermore, the foremost Reformer, Martin Luther, never desired to subvert the authority of the church and Christian tradition. As Paul Althaus explains, Luther

> did not absolutize the Bible in opposition to tradition. He limits neither Christian dogma nor the ethical implications of the gospel to what is expressly stated in Scripture. . . . The Holy Spirit led not only the apostles but also Christendom since the time of the apostles. Luther, however, strongly emphasized the difference between the two cases. This establishes the right and the validity of the Christian tradition. It is to be tested only as to whether or not it contradicts the truth of the gospel clearly contained in Scripture. Whatever passes the test should be preserved. (*The Theology of Martin Luther,* trans. Robert C. Schultz [Philadelphia: Fortress Press, 1966], p. 335)

Martin Luther, "can be forced to recognize any authority beyond the sacred scripture, which is exclusively invested with divine right, unless, indeed, there comes a new and attested revelation."[32] While they were seeking to usurp the interpretive authority of the church, Protestants were at the same time promoting the belief that the Holy Spirit would superintend biblical interpretation and guard against error.

As Protestantism gave way to the Enlightenment, however, the Scriptures themselves were supplanted by human reason as the arbiter of truth. In a letter written to Peter Carr in 1787, Thomas Jefferson gives powerful expression to the Enlightenment faith in rationality. Jefferson tells Carr that every human being is endowed with "a sense of right & wrong," a "moral sense [that] is as much a part of a man as his leg or arm." Secure in this moral sense, Carr should "fix reason firmly in her seat, and call to her tribunal every fact, every opinion," and especially the facts and opinions of religious faith. Jefferson urges Carr to "lay aside all prejudice on both sides, & neither believe nor reject anything because any other persons, or description of person have rejected or believed it. Your own reason is the only oracle given you by heaven."[33] In Jefferson's Enlightenment scheme, neither the Bible nor the church has legitimate authority in matters of belief and practice. Lonely Reason sits on her throne, dispensing her judgments about the true, the beautiful, and the good.

Gadamer correctly observes that "the real consequence of the Enlightenment" was the "subjection of all authority to reason."[34] While Gadamer holds the distinction "between faith in authority and using one's own reason" to be legitimate, he questions the denigration of all authority in the Enlightenment tradition. To many who hold to Enlightenment ideals it never seems to occur that some prejudices might actually be true, that there might be validity to some things believed on the authority of others. We fail to recognize the legitimacy of prejudice and authority because we are confused about the essence of authority. We incorrectly believe obedience to authority to be nothing less than abject capitulation to irrationality. But Gadamer argues that the authority of persons is not

32. Luther, quoted in Robert M. Grant, *A Short History of the Interpretation of the Bible* (New York: Macmillan, 1963), pp. 129-30.

33. Jefferson to Peter Carr, 10 August 1787, in *Thomas Jefferson: Writings*, ed. Merrill D. Peterson (New York: Library of America, 1984), pp. 901-4.

34. Hans-Georg Gadamer, *Truth and Method*, 2nd rev. ed., trans. Joel Weinsheimer and Donald G. Marshall (New York: Crossroad, 1989), p. 278.

based "on the subjection and abdication of reason but on an act of acknowledgment and knowledge — the knowledge, namely, that the other is superior to oneself in judgment and insight."[35]

It is authority in this guise to which the character of Kent refers in *King Lear*. Shakespeare wrote this work around 1603, a time of great uneasiness about authority, when Elizabeth I died childless, leaving no clear successor to her throne. At the beginning of the play, the aging Lear is attempting to head off his own crisis of succession by dividing his kingdom among his three daughters before his death. When one of his earls, Kent, opposes his decisions, Lear angrily banishes him. Undaunted, Kent returns in disguise to serve his king. Without recognizing the man before him, Lear asks him what he would like to do:

> Kent: Service.
> Lear: Who wouldst thou serve?
> Kent: You.
> Lear: Dost thou know me, fellow?
> Kent: No, sir, but you have that in your countenance which I would fain call master.
> Lear: What's that?
> Kent: Authority.[36]

By creating an antithesis between authority and reason, the Enlightenment discredited authority so thoroughly that when reason itself began to come under attack in the late nineteenth century, authority emerged again, but unmistakably on the side of unreason. For a person of the Enlightenment such as Jefferson, it seemed feasible that people free from authority would be protected from anarchy by the rational or moral sense within them; but the attacks upon reason in modernity have destroyed confidence of the sort held by Jefferson. As a consequence, the vacuum created by the exhaustion of reason has been filled by desire, which has rushed to establish itself as the arbiter of values and beliefs. To paraphrase Jefferson, for many therapeutic Americans preferences and desires are the only oracles and authorities given to us by heaven.

---

35. Gadamer, *Truth and Method*, p. 279.

36. Shakespeare, *King Lear*, act 1, scene 4, ll. 22-29, in *William Shakespeare: The Complete Works*, rev. ed., ed. Alfred Harbage (New York: Penguin Books, 1969), p. 1071.

Auden and Authority

Half a century ago, W. H. Auden divined the consequences of the decline of authority and the rise of a therapeutic culture and responded to the challenge with clarity, courage, and cunning. But he did so only after having experimented with a number of early varieties of the therapeutic gospels so common in the twentieth century. Whether selecting his ideas from the fiction of D. H. Lawrence, the writings of Freud, or some obscure cultural or psychological theorist, Auden fashioned his own unique doctrine of psychological and cultural health in the first decade of his poetic career. Journal entries from the early 1930s clearly indicate his bias toward the therapeutic understanding of the self:

It is the body's job to make, the mind's to destroy.

Man is a product of the refined disintegration of nature by time.

Only body can be communicated.

The essence of creation is doing things for no reason; it is pointless. Possessive pleasure is always rational.

"Be good and you will be happy" is a dangerous inversion. "Be happy and you will be good" is the truth.

The only good reason for doing anything is for fun.[37]

Auden dreamed of the advent of a utopia of emotional, sexual, and economic fulfillment, and for the better part of the 1930s he sought to make his art serve the new order of gratified desire. Yet he rather quickly concluded that his dreams were barren and that no gratifying or innocent era would ever be born in history. As the decade progressed, love gradually replaced gratification as a central category of Auden's poetry, and by the end of the 1930s "he finally discarded . . . physical metaphors of health and disease in favor of ethical metaphors of knowledge and authority."[38]

The change in Auden's metaphors is obvious in the poetry written

37. *The English Auden: Poems, Essays and Dramatic Writings: 1927-1939*, ed. Edward Mendelson (London: Faber and Faber, 1978), pp. 298-300.

38. Edward Mendelson, *Early Auden* (New York: Viking Press, 1981), p. 350.

shortly after his return to the Anglican faith, but it can also be detected in the sonnet sequence *In Time of War*, which was written when Auden was on the brink of Christian commitment. In this series of poems, which grew out of the poet's experience as an observer of the Sino-Japanese war, Auden abandoned two of his favorite romantic beliefs: the conviction that history is an impersonal process that turns all individuals into victims, and the belief that "in a world without moral absolutes our sense of nature might serve as a criterion for action."[39]

"Yes, we are going to suffer, now; the sky / Throbs like a feverish forehead; pain is real," one of the sonnets begins.[40] We are going to suffer, not because we are victims of a blind process, but because we are ethical agents who bear responsibility for the very evil we suffer and endure:

> The mountains cannot judge us when we lie:
> We dwell upon the earth; the earth obeys
> The intelligent and evil till they die.[41]

Near the end of *In Time of War*, Auden affirms that in spite of the great evil at work in the world, the quiet labors of love go on. While the brutal conflicts of history rage, "far from the centre of our names, / The little workshop of love" continues its work. "We can't believe that we ourselves designed it, / A minor item of our daring plan," and yet when "Disaster comes"

>   we're amazed to find it
> The single project that since work began
> Through all the cycles showed a steady profit.[42]

In the last sonnet of the sequence, Auden concludes that though we dream of timeless innocence, we live in fallen history:

> Wandering lost upon the mountains of our choice,
> Again and again we sigh for an ancient South,

39. Mendelson, *Early Auden*, p. 354.
40. Auden, *In Time of War*, in *Selected Poems*, ed. Edward Mendelson (London: Faber and Faber, 1979), p. 71. In *Collected Poems*, the sonnet sequence is significantly changed and given the new title *Sonnets from China*. I am quoting from the earlier, original version.
41. Auden, *In Time of War*, p. 71.
42. Auden, *In Time of War*, p. 77.

For the warm nude ages of instinctive poise,
For the taste of joy in the innocent mouth.

. . . .

We envy streams and houses that are sure:
But we are articled to error; we
Were never nude and calm like a great door,

And never will be perfect like the fountains;
We live in freedom by necessity,
A mountain people dwelling among mountains.[43]

In writing *In Time of War,* Auden was effectively rejecting his conviction that our natural innocence has been sullied by the repressive authorities of psyche and state. A few years before he composed the sonnet sequence, Auden had written that our biological ancestors "were meek and sociable, and cruelty, violence, war, all the so-called primitive instincts, do not appear until civilisation has reached a high level. A golden age, comparatively speaking (and anthropological research tends to confirm this), is an historical fact."[44] To his earlier folly, Auden's rejoinder is simple: "We are articled to error . . . and never will be perfect." From this point on, Auden abandons metaphors of health and perception in favor of "ethical metaphors of knowledge and authority."

Auden's most profound meditation upon knowledge and authority was perhaps *The Sea and the Mirror,* a major poem he wrote not long after his return to Christian faith and practice. "O what authority gives / Existence its surprise?" the opening section of the poem asks.

Science is happy to answer
That the ghosts who haunt our lives
Are handy with mirrors and wire,
That song and sugar and fire,
Courage and come-hither eyes
Have a genius for taking pains.
But how does one think up a habit?
Our wonder, our terror remains.[45]

43. Auden, *In Time of War,* p. 78.
44. *The English Auden,* p. 340.
45. Auden, *The Sea and the Mirror,* in *Collected Poems,* ed. Edward Mendelson (New York: Random House, 1976), p. 311.

Auden gave to *The Sea and the Mirror* the subtitle "A Commentary on Shakespeare's *The Tempest.*" The longest section of the poem is a dramatic monologue in prose, in which one of the characters from *The Tempest*, Caliban, addresses the audience one evening after a production of Shakespeare's play. Caliban tells them that they have come in search of enchantment, because each one of them has experienced the breaking of the "childish spell in which . . . everything that happened was a miracle." The child has no doubts about which "authority gives / Existence its surprise," for it believes in itself as the center of power. "It was therefore only necessary for you to presuppose one genius, one unrivalled I to wish these wonders in all their endless plenitude and novelty to be."[46] The child is a "sobbing dwarf" whose deepest desire is to "usurp the popular earth and blot for ever / The gross insult of being a mere one among many." With age, however, comes the inevitable disillusionment. Only when their "singular transparent globes of enchantment" had "shattered one by one" were the audience members driven to the theater in their search for comfort.[47]

Caliban describes for his audience the implications of their fantasies of autonomy. He warns them that in their disillusionment they are bound to submit on "the Journey of life" to one of two authorities — either to himself or to his counterpart, Ariel. Caliban represents the world of the body; he is the state of nature prior to consciousness and language, and as such he is a variation upon the instinctual ideal that Auden himself had so avidly promoted in the 1930s. Ariel speaks for the world of creative spirit, that realm of self-conscious creation that is the province of the artist and other imaginative types.

In worshiping either their own bodies or their own minds, the members of the audience fantasize that they are exercising their freedom, but Caliban tells them that they are simply submitting to the tyranny of a facet of themselves. Caliban tells them that, within the confines of the theater, "at least I, and Ariel too, are free to warn you not . . . to engage either of us as your guide, but there we shall no longer be able to refuse you." Outside the artifice of the theater, Caliban and Ariel will have no alternative but to "say nothing and obey your fatal foolish commands."[48] While he still has them as a captive audience, Caliban wants to let these

46. Auden, *The Sea and the Mirror*, p. 334.
47. Auden, *The Sea and the Mirror*, pp. 312, 334.
48. Auden, *The Sea and the Mirror*, p. 335.

"assorted, consorted specimens of the general popular type" know what will happen "if at our next meeting you should insist . . . on putting one of us in charge."[49]

Caliban informs those who choose him that they are nostalgic souls seeking to return to the innocence prior to the wounds, divisions, and pains of consciousness. He imagines those who follow him crying out, "Release us from our minor roles. Carry me back, Master, to the cathedral town where the canons run through the water meadows with butterfly nets and the old women keep sweet-shops in the cobbled side streets." Caliban's conscripts beg him: "Give me my passage home, let me see that harbour once again just as it was before I learned the bad words." His charges crave the innocent freedom of a pastoral Eden: "O take us home . . . to your promiscuous pastures where the minotaur of authority is just a roly-poly ruminant and nothing is at stake." This Eden, where authority does nothing but chew its cud and give its blessing to license, is what the worshipers of nature conceive of as the "ultimately liberal condition."[50]

Caliban can do nothing but bring those he serves to the place they desire. But that ideal place proves to be not a "cathedral town or mill town or harbour or hillside or jungle or other specific Eden" but "that downright state itself." Here at last, Caliban tells those who have submitted to his authority,

> you are, as you have asked to be, the only subject. . . . You have indeed come all the way to the end of your bachelor's journey where Liberty stands with her hands behind her back, not caring, not minding *anything*. Confronted by a straight and snubbing stare to which mythology is bosh, surrounded by an infinite passivity and purely arithmetical disorder which is only open to perception, and with nowhere to go on to, your existence is indeed free at last to choose its own meaning, that is, to plunge headlong into despair and fall through silence fathomless and dry, all fact your single drop, all value your pure alas.[51]

In this kingdom, where you are the only subject and nothing separates you from what you desire, authority cannot deny you the right to anything — "Liberty stands with her hands behind her back, not caring, not minding *anything*" — and the meaning of your life is yours to choose. Like the

49. Auden, *The Sea and the Mirror*, pp. 334-35.
50. Auden, *The Sea and the Mirror*, p. 336.
51. Auden, *The Sea and the Mirror*, pp. 336-37.

damned souls in Dante's Hell, Caliban's followers receive exactly what they desired in craving the "ultimately liberal condition," even though it hardly turns out to be what they had imagined.

Ariel, Caliban's "more spiritual colleague," is chosen as leader by a "smaller but doubtless finer group" of "important persons at the top of the ladder." These are the spiritual individuals tired of doing good for a world that does not appreciate them. They pray to Ariel, "Deliver us from these helpless agglomerations of dishevelled creatures with their bed-wetting, vomiting, weeping bodies, their giggling, fugitive, disappointing hearts, and scrawling, blotted, misspelt minds, to whom we have so foolishly tried to bring the light they did not want." Caliban tells the audience that the requests of Ariel's followers betray a "wish for freedom to transcend *any* condition, for direct unentailed power without *any* . . . obligation to inherit or transmit." When he obeys their commands, Ariel transports his followers "into a nightmare which has all the wealth of exciting action and all the emotional poverty of an adventure story for boys, a state of perpetual emergency and everlasting improvisation where all is need and change."[52]

In Ariel's realm of absolute spiritual freedom, "all the voluntary movements are possible" and "all the modes of transport . . . are available, but any sense of direction, any knowledge of where on earth one has come from or where on earth one is going to is completely absent." Ariel rules a world where "everything . . . suggests Mind," yet "the heart feels nothing but a dull percussion of conceptual foreboding."

> And from this nightmare of public solitude, this everlasting Not Yet, what relief have you but in an ever giddier collective gallop . . . toward the grey horizon of the bleaker vision, . . . what goal but the Black Stone on which the bones are cracked, for only there in its cry of agony can your existence find at last an unequivocal meaning and your refusal to be yourself become a serious despair, the love nothing, the fear all?[53]

"Such are the alternative routes," Caliban concludes, "the facile glad-handed highway or the virtuous averted track, by which the human effort to make its own fortune arrives all eager at its abruptly dreadful end."[54] When they cannot abide an authority external to the self, modern individuals inevitably choose to make either the body or the mind their

52. Auden, *The Sea and the Mirror*, pp. 337-38.
53. Auden, *The Sea and the Mirror*, pp. 338-39.
54. Auden, *The Sea and the Mirror*, p. 339.

lord and guide. Either way, however, they eventually arrive at a state in which they have become the only subjects in the world and are alienated from nature and humanity.

As his address to the audience draws to a close, Caliban tells them that the dramatist faces a terrible dilemma. If he paints the estrangement of humanity vividly, then "the less clearly can he indicate the truth from which it is estranged." Yet "the brighter his revelation of the truth in its order, its justice, its joy, the fainter shows his picture of your actual condition." According to Caliban, the dramatist's only hope is that somehow we will "see ourselves as we are, neither cosy nor playful, but swaying out on the ultimate wind-whipped cornice that overhangs the unabiding void." Only then might we realize that "there is nothing to say. . . . There never was, — it is at this moment that for the first time in our lives we hear . . . the real Word which is our only *raison d'être*. . . . [I]t is just here, among the ruins and the bones, that we may rejoice in the perfected Work which is not ours."[55]

But what would it mean to "rejoice in a perfected Work" not of our own devising? How can self-reliant, postmodern American individualists respond to a promise that, because of their deepest desires for autonomy, must seem to threaten all that they treasure? The answers to these questions are difficult for us to conceive of, since we have become so accustomed to imagining the self in an antagonistic relationship to authority and tradition. As Gadamer explains, the Enlightenment's diametric opposition between authority and freedom is one of its most dubious and lamentable legacies. In its inability to see the acknowledgment of authority as a recognition "that the other is superior to oneself in judgment and insight," the Enlightenment tradition has made it extraordinarily difficult for the modern mind to accept with gratitude what has come before it and what has been done on its behalf.[56]

The call to "rejoice in the perfected Work which is not ours" is also likely to seem preposterous because of contemporary America's profound aversion to the tragic vision. For the Christian faith, the events of the Passion week show human experience — and the experience of Jesus himself — to be a tragedy encompassed by a comedy. The final word of the Christian faith is a decidedly comic one. The gospel is a ringing word of affirmation, proclaiming the love of God, his power over sin and death,

55. Auden, *The Sea and the Mirror*, pp. 339-40.
56. Gadamer, *Truth and Method*, p. 279.

and the final reconciliation of humanity with its Creator. As the apostle Paul writes in his second letter to the Corinthians, "the Son of God, Christ Jesus, . . . was not a mixture of Yes and No. With him it is always Yes" (2 Cor. 1:19, REB).

Nevertheless, in the Christian gospel the final victories come only after the decisive battles have been fought. There is in the Christian faith an ineluctable pattern of guilt *and* grace, sin *and* forgiveness, death *and* resurrection. The gospel is always about both sides of these dramatic equations, never simply about one or the other. A faith that looks back to Good Friday only is a faith of despair, a faith that resigns itself to the brutal indifference of the forces that govern and destroy human life. A faith that only celebrates the resurrection is a shallow faith, a faith that is not true to the terrible realities of suffering and death. Versions of the Christian faith that ignore or trivialize those realities may have initial appeal and a strong marketing draw, but they rarely have the power to sustain the afflicted soul through grief and sorrow.

Resurrection without the cross and glory without suffering have become integral elements in the creed of contemporary America. John Updike writes of Rabbit Angstrom, the central character of his four *Rabbit* novels, that he "has no taste for the dark, tangled, visceral aspect of Christianity, the *going through* quality of it, the passage *into* death and suffering that redeems and inverts these things, like an umbrella blowing inside out. . . . His eyes turn toward the light however it glances into his retina."[57] Rabbit is a manifestation in the common culture of a blithe, pragmatic optimism that we have seen to have its powerful advocates in the contemporary intellectual world.

For the proclamation of Christian truth to have power in the postmodern era, in short, that truth must come to contemporary persons as a promise of redemption for a troubled world, not as a therapeutic message of happiness denying the pain and promise of suffering and death. Christians who seek to reach the "cultured despisers" with the challenge and comfort of Christ must counter the therapeutic culture's gospel — what Caliban calls the "cosy and playful"; they must do so by insisting that we "see ourselves as we are, . . . swaying out on the ultimate wind-whipped cornice that overhangs the unabiding void." It is a grievous error and a profound injustice to tell the citizens of the culture of interpretation anything less than the truth, when that truth is one of

57. Updike, *Rabbit, Run* (New York: Fawcett Crest, 1960), p. 219.

trials that issue in delights, of sorrows that give way to joy, of death that submits to life.

> God will cheat no one, not even the world of its triumph.
>
> He is the Way.
> Follow Him through the Land of Unlikeness;
> You will see rare beasts, and have unique adventures.
>
> He is the Truth.
> Seek Him in the Kingdom of Anxiety;
> You will come to a great city that has expected your return for years.
>
> He is the Life.
> Love Him in the World of the Flesh;
> And at your marriage all its occasions shall dance for joy.[58]

If Auden is right in making these audacious assertions — and indeed, the Gospels promise precisely what he imagines — how can the Christian church be content to preach a gospel of comfort and ease? If God will not cheat the world of its tragedy and its triumph, what possible right does the Christian interpreter of culture have to do so?

58. Auden, *For the Time Being,* in *Collected Poems,* p. 308.

INDEX

Abrams, M. H., 59n.12, 65n.26, 67, 178-79, 181

Adams, John, 112

Aesthetics: Christian, 225-35; influence of Kant on, 49-52; modernist, 62-63; in the romantic age, 53-60; Victorian, 60-62

Ahlstrom, Sydney, 144

Allen, Gay Wilson, 112-13

Althaus, Paul, 224, 254n.31

America: banishment and exclusion in, 157-60; the centrality of Cartesianism in, 105-10; and Christian theories of the arts, 225-35; the conflict of interpretations in, 149-57; the place of tradition in, 137-41; and the question of identity, 116-19, 144-49; the rise of literary culture in, 124-26

Anderson, Quentin, 105, 149

Appleby, Joyce, 73

Aquinas, St. Thomas, 85, 98, 211, 212

Aristotle, 85, 244, 254

Arnold, Matthew, 181; on literature and the transformation of culture, 60-63, 107, 172-73; on literature as a replacement for religion, 33-34, 179

Aronov, Aaron, 31-32

Auden, W. H.: assessment of American culture by, 139-40; on authority, 257-65; and critique of romanticism, 129, 134-35; critique of the Enlightenment by, 27-30; response to modernism by, 183-84. Works: *For the Time Being*, 27-30, 265; *In Time of War*, 258-59; "Precious Five," 135; *The Sea and the Mirror*, 259-65

Augustine, St., 80, 85, 98, 212; on language, 244-45; as source of aesthetic doctrines, 52; views of the self and sin, 138, 206-9, 211. Works: *Confessions*, 207, 244; *On Christian Doctrine*, 52

Authority, 253-65

Bacon, Francis, 53

Bakhtin, Mikhail, 93n.37

Barth, Karl, 202, 204n.40, 206; assessment of Enlightenment by, 82-83; critique of Schleiermacher by, 70, 78-79

Barthes, Roland, 205

Behler, Ernst, 50

Bellah, Robert, 132-33, 140-41, 200-201